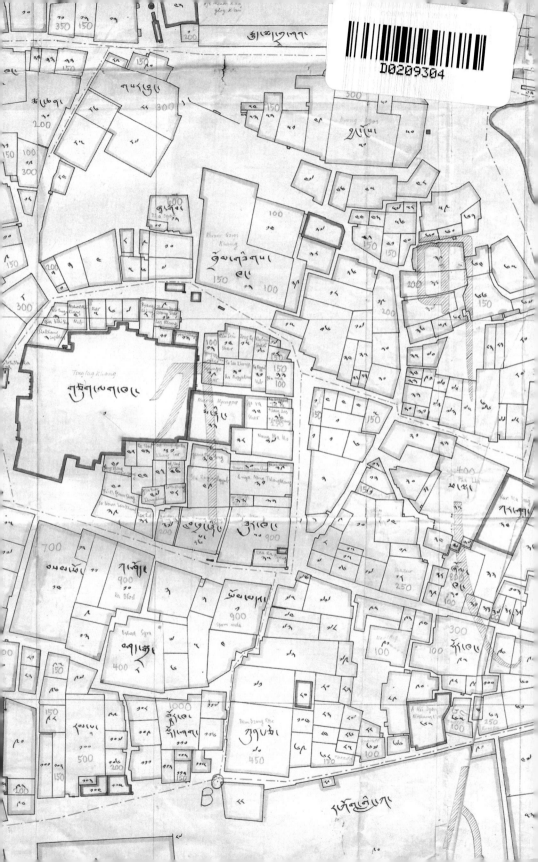

ASIA PERSPECTIVES

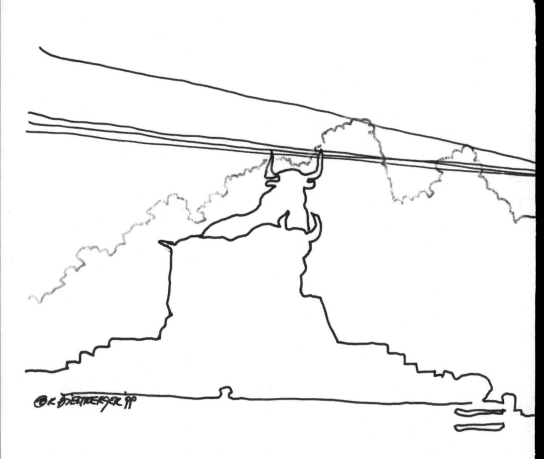

COLUMBIA UNIVERSITY PRESS   NEW YORK

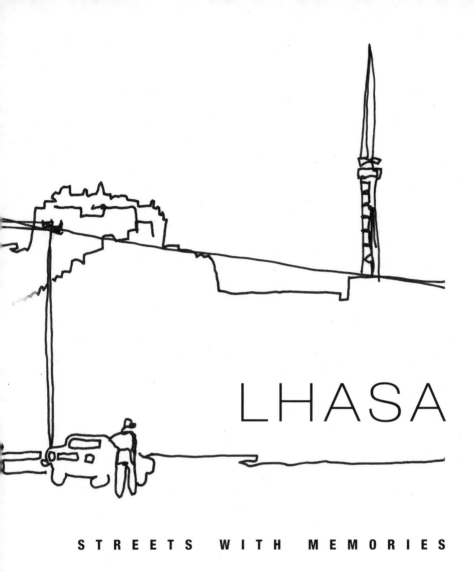

LHASA

STREETS WITH MEMORIES

ROBERT BARNETT

Columbia University Press
Publishers Since 1893
New York
Copyright © 2006 by Robert Barnett
Illustrations copyright © 2006 by Karen Diemberger
Endpaper illustration from a section of the map of Lhasa
produced by Peter Aufschnaiter, 1947–48. Reproduced with
the permission of the Museum of Ethnography, University of
Zürich through the generous assistance of Dr. Martin Brauen.
Plan of Lhasa (pp. xxx–xxxii) by L. A. Waddell, Lt Colonel, I.M.S.
First published in L. Austine Waddell, *Lhasa and Its Mysteries:
With a Record of the Expedition of 1903–1904* (London: John
Murray, 1905 and New York: Dutton, 1905).

An abridged version of this book was published in French in Katia Buffetrille and Charles
Ramble, eds., *Tibétains: 1959–1999, quarante ans de colonisation* (Paris: Éditions Autrement,
1998). Another version was published in Italian as *La città illeggibile, Storie narrate dalle
strade di Lhasa* (Milano: CDA, 1999). Part of "*Mestizo*" was first published in James O'Reilly
and Larry Habegger, eds., *Travelers' Tales from Tibet* (San Francisco: Travelers' Tales, 2002).

Library of Congress Cataloging-in-Publication Data
Barnett, Robert, 1953–
Lhasa : streets with memories / Robert Barnett.
　　p.　　cm. — (Asia perspectives)
Includes index.
ISBN 0–231–13680–3 (cloth) — ISBN 0–231–51011–X (electronic)
1. Lhasa (China). 2. Lhasa (China)—Description and travel. I. Title. II. Series.
DS797.82.L537B37　2006
951'.5—dc22　　　　　　　　　　　　　　　　　　　　2005048412

∞

Columbia University Press books are printed on permanent and durable acid-free paper.
Printed in the United States of America
c 10 9 8 7 6 5 4 3 2 1

For Bolor and RY

The City . . . does not tell its past, but contains it like the lines of a hand, written in the corners of the streets, the gratings of the windows, the banisters of the steps, the antennae of the lightning rods, the poles of the flags, every segment marked in turn with scratches, indentations, scrolls.

—Italo Calvino (*Invisible Cities*, 1974)

We construct, we make every city a little in the image of the ship *Argo*, whose every piece was no longer the original piece but which still remained the ship *Argo*, that is, a set of significations easily readable and recognizable. In this attempt at a semantic approach to the city we should try to understand the play of signs, to understand that any city is a structure, but that we must never try and we must never want to fill in this structure.

—Roland Barthes (*Semiology and the Urban*, 1971)

You will not find new lands or sail other seas.
Your city will pursue you. Streets you'll walk along
Will be the same. You'll age in the same neighborhoods,
Grow gray in these same houses.
This city is where you'll arrive. Always. A different land? No hope.
There is no ship for you, there is no road.

—Constantine P. Cavafy (*The City*, 1910)

CONTENTS

Returning to London after some years away, I am struck by the way each street evokes specific memories and sometimes poignant feelings. I sit on the upper deck of the No. 55 bus and look over the iron railings and the walls that shield Gray's Inn Fields. I see the windows of an office once occupied by a leading politician, and the blue plaque that marks the house in Doughty Street where Dickens lived. A thickly varnished door leads to the former rooms of a lawyer friend paralyzed in a car crash two decades ago. I can see the entrance to a dentist's clinic I used to visit. A party that I once attended in the mews behind it just after I finished university comes hazily to my mind.

Later, driving through Southwark, on the south side of the Thames, I pass streets named after the bear gardens and the playhouse where Shakespeare worked. I recognize the site of the tavern where Marlowe is said to have been murdered. I pass a lavish theater thronged with tourists; I worked on that site before the theater was built, setting up stalls for tourists at the time of the Silver Jubilee. On the overground train to Blackheath, I can see where Watt Tyler and the Peasant's Revolt were halted in 1381, and I glimpse the observatory where Newton worked. Near my sister's house in Holloway, not far from the prison, I pass 39 Hill-drop Crescent, where Dr. Crippen disposed of his wife before attempting to flee on the S.S. *Montrose* to America. Behind the crescent is the house where the famous lyricist Michael Flanders once had me sing a song while he accompanied me on the piano. It was doubly memorable, because I cannot sing.

Some of these associations mark moments that are significant only to me, while others might be relevant to a larger community. Some derive their potency from something I have read or heard, a film I have seen, or scraps of conversation that I cannot quite recall. They are triggered by the sight of memorable buildings and places that I pass.

Such an affective conglomeration is available around every place where we have lived or to which we have nurtured a connection. It is a form of history, and an important one. I do not have access to this kind of knowledge in New York, because I know so little about it, or in Beijing, which I have only visited occasionally for meetings, and of which the little history I know is drawn from guidebooks and the press. In those places, the streets and buildings are largely empty of rich association for me. They inspire feelings, of course, and analogies with other experiences that I might be tempted to apply, but none will be tied to that particular place or be a part of its communal history. Unless I remember to question them, many of these associations are likely to mislead me.

This book is an attempt to scrape a little of the topsoil off the affective history of a city, Lhasa, that is not my own. It seeks to excavate the stories that can be told by the city's buildings and its streets and to distinguish them from the tensions and counternarratives produced by the interventions of outsiders. Such stories, however, cannot be single or coherent, composed as they are of countless, changing elements that I and most outsiders cannot know. At first I think of the task as a kind of archaeology of sentiment, like uncovering the layers of a medieval palimpsest or peeling away layers on a master's painting to reveal what Lillian Hellman called a pentimento. But it is neither, because some of the elements that I will find will turn out in time to be my own invention, or to be irrelevant to the web of associations most valued by the inhabitants or even damaging to their interests. Instead of seeking some treasure beneath the surface, my interest is in the convergence of memories, some of which may be unrecorded, that form critical junctures in the historical understanding of a city by its residents and that contribute to the essential illegibility of a city to its foreign visitors.

These recollections are therefore not like Proust's *madeleines* or the turtle-walkers whom Walter Benjamin recalled in the Arcades of Paris, which were offered in discussions of the aesthetics of memory and nostalgia and as studies of cultural production. My inquiry is about the effort to know through memories the inner language of a foreign city. This becomes more important and more problematic in a place where certain topics may not be discussed, and where the insertion of foreign notions into the narrative becomes highly probable. A foreigner always has limited access to the associations that hover around the streets and buildings of another people's city, but in Tibet even visitors fluent in the language are left to guess whether their more political conceptions are shared by local people.

So a study of this kind cannot just mine histories and writings by contemporary Tibetans, or wait to have unfettered discussions with the residents. Instead it looks at Tibetan writings from earlier times that might give clues to local ways of thinking about Lhasa, at foreign writings about the city, and at my own interactions with the place. The last two are scarred by histories of misreading that became apparent only afterward, long before issues of restricted speech arose to complicate matters further.

I do not attempt to be complete or scientific in dealing with the question of foreign interpretations of Tibet, since misrepresentation is so familiar a device now in writings about foreign places, thanks in large part to Edward Saïd and the scholars and critical ethnographers who have followed him. In the case of Tibet, much was done by Peter Bishop in a book called *The Myth of Shangri-la*, and later a similar task was performed by Donald Lopez in his *Prisoners of Shangri-la*. Both were following the lesser-known work of an Austrian Buddhologist, Agehananda Bharati, not to mention a long history of awareness in Western, Indian, and Arabic literatures that many writings about Tibet were literally fantastic. Given this history, it was somewhat ironic that in the late 1990s a series of writers and journalists produced articles claiming to show that earlier Western writers on the subject of Tibet knew little of what they described. CLINTON TO FIND NO SHANGRI-LA ON TIBET, announced a headline on a Reuters article in June 1998; THE SHANGRI-LA THAT NEVER WAS, declared *The New York Times* the following week, as if the press was about to reveal to the U.S. president and people that the novelist James Hilton had deceived them after all.

This school of writing, which was taken up by several scholars too, rests in part on an interesting but concealed device that is integral to the work of stage magicians: most of the audience already knows what is about to be revealed but cooperates in the pretense anyway, so as to revel in the perception that they are among the elite with prior knowledge. There were likely then, as now, few readers of such pieces who were not already well aware of the fantasticalness of many writings about Tibet, and fewer, apart from devotees themselves—and even that is arguable—who did not view the associated mystical contestations as highly speculative or aspirational. The same was true of earlier generations: when Annie Besant, a prominent socialist leader and labor activist in 1880s London, shifted to being a devotee of Madame Blavatsky in India and of the Great White Lodge supposedly denizened in Tibet, her sanity was widely doubted. Conversely, when Roosevelt named his summer residence after Hilton's imaginary Shangri-la, no one thought that he had mistaken the novel *Lost Horizon* for a travel guide. Everyone had seen Ronald Coleman playing the male lead in the cinematic fantasy of that name, and there was no difficulty in distinguishing filmic fiction from documentary, at least in its general features.

My intention therefore is not to add to the works of earlier writers on this subject, or to add to celebrations of the supposed evolving enlightenment of the West in detecting, as if for the first time, its own earlier presumptuousness in describing foreign places. Neither is it to support the implication that there is a significant body of "uneducated" readers who are unable to distinguish fact from fiction. I include accounts of earlier foreign interactions with the city to provide a baseline for critical reflexivity, a benchmark for assessing the contemporary repetition of previous histories, and a lever to open up my own experiences in Tibet.

In looking at Lhasa and at foreign writings about it, I have therefore not attempted to be systematic or complete. Much has been omitted, since I am primarily interested in that kind of elusive and nonlinear history of associations that does not have a place in more conventional accounts. I have not used the word "foreign" to mean Western, and so refer to some writers who are from other areas, as well as exiles who became foreign only by having had to remain abroad for several decades, so that they were excluded from direct involvement in the history of their city and often found themselves writing in a hegemonic language not their own. I have also included Chinese who traveled to Tibet after 1950 as foreigners in some sense, not always much different from Westerners engaged in similar encounters.

The word "foreign" is therefore not used here as a political or a racial term. Rather, it implies exclusion from the process of making the collectively remembered history of a place, and thus an inability to comprehend that history. It means not to be a partaker in the thick tangle of historical and personal associations with which each place is imbued. Even those who are resident for a lengthy period may not gain access to the previous history or histories that they are changing, and so will be excluded necessarily from comprehending them, even if these residents are the driving force and power that wishes to redesign that history. It may be said of both the British and the Chinese in Tibet that to the extent to which they were involved in seeking to change or even to celebrate its future, they became inevitably involved in fantastical or didactic reconstructions of its past and present, and thus excluded from the ability to read or know its histories. The Tibetan exiles too, although deeply imbricated with the past of that place, suffered exclusion in an inverse and tragically equivalent way by being cut off or by shutting themselves off from its unfolding present.

By contrast, I have often wondered whether the Europeans Aufschnaiter, Harrer, and Ford, and maybe Richardson and Fox, long-term residents of Lhasa in the 1940s, and later perhaps Bass in the 1980s, became conceptually conversant with their host communities in terms of their memories and thoughts about the city. They knew the language, and perhaps more important, they were in the city at times when the imperialist aspirations of their parent states had waned and had lost their moral authority. So perhaps they no longer sought to reconfigure the Tibet in which they found themselves and became to a considerable extent able to share in and to communicate something of its felt history. Certainly this can be said of the Japanese spy Kimura, even though his parent empire only imploded, unbeknown to him, while he was resident *sub rosa* in the Tibetan capital.

In contemporary Tibet there are no published rules forbidding conversations with foreigners. Officials do not intervene at the first sign of interaction, and local scholars are not automatically forbidden to travel to conferences abroad. Such conditions had existed in Tibet until well beyond the end of the 1970s, but had been modified significantly in the 1980s. Tourism was allowed, scholars invited, and some foreign books translated, so that the possibilities of interaction changed dramatically. But, just as most historical documents in Lhasa are still kept secret from foreign and even local view, there remains a line beyond which Tibetans cannot safely cross in conversation with others. Where that line lies is a matter of contention, and it changes from time to time, according to political conditions, the temperament of certain leaders, individual interpretations, and, most dangerously, erroneous calculation of risk.

There are foreigners in Lhasa who successfully avoid difficulties with the state, and scholars whose knowledge and intellectual discipline enable them to avoid such entanglements. But one of the peculiar problems for visitors to Lhasa (other than those of Chinese or Tibetan descent) is that if they cross that unknown line, the consequences will tend to fall entirely on the local residents, and usually only after the visitors have left. For diplomatic reasons, the old imperialist practice of extraterritoriality remains in place in modern Tibet, so that foreigners, or at least Westerners, will not usually know when they have caused harm. For quite different reasons, earlier generations of outsiders in Tibet also thought they were doing good, only to be judged otherwise by history. Without giving details that might create further problems for the people involved, this book therefore reproduces minute interactions where foreign readings of a situation, like miniature repetitions of earlier history, seemed at one time positive but later were invalidated.

This is thus a book that looks two ways. In the past it looks at some underlying themes in Tibetan myths and histories that might give broad clues to the ways Lhasa's residents think about their city. In the present it looks at buildings and the layout of the city streets, seeing these as a kind of concrete spelling out of the dreams and aspirations of the state or the people who had them built. Scholars of urban studies, geography, and architecture have illuminated the possibilities of studying buildings and the ways in which cities are constructed, teaching us to read them as texts, while archaeologists and historians have in recent times done something similar with much smaller objects of everyday use in the study of material culture. The physical fabric of Lhasa offers clues to a similar kind of history that might be closer to that experienced by its inhabitants, carrying signs of its past, its changes, failed hopes, and erasures.

Ideally, I would have taken an individual building, like the former aristocratic mansion of Kyitöpa where Chinese officials and underground Tibetan communists worked in the 1940s, and excavated all the stages of its history, occupation, associations—the things that it housed and witnessed; the people who lived there or passed by; the events that swirled around it; the changes in its fittings and façades; and the parties, arguments, and revelries within it, to produce a sense of the multilayered associations that Lhasans of a certain age and knowledge might experience when they pass by. I have hinted at the possibilities of such an approach, and have paired it with a set of questions about streets rather than individual buildings.

When a whole street or city area is constructed or revamped and a particular style invoked, its buildings become monuments to the aspirations of the builders or designers and their ideologies. For people living in or near them, they might become beacons of hope for a better future, memorials to something that was demolished to make way for them, or future epitaphs to the eventual failures of those who built them. As the functions of a street or building change over time, they might leave traces in the layered memories older citizens recall when they walk by. Using the buildings and the layout of the city as textual fragments available to be read, but not necessarily understood, by all, this work tries to glean some at least of the stratified associations hovering around the stones and thoroughfares of the Tibetan capital.

When I first saw the streets of Lhasa, after months touring by bus through southern and western China, the issue that struck me as most prominent was nausea. The mountains around me were inspiring and the vivid azure of the sky was impressive, but the effects of altitude were more preoccupying. Still, this trip was my reward after a not entirely successful summer working in Hong Kong, and my reason for traveling rough across China, like most backpackers there, was to show my innate ability to overcome mere externalities such as height and distance. I intended to have inner experiences that would prove that as a traveler I was superior to my compatriots at home, and especially to such low breeds as actors, businessmen, and tourists.

So I had resolved to go and practice meditation. On the eve of October 1, 1987, I had concluded a deal in the forecourt of the Yak Hotel with an English girl called Kate, who sold me a sleeping bag and a small gas stove. Kate knew a thing or two about Buddhism from an expatriate lama she had studied with in Oxford, including the location of a cave a few hours' drive from Lhasa that the *Lonely Planet* travel guide confirmed as suitable for such endeavors. I didn't know how to meditate, not having tried since more youthful days in India some 15 years before, but Kate didn't seem to think that mattered greatly, and neither did I. Anyway, I only planned to be a hermit for a week or so before, significantly enlightened, I would head south toward India and my plane ride back to London. It was only as a concession to touristic obligations that at about 9 the following morning I decided, before leaving the city, to make my first visit to the Jokhang temple in the heart of the old town, some 500 yards from the hotel where I was staying.

I never got to the cave, and never learned to meditate again. The English girl spoke to me only once more, to express contempt at my cancellation of the pilgrimage and my lack of spiritual resolve. As I had entered the square in front of the Jokhang, I had seen a crowd gathering in the street and armed police already driving up in open trucks along the far side of the square. An official was hectoring the throng, a large stone in his hand. An American tourist lurched through the crowd, heading toward the hotel. He told me he had been dragged briefly into a nearby police station for taking photographs of a small protest earlier, and in the courtyard had seen monks from that demonstration being pummeled with spades by police. The crowd, he said, was demanding that the police release the Tibetan prisoners, as they had released him. He and I, and maybe fifty other tourists in the square that morning, had ended up as witnesses to the first major protest in Tibet to be seen by foreigners.

The events of that day are relatively well known—the deaths, the arrests, and the momentary turmoil as China sought to deal with major opposition to its rule in Tibet for the first time in front of foreign eyes. I was only a tiny part of those events, and only one of many who tried to make sense of what we saw and heard, to tell others what we had seen, and to help the wounded where we could. A few of us stayed for a while in the hope that an alien presence would act as a deterrent to further violence, until we realized that we had become irrelevant or damaging.

After returning to London, I went back to my old work in theater as before, and continued it for the next ten years. But in my spare time, since there was little available on the subject, I started to write about current events in Tibet. With the help and advice of many others, I also set up a research project that published reports and analyses of those events. Those reports are widely available and indicate well enough the scope of the work we did, although nothing can measure or repay the skill and dedication of the people who made them possible. In 1998 I moved to Columbia University in New York to work on academic aspects of the issue.

Eventually I became one of those who, through the intricacies of bureaucratic calculus, was allowed to spend several months in Lhasa every year, in my case as a teacher and a scholar. I get to see my hosts and students enjoy the glittering appeal of streets lined with shopping malls and boutiques while together we frequent the Internet salons, bars, and restaurants of the city, read books in Tibetan, or watch one of the sixty domestic channels available on our television sets. Yet I for one do not know what attitude they or other Tibetans have about the situation in which they find themselves. I cannot know for sure what is the collective rationale of the inhabitants of the city, or even how it varies among different groups and individuals. In the days of open protest, everything seemed clear. But Lhasa became again a city where the spoken word is far removed from what is thought, where all around the signs speak more loudly of the global entrancement of desire than they do of politics, and where the foreigner wanders around in an ignorance that he or she has no sure way to measure. It is a city in which the memories and stories that belong to each street and house still speak, if they can be heard, more audibly than the inhabitants.

It was against this background that this book was written.

A NOTE ON HISTORY

Tibet became a place where residents still speak guardedly with foreign visitors because of a chain of events that can be traced back to a single moment: the British invasion a century ago. In 1903, the Viceroy of India, Lord Curzon, decided that he had identified a *casus belli* for the invasion of Tibet. Some scholars have suggested that he and his underlings, particularly Colonel Francis Younghusband, who was to lead the expedition, were driven by a desire to be the first Westerners to enter openly the fabled city of Lhasa in modern times, or that they wished to perform some act of bravado to ensure public prominence in what they may have sensed to be the final years of British imperial adventurism. They found their excuses for this exercise in accounts of unseen weaponry that posed an imaginary threat: they embellished vague reports of Russian weapons in Tibet so as to suggest that the Tsar might one day move troops through Tibet to the northern border of British India. Using as his immediate reason the refusal of the Tibetan government to answer three letters he had sent, Curzon dispatched Younghusband with an army across the border.

Once out of India, Younghusband refused to negotiate with the Tibetan dignitaries sent to meet him, arguing that only higher-level officials would suffice and meanwhile pushing farther into the Tibetan

heartland. Along the way, as Charles Allen has shown, the British pro-
voked major battles in which their Maxim guns gave them an insuper-
able advantage. They killed some three or four thousand Tibetans, in
many cases in retreat, and lost fewer than forty on the British side. Once
they reached Lhasa, they forced the Tibetans to sign a treaty committing
them to pay a huge indemnity and to trade with the British. Having
thus humiliated the Tibetans, Younghusband promptly returned with
his troops to India.

Whatever the Tibetans thought of being invaded for such a reason
rapidly became of marginal significance, because within six years they
were subject to another invasion, this time from the East. Beijing, well
aware that the British threatened China's long-standing interests in the
region, decided to reframe its claims to Tibet in terms that would be
unmistakable to the international community. By 1906 the Qing government had persuaded London (whose officials had been embarrassed by
the excesses of the Tibet expedition) to sign a treaty limiting any rights
implicitly accorded Tibet by Younghusband's agreement. Beijing then
began to implement a new frontier policy according to which Tibet would
become a Chinese province—in other words, it would be unambiguously
annexed as part of China's integral territory. In 1910 a Chinese military
force entered Lhasa and placed the city under full Chinese military administration. If the Qing dynasty had not collapsed the following year,
leading to decades of instability and civil war in China, Younghusband's
adventurism would have ensured that Tibet remained no more than one
of China's provinces. But the fall of the Qing gave the Tibetans the chance
to rephrase their status in modern terms, and in 1913 the thirteenth Dalai
Lama declared his country to be fully independent.

THE DEBATE OVER STATUS

Tibet had certainly been a nation, though not always a nation-state, for
many centuries; a thousand years earlier it had even been an empire
that had for a time dominated China as well as parts of Central Asia.
Whether it had also been independent before the twentieth century is
harder to say, since its status varied over time and since that term seems
not to have been in use in regional politics until about the time of Younghusband's expedition. In the thirteenth century Tibet had come under
the aegis of the Mongol emperors, some twenty-five years before they

took over China and renamed themselves the Yuan. Tibet was from then on in some sense within the influence of Beijing, and it is from that moment that China today bases its claim to sovereignty over Tibet. That term, however, also seems not to have been used by the Chinese or the Tibetans before the last century, and can be applied only in retrospect and without precision.

Tibetan exiles have argued, for example, that Tibet's previous relations were conducted personally with the Mongol rulers or later with the Manchu emperors, and not with China per se or with the ethnic Chinese dynasties that subsequently replaced both those invaders as rulers in Beijing. Tibetans also claim that the link between Tibet and its overlords was a specifically Buddhist or Inner Asian type of religious compact called by them a *chöd yön* or "priest-patron" relationship, in which the Tibetan lama offered spiritual entitlement to the emperor in return for political protection, implying both parties to be in some sense equivalent. Indeed, Tibetan government documents before the twentieth century always used the term *chöd yön* in correspondence with their neighbor, whose country they referred to as *Gya* or China, a word that specifically did not include themselves. The presence of those three words in Tibetan governmental documents is likely the main reason why most today remain sealed and inaccessible to foreign or local inspection.

By the nineteenth century the situation had become more complex. In 1727, nearly a century after the Manchus had established themselves as the Qing Emperors of China, *amban*s or imperial commissioners were sent to rule alongside the Dalai Lamas, established by Mongol armies since 1642 as the political leaders of Tibet. Luciano Petech and other Western scholars have described Tibet at that time as a protectorate belonging to Beijing, a term that, even in contemporary usage, does not connote the loss of nationhood. The Chinese clearly thought then that Tibet was in some way subservient to them. The relationship between the *amban*s and the Dalai Lamas was unclear: the former claimed authority over the latter but found it increasingly difficult to exercise. By the close of the nineteenth century, Beijing's involvement in Tibet had become somewhat notional, at least as far as outsiders could tell. That changed dramatically with the arrival of the British and its short-lived consequence, the Chinese invasion of 1910.

In 1913, after the collapse of the Qing dynasty, the thirteenth Dalai Lama had his troops oust the occupying Chinese army, together with all civilian Chinese and their allies. Influenced by what he had witnessed in his visits to Mongolia, India, and Beijing, he made the first attempts to move Tibet toward a modern form of nationhood. Besides declaring independence, he liberalized some conditions for the peasantry, set up a standing army, and sent the children of some aristocrats to England for their education. By the time of his death in 1933 these efforts had largely stalled, conservative elements in the monasteries and among the nobles having undermined his attempts to create international connections or to introduce British-style military training and schools. For similar reasons, he and his officials did little to establish internationally their claim to independence, apart from allowing the British to have a legation in Lhasa. The seventeen-year-long regency that followed his death, as it must the passing of each Dalai Lama, led to increased corruption, conservatism, and a reluctance to risk contact with the outside world, despite increasing pressure from individual Tibetans for reforms that would modernize the country's administration and clarify its status.

As a result, when Mao Zedong finally seized power in China in 1949 and declared his plan to reunite Tibet with the motherland, Tibet had most of the trappings of statehood but none of the military wherewithal or international connections to secure it. In October 1950, when Chinese forces crossed for the second time that century into central Tibet, the British, who had never fully acknowledged China's claim to sovereignty, admitting only that China "had a special position there" (an opinion Britain still maintains), asserted that Tibet's status was ambiguous. India under Nehru saw China as an ally against Western domination and did nothing to oppose the annexation. The Americans offered small arms, but would do little of substance without Indian connivance, and in any case the Tibetan leaders vacillated, doubtful of American sincerity.

Mao nevertheless moved cautiously and had his troops wait a year in the eastern Tibetan borderlands, until May 1951, when representatives of the Dalai Lama, led by the controversial *kalön,* or cabinet minister, Ngapö Ngawang Jigme, signed a surrender agreement in Beijing. In that document, known as the Seventeen-Point Agreement, the Tibetans explicitly declared Tibet to be a part of China. Curzon and Younghusband, whose little adventure some five decades earlier had been designed to bulwark Tibetan nationhood and thus keep major foreign powers such as Russia and China far from India's borders, had achieved the opposite of their intent.

Tibet's status continues to be disputed. It is argued by some that the surrender document was signed under duress, or that it became invalid because one or the other side reneged on its obligations, or that a right of self-determination persists irrespective of the agreement. These arguments are legal rather than political. China insists that its claim to ownership of Tibet is absolute and is unaffected by considerations such as the vagueness of the earlier relationship or China's inability to exercise control for some four decades. Whichever of the conflicting positions on this question has validity, it is clear, though it has not been argued by the Tibetan government in exile or its supporters, that until 1910 even China had not suggested that Tibet was an integral part of its realm, and had certainly never claimed Tibet as a province. In modern states the notion of nonintegral territory is obscure, but the condition of a colony may offer an analogy in current terms to the earlier Tibetan relation to China.

Over the last fifty years that relation has continued to be complex. Tibet is termed by China an integral part of its territory, yet has been recognized since 1965 as an autonomous region. Despite some legal provisions, signs of autonomy are not much evident. The Chinese military has retained a compelling presence in Tibet, and the nature of single-party rule in China precludes autonomy in any important areas of political life.

THE PEOPLE'S REPUBLIC

But aggressive forms of policy enforcement are only one part of the Chinese story in contemporary Tibet. There were periods when the Chinese and some Tibetan supporters tried to eliminate traditional culture and society; these are associated nowadays with the Cultural Revolution, a mass movement inspired by Mao initially to unseat lesser party leaders in 1966. It shook most of China for the following ten years (although it was confined to certain areas, and not allowed in border areas), but in Tibet and Inner Mongolia it represented an attack not only on inequality but also on any expression of identity that was not Chinese. From the time when Londoners were raving about the Beatles and Americans were sending men to the moon until the arrival of the Sony Walkman and the Apple II computer, Tibetan clothes and customs were being outlawed, cultural artifacts, temples, and non-Marxist books were being destroyed, religion was forbidden, and those with social status were pilloried in public rallies. Many committed suicide, thousands were imprisoned, and others were persecuted to death.

In 1978, those nationwide attempts to eradicate culture and tradition were recognized by the Chinese leadership as an error of policy and replaced by "liberalization and the open door." That admission referred to "the ten bad years" from 1966 and did not cover earlier campaigns, such as the antirightist movement of 1957–58 or the reforms of the early 1960s. In central Tibet, for example, all but 70 of the 2,500 monasteries had been closed at least three years before the Cultural Revolution began. But the retraction initiated a new era that was not primarily coercive. In the early 1950s, Mao had allowed the Dalai Lama and his government to continue their administrative, religious, and social practices, albeit under Chinese oversight and with significant restrictions, and in the early 1980s, that policy was restored. Many Tibetan religious and traditional customs were allowed again. A significant number of Tibetans were allowed to take up positions of some social status, to obtain education in universities, to study Tibetan culture, to travel abroad, and even, until 1985, to travel to India to meet the Dalai Lama. Tourism was permitted, and the Tibetan language was encouraged in primary schools. Publications in Tibetan boomed, monasteries reopened, and foreign films were shown on television.

The return to a concessional approach and the results of modern technology were widely welcomed in Tibet. But within eight years, Beijing's attempt at concessional rule saw mass protests on the streets of Lhasa calling for the Chinese to leave Tibet, mirroring the events of 1959 when, also after eight years of concessions, an armed uprising had led 80,000 Tibetans to flee with the Dalai Lama to India. Hundreds, if not thousands, of those who remained in 1959 are thought to have been imprisoned for 20 years, if they survived that long, until Deng Xiaoping returned to power in 1978 and reversed many of his predecessors' policies. In 1987 Beijing's second effort at a more moderate form of domination was also reversed as soon as it encountered popular unrest, and it is the reaction of the authorities to that movement that forms the background to this book.

On September 27 that year, a group of 21 monks and half a dozen laypeople staged a small demonstration outside the offices of the local government in Lhasa. They were driven by ideas of democracy, freedom, and Tibetan nationhood. It was a small and peaceful affair, but all were arrested and sent to prison. It was the first protest to have occurred openly in Tibet since foreign tourists had been allowed into the area about six years earlier. Initially some Western commentators endorsed the Chinese claim that the protest had been fomented by exiles, but the cause lay more likely in a campaign of vilification against the Dalai Lama that had been set in motion by local officials just previously, and in a mass sentencing rally held in the Lhasa sports stadium earlier that week. Some 14,000 locals had been required to watch a group of Tibetans being sentenced to death for offenses that seemed unclear, and many saw the executions as official revenge for a visit by the exiled leader to Washington earlier that month. The eras of "soft" rule had always included significant restrictions, but the 1980s concessions may by then have appeared without substance to those who lived under them.

Four days later, on October 1, 1987, about 30 monks staged a protest in the Barkor, the alleyway that runs around the Jokhang, the main temple in Tibet, in the heart of the city of Lhasa. They protested the arrests of four days earlier but were severely beaten by police in full view of the public. About 2,000 Tibetans then besieged the local police station to demand the release of the monks detained inside. Eventually they set fire to the door of the station to enable those prisoners to escape. When the authorities opened fire on the crowd, around ten people were shot dead, including children, with several times that number wounded. Over the next three years there were three more protests in Lhasa involving thousands of participants, with perhaps 75 or more deaths from police gunfire, and some 3,000 arrests. Extreme forms of torture were regularly used on detainees throughout this period.

About 200 smaller demonstrations took place in Lhasa and many other towns and villages of Tibet in the following nine years, often involving less than a dozen people, always ending in the arrests of any participants who could be caught. Those arrested for such offenses, for putting up pro-independence posters, or for possessing books or cassette tapes obtained from the exiles in India were sentenced on average to six to seven years' imprisonment.

By 1993, security policy had changed. The funding and power of China's State Security Bureau were increased, and control of information flow, in both directions, was made its main priority. On the streets of Lhasa, police techniques moved from what the authorities described as "passive" to "active": instead of shooting or arresting demonstrators, police aimed to capture them before incidents began through the improved use of informants, or within seconds of an incident beginning through plainclothes snatch squads positioned around the city center. In any case, the certainty of years in prison became effective as a deterrent, and, increasingly, discontented Tibetans fled into exile rather than remain to express dissent. Protests continued to occur all over the Tibetan-inhabited areas from time to time, and people disappeared into prisons for unknown offenses, usually related to having some forbidden book or photograph from India, printing a dissident leaflet, or planning a minor street protest. But the number of prisoners became far fewer and news about such events became infrequent, and more dangerous for Tibetans who wanted to communicate it.

There was a bigger change under way in Lhasa. Before 1987 the Chinese authorities had begun to retract some of the concessions offered in the early 1980s, but it took much of the next decade for them to be reversed without explosive consequences. Selected sectors of the Tibetan population, such as monks and nuns, government employees, those returning from illegal studies in India, and sometimes scholars trained in traditional culture, were targeted for more rigorous controls. The leadership combined this with a new policy that seemed an unlikely choice for socialists: taking advantage of a movement initiated by Deng Xiaoping in southern China in 1992, the apparatchiks in Tibet turned to the market system to accelerate development and "stability."

The new policy aimed to integrate the local economy rapidly with that of inland China, and to stem dissent by increasing infrastructural expansion, urban wealth, and consumer satisfaction. The policy depended, as before, on central government subsidies but included encouraging Chinese migrants to open private shops and businesses in Tibet in the name of "deepening reform." This led to a rapid increase in the availability of consumer goods in Tibetan towns, accelerated construction, a surge in Chinese migration into urban areas, and a GDP increase of around 12 percent per year.

Contemporary Lhasa offers ample facilities for those who can afford them, and a newly enriched Tibetan middle class receives inflated salaries in government positions. The growth is mainly urban, and development in the rural areas is falling farther and farther behind the towns. Political arrests still take place but are unlikely to be known about by others. Access to computers is available everywhere in the urban areas, although an identity card is required to use the Internet. The educated elite has less and less command of written Tibetan, especially if they come from the eastern areas. The most able of them have spent their teenage years in schools in inland China, and all education in Tibet for those above the age of 13 is conducted in Chinese. Not all these changes are unwelcome, and some might have come anyway through global pressures and modernization, irrespective of Beijing's policies, but many are distinctly problematic amid a crisis of culture and identity.

Religion, the Tibetan language, and tradition are increasingly associated with the countryside, the poor, the "uneducated," and the elderly, who throng the remaining monasteries and temples. Controls are not usually visible, as in most societies. Those who work in government bodies and those who study in schools know that they are not supposed to visit a monastery or practice any form of religion, if they are Tibetan and the religion is Buddhism. But the casual observer will not notice their absence from religious sites, and is unlikely to be told about it.

From the mid–1990s, the culture once reviled as feudal and barbaric became a tourist attraction for wealthier Chinese, with nearly a million a year visiting Tibet to enjoy its exotic architecture, customs, and religious traditions. By the end of the century they outnumbered Western tourists by ten to one. At about the same time, much of the old city of Lhasa was torn down to make way for new developments, and in 1999, Beijing announced the construction of a railway linking Lhasa directly to inland China. Air-conditioned passenger trains are scheduled to begin regular service in 2006. Officials, it is said, expect the population of the city to double once the trains arrive.

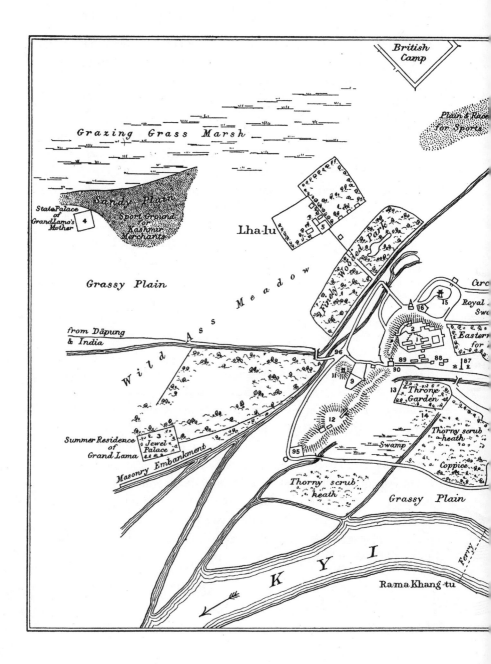

British
Camp

Plain & Race
for Sports

Grazing Grass Marsh

Sandy Plain
State Palace
of
Grand Lama's Mother
Sport Ground
of
Kashmir
Merchants

Lha-lu

5

Finely Wooded Park

Grassy Plain

Circ

15

Royal
Swo

16

Wild Ass Meadow

from Dāpung
& India

2

Eastern
for

96

89   88

87

90

11

9

13   Throne
Garden

12

14

Summer Residence
of
Grand Lama

3
Jewel
Palace

95

Swamp

Thorny scrub
-heath

Coppice

Masonry Embankment

Thorny scrub
heath

Grassy Plain

K   Y   I

Ferry

Rama Khang-tu

Plan of

LHASA

by

L.A.WADDELL´, Lᵗ COLONEL, I.M.S..

Scale of Miles

REFERENCES TO
LIEUT.-COLONEL L. A. WADDELL'S
PLAN OF LHASA.

1. The Great Cathedral, the true "*Lhasa*" or "Place of the Gods."
2. Grand Lama's Palace on Potala Hill.
3.   Do.   Summer Palace (*Norbu Ling*).
4.   Do.   Mother's Palace, for Receptions.
5.   Do.   Parents' Palace, or Paradise (*Lha-lu*).
6. Ex-Prime Minister Yutok's House.
7. Residence of the deposed King-Regent (*gyal-po*).
8.   Do.   Ex-Regent of *Tso-mo-ling*.
9.   Do.   Do.   of *Kun-de-ling*.
10. Chinese Residency of the Ambans.
11. Ba - mo (*Bong - ba*) Hill, surmounted by Chinese temple to Kesar.
12. Chag-ga or Chag-pa Hill, surmounted by Temple of Medicine.
13. Throne Garden, with a stone or brick seat for Grand Lama.
14. A heath, called the "Centre Snake-waiting," alleged to have been visited by Buddha Sakya Muni.
15. A Snake-Dragon Temple, surrounded by a moat, and connected by a lock with marsh to the east.
16. Elephant stable of Dalai Lama.
17. Camping Ground for troops going to the Race-course and Sports in first month of year.
18. Ra-mo-che Temple, alleged to be erected by the Chinese Princess Konjo or Tara (*Dol-tang*) in seventh century A.D.
19. Upper School of Mysticism.
20. Temple of the Buddha of Boundless Life.
21. *Kang-da K'hang Sar*, Palace of former lay "Kings."
22. Residence of the late deposed Regent Re-ting, a Lama of Se-ra, who died in banishment to China, about 1860. Now used as an Academy.
23. Assembly Hall of Turki merchants.
24. "Nam-de-le" cross-roads.
25. Residence of Dowager Mother of (previous) Grand Lama.
26. Cháng lo-chen.
27. Chinese Restaurant.
28. Tibetan Restaurant.
29. Jail.
30. Chinese torture-chamber.
31. Pottery Market.
32. Chinese *Gya-bum-kang chorten*, and by its side a temple erected 1891.
33. Lower School of Mysticism and Printing-house.
34. Muru Monastery.
35. Residence of the General (*Dah - pon*) who visited Darjeeling in 1892 (Nga- pŏ-sa).
36. Guard-house
37. Tannery.
38. *Phun-kang chorten.*
39. Oracle of Darboling.
40. Saddlery and Harness Bazaar from Eastern Tibet.
41. Salutation Point (as here the Pilgrims by the Circular Road catch a glimpse of the Grand Lama's Palace of Pota-la, which they salute).
42. Chinese "Valley" (*Gya-mo-rong*).
43. Grass Market.
44. Nuns' Restaurant.
45. Chinese Drug Shop.
46. Eating House.
47. Inner Chinese Meat Market with double row of stalls entered through Chinese arch.
48. Shops of Newars from Nepal.
49. Rice Market and large Prayer Flag.
50. Mohamedan Chinese Eating House.
51. Bhotanese and Chumbi Shops.
52. Summary Magistrates' Court for Disputes.
53. *Su-khang.*
54. *Sur-gyar-khang.*
55. Large Prayer Flag, "the Eastern Mountain."
56. Chinese Eating House.
57. Bankye-Shag (*Phala*) Palace.
58. Karmashar Oracle.
59. Horse Market.
60. Chinese Military Paymaster.
61. Slaughter House.
62. Gye-ton Jong-pŏn.
63. House of Kashmiri Magistrate for Mahomedan Disputes.
64. *Rab-sal.*
65. *Kun-sang-tse.*
66. Shata Palace.
67. The Lama-Defender of Religion.
68. Shata-ling.
69. Nepalese Consul's Summer House.
70. *Sam-dub* Palace.
71. Old Palace.
72. *Kah-shag.*
73. *Gah-ru shar.*
74. Square of *Song-cho ra* where Thanksgiving is held in first month and where Whipping is inflicted for thieving, etc.
75. Meat and Leather Market.
76. Rag-ga-Shag.
77. Edict Pillar.
78. White Tara's Shrine.
79. Dancing Hall.
80. Lodging House for Tashilhumpo people.
81. Mi-sad Bridge and Chinese Arch.
82. Fairy spring of Chinese princess.
83. Triad Chaitya, *chorten.*
84. Turquoise-tiled bridge (*Yutok sampa*).
85. Summer Garden for Ministers and Civil Officers.
86.   Do.   for Lamas.
87. Edict pillar.
88. Bazaar and Foundry.
89. Grand Lama's Stable.
90. Gateway of *Pargo-kaling.*
91. Temple of the three Lords.
92. Council Chamber.
93. Nepalese Consulate.
94. Four-doored *chorten.*
95. Gallery of Rock Paintings on Medical College Hill.
96. Beggar's Horn Huts.

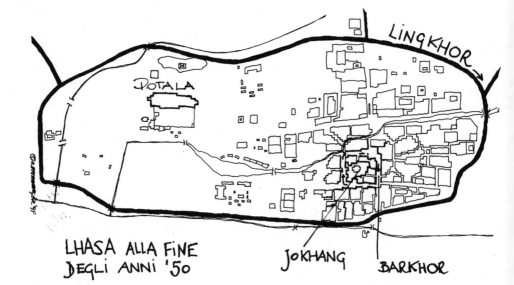

LINGKHOR

POTALA

LHASA ALLA FINE
DEGLI ANNI '50

JOKHANG

BARKHOR

A NOTE ON TERMINOLOGY

In this book I have taken some liberties with the uses and spellings of Tibetan words. There is no standard for romanizing Tibetan words phonetically, and I have tried to spell them in ways that standard English speakers will find manageable, without straying too far from the Tibetan.

More complex issues arise with political terms like "Tibet," which the Chinese authorities have used since 1965 to mean the Tibet Autonomous Region, or the TAR. This is more or less equivalent to the central and western part of the Tibetan plateau, which was the approximate area ruled by the Dalai Lama's government in the late 1940s. Others use "Tibet" to describe the whole plateau, including the eastern and northeastern areas of Kham and Amdo, where more than half of the Tibetan people live, mainly in "Tibetan autonomous prefectures." I have used the term loosely here, but not in order to make any political point. When speaking about administration or policies after 1950, I use "Tibet" generally in the former, narrower sense, since policies in the TAR are different from those in the other Tibetan areas.

I have sometimes used terms that the Chinese authorities regard as contentious, such as "country," "state," and "nation," for Tibet, because at many times it was one or all of these, though not necessarily in the modern sense. When I use the terms "invasion" and "colonial" for the events of 1910 and 1950 and their aftermaths, it is not designed to antagonize the Chinese government, whose intellectual positions are sometimes more worthy of serious attention than is usually acknowledged, but because those events are and were perceived in that way by many people in Tibet.

The notes are offered to indicate my debts to the scholarly literature that exists on many issues raised in the book. I have not attempted to supply references for every citation or remark.

Specific details of personal encounters in Tibet have been altered in order to protect the individuals involved. No one described in these encounters is now traceable or still in Tibet.

པ་དུར་ཅུ་རྡུ་ལམས་ག་ཤེར་པ་ཤེ་མར་དང་དེ།　ཆེ་ར་གུ་ན་རྡུ་ལ་སུ་མེ་ཚོ་ལ་ཁུལ།

མར་ཅི་དེ་ཀི་ཤེ་ད་ར་པར་ཤེ་མས།　ཇེ་ཡ་ཚོ་ག་ཡ་མ།

ག་ཡོ་ག་སྐུ་རེ་ག་སྒྲུ་རོ།　ག་ཡ་མ། ཁ་ད་ཀྱེ་ན།

ད་དར་ཡ་གྱུར།　ཐ་ཡེ་ཀྱི་བ་ཆུ་གས།

ར་དག་ག་ཤ་ཡོ་བྱུར་རོ།　ཅེ་དོ་ག་ད་ཆོ་ན།

པ། ཅེ་ལ་ཡོ་ངོ་ར་དུ་ར་མ་མུ་ད་དོག།　ཧྲུ་ད་པ་བྱུན་ག་པ་ཉོ་རྒྱལ།

ACKNOWLEDGMENTS

This book began in 1998 at the insistence of Katia Bouffetrille and Charles Ramble, who asked me to write a piece for their collected volume, *Tibétains*, which was published in French by *Autrement* that year. A second, longer version was published in Italian in 1999 by CDA, thanks to the extraordinary energies of Maria-Antonia Sironi and her remarkable family. Most of chapter 8 exists due to the generosity and charm of Kim Morris and James O'Reilly, for whom it was first written. The English-language version has been rewritten, updated, and expanded, and exists thanks to the professionalism, patience, and insight of my editor, Anne Routon, and manuscript editor, Leslie Kriesel, at Columbia University Press in New York, together with the support of Michael Dwyer of C. Hurst & Co. in London. I am especially grateful to Hildegard Diemberger at Cambridge, Melvyn Goldstein at Case Western Reserve University, and Charles Ramble at Oxford, as always, for their invaluable criticisms and advice, and to the helpful suggestions of an anonymous reviewer. Karen Diemberger showed endless sensitivity and understanding in preparing the illustrations.

I owe debts that cannot be repaid for the insights, tolerance, brilliance, and advice of many people who gave help and guidance throughout this period of travel and writing, including Ron Schwartz, Ravina

Aggarwal, Isabel Hilton, Matthew Akester, Frances Howland, Gendun Rinchen, Luca and Camilla Corona, Françoise Pommaret, Tsering Yang-kyi, Phuni Meston, and Daniel Alberman. I especially want to thank Lhamo and Tsamchoe, and to mention the pioneering work done by Tsering Shakya in his writings, as well as to thank him for all his encouragement and help over the years. Special tribute and admiration are due for the extraordinary work that Andre Alexander, Pimpim De Azevedo, Lharitso, and others have done with the Tibet Heritage Fund. No less can be said for the exceptional work of Francesca van Holthoon, Marion Jaffret, Kathy Rogers, Jan Willem, Kate Saunders, Palden Gyal, Jamyang Choegyal, Torty Conner, Clare Wilshaw, Katrina Edwards, Liu Hong, Sarah Cooke, and the many others who worked so hard and with such brilliance. Thanks also to Eileen and Gonkar for their support. Jane Woolley gave me constant encouragement and support in this project, and Dinah Kung helped enormously for no reason except generosity of spirit, while Nancy Li, Philip Baker, Susan Whitfield, and Nicolas Becquelin always took time to make the rest of us laugh.

Guy Dinmore, Jasper Becker, Simon Long, Tim Luard, Angela Knox, Sophia Woodman, John Gittings, Andy Higgins, Jonathan Mirsky, and many others shared unsparingly their inspiring knowledge and expertise in their field, and I learned more than I can say. Later I had the extraordinary good fortune of learning from luminaries like Gene Smith, Alak Zenkar, Heather Stoddard, Samten Karmay, Per Kvaerne, Ernst Steinkellner, David Germano, Dawa Norbu, Elliot Sperling, Amy Heller, Pema Bhum, Lauran Hartley, and others. I am sure in Tibetan there is some suitable phrase to describe these people and their fellow scholars, something like a shining galaxy of Tibet scholars brightening the sky while I, the lowly yak, chew grass.

A special word of appreciation is due to those who worked so hard in the late 1980s and afterward to try to make something valuable come out of our chance encounters. Among them are Julie Brittain, Steve Lehman, Christa Mairitsch, Barbara Guenther Seggl, Althea Maddrell, Rupert Wolfe Murray, Malachy Duffy, Christa Meindersma, Anders Andersen, Jane Peek, Gabi Schich, Terry Wray, Richie Boele, John Ackerly, Nick Howen, and later, Chope Paljor Tsering and Ngawang Rabgyal, to name only a few. Suzette Cooke, Steve Marshall, and many others later on did especially impressive work.

I want to thank also Wangchuk Tsering, Mrs. Kelsang Takla, Phuntsog Wangyal, Lodi Gyari, Tashi Wangdu, Tenzin Gyeche, Lobsang Nyandak, and their colleagues for their support and forbearance with all my questions and annoyances, for which I am more grateful than I can say.

As in all books that touch upon political realities in places like Tibet, there are many people to whom I owe a great debt for their help and tolerance, but who have to remain unnamed. I want to pay special tribute to them, especially those who worked with extraordinary skill, courage, and attention to detail, whom I know as TK, Queen, Princess, Fever, Lu, Charl, Fs, Polly, Gondola, Shoulder, Raymon, Ru, String, Gin, Cookie, and Pistachio. Without them, my efforts would have been of little value and of dubious quality. I hope somehow it has helped.

I owe special thanks to Jim Seymour, Andy Nathan, and John Dolfin for getting me to New York; to Madeleine Zelin, Robert Thurman, Carol Gluck, and Lu Xiaobo for their support and hospitality; and to Waichi Ho, Elizabeth Dimissie, Susan Greenfield, Janice Duffin, Tenzin Norbu, Mickey Spiegel, Jeanne Marie Gilbert, Elise Frick, and Katie Grover for putting up with me and helping me in so many ways once I got there. Thanks too to Tracy Zhang, Erin Burke, Anabella Pitkin, Zoran Lazovic, Julia Famularo, Dana Sommers, Anna Stirr, and Tina Harris for all their help.

I owe much gratitude to Barbara, Celia, Colin, Hannah, and Loz for all those years, and to my late father and Helen, for all they taught me; I remember them with love and wish I had listened more carefully. I want to express my special admiration and esteem to RY and my deep thanks to YQ, for providing hope.

While the views expressed here remain mine alone, it has been a privilege to collaborate with such people, and it is sad that not all can be thanked by name.

Research for this book was carried out with the generous assistance of the Weatherhead East Asian Institute of Columbia University, the Österreichischen Fonds zur Förderung der wissenchaftlichen Forschung, and an anonymous donor who helped me to get back to Lhasa.

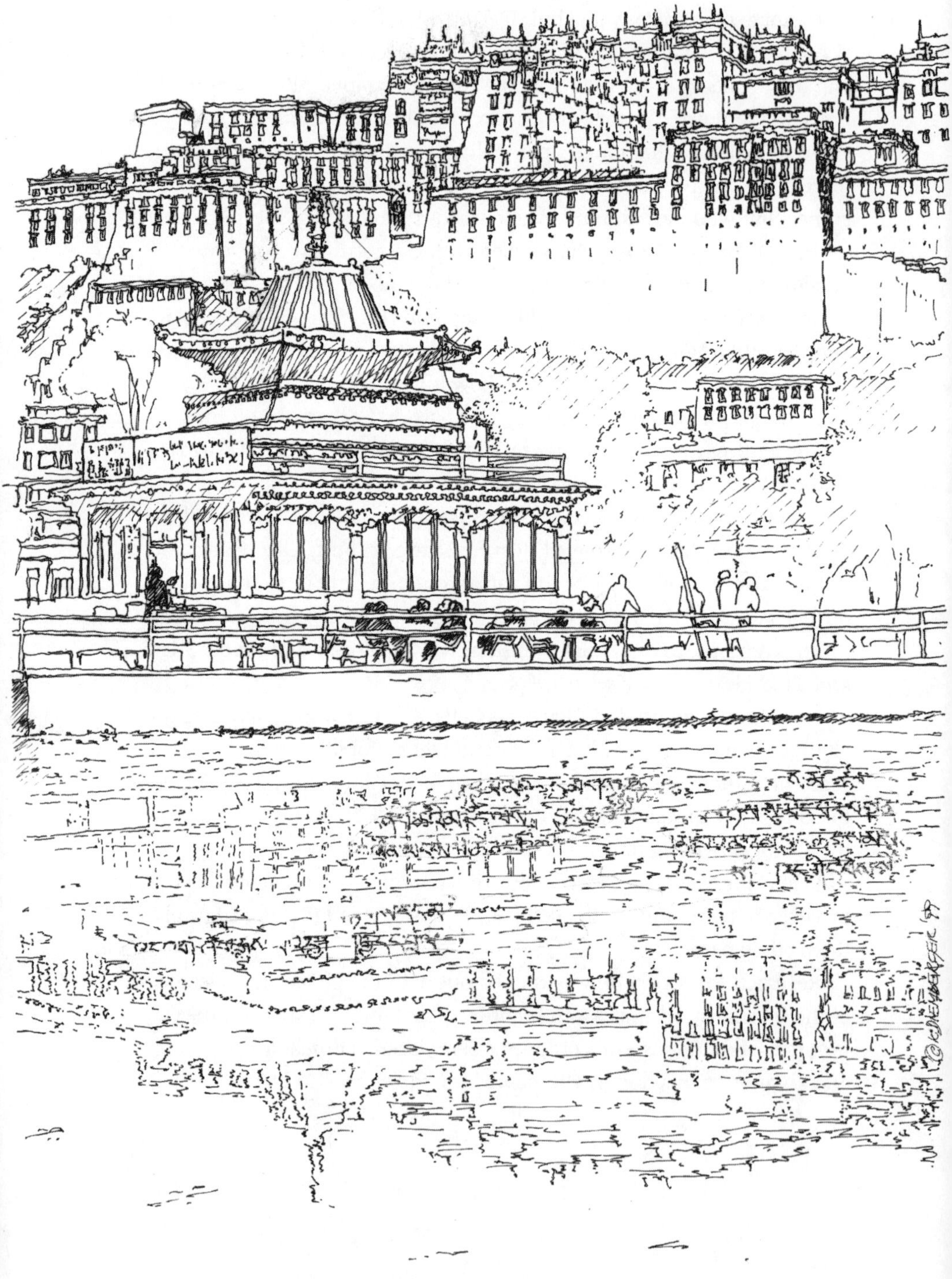

From the peak of the Red Hill, the Potala Palace still looks down upon the city 300 feet below, and the Jokhang temple is still, for pilgrims, the destination of their journeys and the heart of the city, perhaps of their life aspirations. Drepung, Sera, and Ganden, the three great monasteries whose names mean the Grove of Wild Roses, the Heap of Rice, and the Place of Bliss, stand like sentinels in a giant circle on the mountain slopes around or beyond the city. On the western outskirts, white scarves have been left by devotees at the gates of the Norbulingka, as though the Dalai Lama is about to resume his residence at the Summer Palace. And the Barkor, the ring of alleyways along which the pilgrims walk in their endless circumambulations of the Jokhang, is crowded with prostrators, pilgrims, hawkers, and businessmen, much as it has been for 500 or perhaps 1,000 years.

But other things have changed since the Chinese arrived five decades ago. Lhasa today is a city of some 200,000 people, more than six times the number in 1950, and the city now sprawls across an area some 20 times greater than the one square mile it covered during the centuries before Mao's Peaceful Liberation. The highest building is no longer the Ramoche temple or the Jokhang, but the 13-story Public Security Building on the road to Sera monastery; when the new hotel is completed on the former picnic site on Thieves' Island, even that edifice may be dwarfed. These buildings have been deposited by two great waves that during the past quarter century have swept over the city and transformed its history, perhaps faster than any other process since the fifteenth century. One of those waves is the Chinese state; the other is modernity.

If we wish to read the text that is formed by the streets and stones of this modern Lhasa, we must turn first to history, and then to other forms of story. In principle our task should not be too difficult: Lhasa is small for a city of such fame, its population one fiftieth that of London or Beijing. And it belongs to an older world, one that is generally seen by outsiders in the way we see many ancient things: as unitary, undivided, and homogeneous. Compared to other capitals of such repute, Lhasa is hardly even the size of a county town. It should therefore be relatively easy to describe.

THE UNITARY VIEW

 Many of the descriptions of Lhasa offered to foreign readers hzave demanded little intellectual effort for their comprehension. The literature of exiled Tibetans, those who fled to India and elsewhere after the Chinese crushed the uprising of 1959, for example, speaks of a world that was, in their description, focused on the twin certainties of religion and tradition. Where other things are mentioned, it is in simple terms. "Lhasa is known all over Tibet for its easygoing and carefree way of life," wrote the noblewoman Dorje Yuthok in her autobiography, recalling the city as it had been in the 1940s. "Very sympathetic, honest, cheerful, and satisfied with their lot," said W. T. Shakabpa, for twenty years a *tsipön* or finance minister of Tibet, about his fellow countrymen, whom he described as "loyal, open, gentle, and kind." Where complexity is spoken of in such accounts, it is to be found in the elaboration of detail, not in the suggestion of ambiguity or contradiction. In Lady Yuthok's account of Lhasa before 1959, three kinds of event stand out: religious festivals, picnics, and parties. The latter were not insignificant occasions, at least among the elite: "Usually the parties lasted for seven days, but at the end if food still remained they would sometimes extend the party a few more days," she recalled of the time before 1959 when

the Chinese authorities took over the direct running of Tibet's administration, of which her brother had been one of the last *kalöns* or cabinet
ministers. Less elaborate "but also festive" food was given to the servants, she adds, concluding that "all Tibetans enjoyed a slow pace and
had a happy outlook on life."

In these accounts Lhasa became a place about which generalizations
could thus be made with relative ease. Such statements, relying on what
could be called the device of collective sentiment, are frequent in writing
of this kind, yielding depictions of Tibetans as a happy people and Lhasa
as a peaceful city where people wore gaily colored clothes, where everyone was religious, and where the citizens were generous and kind. The
exiles' use of this device represents not naïveté or a desire to mislead,
but a natural flattening of memory, an understandable form of evocation by people forced to abandon their homeland, and a counter to over-
stated, opposing claims by those who had usurped their positions and
ridiculed their legacy; it is no coincidence that this genre emerged at the
time that Western writings were replete with the simplifications of Cold
War rhetoric. But its principal significance is not its content but its context: the device appeared in exile writings in English, those intended for
foreigners. In the minds of the authors, for whom the multiplicity of
lived experience would have been self-evident, beautification offered a
rhetorical strategy to explain something highly complex to those who
had neither time nor inclination to listen to more layered narratives.

Such a choice was rooted in historical experience. Tibetans had already known for some decades that the self-ethnographic project, the
effort to describe oneself to others, was restricted by the emotional capacity of the audience, and that Westerners, at least in Tibet's case, had
no appetite for complexity. "I suppose our distant country holds little of
interest for your public except for what of the strange can be written
about it," wrote Rinchen Lhamo after her arrival in London in the 1920s
as the wife of a British diplomat she had met in western China. "The
most absurd and the most scandalous things are said about us, and
there is no one to contradict them," she observed. Her literary boldness
must have been predicated on the knowledge that she had a largely independent country to return to if she wished: nationalist assertion may
seem imaginary to philosophers, but it rests on practical considerations.
When the exiled aristocrats began to tell their stories to foreign intermediaries fifty or so years later, they were in no position to hector their

prospective listeners. It is anyway unlikely that the Westerners who were their scribes would have sought out or recorded the public expression of critical sentiments, if indeed they had been willing to hear or understand them, since they did not speak Tibetan and relied upon translators. So it is not surprising that these texts offer outsiders a unitary view of Tibetan life, of the kind one might expect when spoken to concerning that of which one patently knows little.

We do not have to be deconstructionists to doubt descriptions of this kind. By their nature they are dubious, impossible to verify and uncertain in meaning. Does a "happy, peaceful" people, for example, mean a people who never cry or fight, or a people who rage and weep sometimes but not for more than, say, twenty minutes a day? And how would anyone, even the enlightened, know whether some of these people somewhere cried in secret, or what percentage smiled out of custom or from fear?

The answer is, of course, that such remarks are intended not as serious description, but as a gentle form of persuasive education. Such an explanation, however, becomes insufficient when the device of describing a city's population as happy, or as having any particular emotion, is used by foreigners or applied to contemporary times; shorn of a nostalgic hue, it acquires a problematic tone. "They are enthusiastic and open-minded and good at singing and dancing," says an official Chinese handbook of the Tibetan people. The remark, a staple of modern Chinese accounts of their non-Chinese nationalities, sounds condescending when uttered by an outsider and lacks the detail essential for credibility. It is not in fact much less meaningful than generalizations made by deposed aristocrats, but it belongs to a different discourse universe, in which power, not the loss of it, is idealized. It hints at not a world that is being reduced rhetorically, but one in which the experience of the Other seems to have been, for want of a better word, flat. This may not be the case, but it is as if for Chinese officials and their cohort the encounter with Tibet was one-dimensional and principally visual.

Indeed, the visual has seemed primary for the most recent Chinese rulers of Tibet. For fifty years after their arrival there, propaganda experts in China believed that publishing the seen impressions of foreign visitors to that region was the key to persuading the world of the rightness of their rule. In 1997, for example, officials in Beijing reported that a Mexican senator had declared, after five days in the city as a guest of the government, that "people in Tibet are happy and keeping pace with modern times." China's official news agency, in publishing his remark, perhaps sensing a need to explain how the senator had reached this conclusion, added that "happy smiles on their faces served as a true indication of their happy lives." The evidence was there to be seen, this seems to say, as if the city streets and the faces of the citizens were transparent: they could be read by foreigners like the pages of an open picture book.

In a pile of rags in the corner of the alcove an elderly woman lay curled up, ill, emaciated, haggard, close to death. Her final home, which for many days had probably been unvisited, was invaded by a horde of rushing feet, of people standing with their backs to her, peering out toward the square. She sobbed. Perhaps it was the shock of change and the commotion.

I gave her a strip of dried apricot I had bought in Chengdu four weeks earlier; dried apricot was meant to be a cure for altitude sickness. Maybe it would work for whatever was making her cry.

I don't remember now if she ate it, I only remember that she cried and no one around us noticed. They were busy passing out the paving stones that had been stacked within the courtyard of the Jokhang for some new construction there. The broken slabs were now flying in parabolas above the crowd, toward the soldiers fleeing from the square.

The western frontage of the Jokhang is long, white, and interrupted at its center by the giant porch that leads to the great door of the temple. Before this doorway pilgrims perform prostrations for hour after hour, facing the statue of the Buddha unseen within the building. But some 50 yards to the right as you face the great entrance to the temple, just before you reach the old debating courtyard of the Sungchöra on the southern side of the complex, there is a second, smaller doorway set into the front wall of the temple. That was where I had taken shelter, that morning of October 1.

I had not noticed that doorway before, but I had only been in Lhasa for four days. For the first two of these I had felt too nauseated from the altitude to move, and on the third day I had been to visit the Potala. The fourth day, it was nine in the morning and it was my day to visit the Jokhang. That is why I was there. That was why the new plaza had been built, so that we tourists could gaze at the 1,400-year-old temple with an uninterrupted view. There had been 47,000 foreign tourists that year in Lhasa, I had read somewhere, and the opening up of the new square meant that we could sit on the veranda of the Barkor cafe and gaze uninterruptedly at the Jokhang through the lenses of our cameras.

47,000 *was the highest the number of visitors had ever been for a single year, or would be for ten years afterward. I liked the view of the Jokhang from the square. I did not know what had been cleared away to give us that view. I was there to look at the temple, not at what had been there before. But that was before nine o'clock on October 1.*

I moved quickly toward the smaller door; it seemed safer there. It is set in an alcove some 15 or 20 feet deep within the great outer walls of the temple. It is called the Shingra Door, because in the old days at the time of the Monlam festival the poor could go there to receive alms of wood from the monks, and that's what shingra *means—place of wood. Of course I didn't know that then, and anyway that day, when I took shelter in the doorway, the monks were passing out stones, not wood. It was 1987, the year of the Fire Hare. It was the year the monks passed out stones, not wood.*

I couldn't see the monks inside; only their bare arms appeared through the crack in the door as they passed the broken pieces of paving stone to the women in the alcove. They gathered the debris in their striped aprons—they must have been married, since the aprons are meant to be a sign of matrimony, and they were of a certain age, no doubt with children already in their teens. Without speaking, the women, holding their aprons, sagging with the weight of rocks, by the corners, slipped quietly out of the alcove into the crowd gathered beside the Sungchöra, opposite the police station.

In front of us, not sheltering but within the crowd itself, I could see another woman sobbing. She was neither young nor emaciated, and she was not passing out stones to be hurled at the troops. She simply stood and watched and cried.

This was really strange. This I really could not understand. The soldiers were fleeing across the square in disarray, an abandoned rifle was being smashed by the children in front of the crowd, and the snatch squads had given up attempts to grab demonstrators from the throng. So this woman's tears could not be the result of grief. There was no reason for her to cry. She was witnessing an epic moment, when the police had been routed without loss and when, for the first time in 30 years, the Barkor Square and the streets of Lhasa had been reclaimed by their inhabitants. Her tears could only have been tears of relief or happiness.

Literary effusions about the happiness of Tibetans before the Chinese invasion do not always cohere with the stories in which they appear: the texts, we could say, communicate more meanings than their authors deign to speak of. Even the autobiography of the present Dalai Lama, the

fourteenth of his line, sometimes tells of incidents that, although small, jar with the collective myth: the sweepers at the main temple are caught stealing the golden offering bowls from his private rooms, the monks in the main temple fight among themselves when they are meant to be praying, and many of the officials he meets are irritable or bad-tempered. Had he wished, he could have told worse stories of monkish misbehavior. In 1921, for example, the monks of Loseling, a college in the great monastery of Drepung, the Heap of Rice, had urinated and defecated in the gardens of his predecessor, the Great Thirteenth, because they disapproved of his antipathy to China. At that time, it seems, not even distrust of Beijing or reverence for the Tibetan leader had been collective sentiments.

The exiled aristocrats also concede more in the minutiae of their texts than their generalizations admit. Jamyang Sakya, another lady of the highest social standing, describes in her memoir the endless fighting in the 1940s between the different branches of her husband's family as they struggled to get control of the Sakya dynasty and its treasures; in these battles, the combatants were not laymen but lamas of the highest rank. Dorje Yuthok mentions the sexual adventures of her husband, onetime governor of Tibet's eastern province of Kham, and his frequent desertion of her for other women, but our own connivance as outsiders in the manufacture of Tibetan myths should not be forgotten: the more salacious parts of her account were removed, it is rumored, by her American amanuensis, who was reportedly more intent than she on preserving an image of a Tibet unblemished by unsavory desire before the dark days of invasion.

But there are more serious issues than philandering or family arguments that undermine the perception of Lhasa as a single story. Let us take three of the most controversial examples: the sacking of Tengyeling, the blinding of Lungshar, and the prison death of Retring. In terms of social conflict or brutality, those episodes scarcely merit mention if compared to the levels of endemic violence and abuse in China and elsewhere at that time, or perhaps even now. But locally they were of importance and must be woven into the tapestry of the city's recollections.

In 1912 the monastery of Tengyeling gave shelter to Chinese troops during the Tibetan government's attempt to wrest back Lhasa from the Chinese army that had seized the city two years earlier—Beijing's response to the punitive invasion by the British earlier that decade. Tengyeling was one of the highest monasteries in the land, and its chief incumbent, Demo *hutuktu*, was one of only eight lamas in central Tibet entitled to serve as a regent in the inevitable minority of a Dalai Lama. It was not its first instance of perfidiousness: twenty years earlier, the attendants of Demo *hutuktu* had conspired to assassinate the thirteenth Dalai Lama, and had sewn evil incantations against him into the boot soles of a sorcerer, a method reputed to intensify the potency of curses. When the Chinese troops had taken Lhasa in 1910 and the Thirteenth had fled to India, the monks of Tengyeling sided with the new rulers, not foreseeing that the fall of the dynasty in Beijing would result in the Chinese troops being ousted from Tibet two years later. For that offense the monastery was stripped of its possessions, and six government officials who had allied with its monks were killed or executed; the Demo was banned from recognition in future incarnations, and many of his monks fled to China.

That same year Charles Bell, the British envoy in Lhasa, capitalized on his encounters with the thirteenth Dalai Lama during his exile in India, the first time any ruler of Tibet had visited a territory ruled by Westerners. Bell persuaded the Dalai Lama to allow four Tibetan youths of noble birth to travel to England to attend the British public school of Rugby, with a Tibetan aristocrat, a senior official by the name of Lungshar, accompanying them as their guardian. The boys returned to Tibet in due course as technicians and engineers to plant what were meant to be, in the eyes of the Dalai Lama and his British advisor respectively, seeds of either progress or British dependency. One of the Rugby graduates later constructed the first electric generator in Lhasa; another worked briefly at making maps. Lungshar, however, returned with no affection for the British at all, an ingratitude they did not forget, and with notions of modernity rather more substantial than the provision of electric light. By 1933 he had founded a group in Lhasa called the *Kyicho Kuntun*—"those who are all united on the side of happiness"—which attracted a hundred or more members and was dedicated to introducing parliamentary democracy, a constitutional monarchy, and a modernized civil service. Not without the tacit approval of the British, Lungshar's enemies persuaded the Tibetan government and the monastic leaders that his tentative efforts at constitutional reform concealed such intentions as a Bolshevik plot to overthrow the regime. He was sentenced to have his eyes gouged out.

The blinding of Lungshar was exceptional, so much so that no one living could be found who knew from experience how to do it. The

Tibetan who ended up with the task had to rely on half-remembered recollections of his predecessors' technique, which was to strap the knuckle bones of a yak into the eye sockets and so tighten the thongs around the head that the eyeballs would pop out. In the event, the technique worked with only one eye; the other had to be carved out with a knife, causing even more than the expected pain to the former official, who was not helped by the fact that the sedatives he had been administered were largely ineffective, so that he remained conscious throughout the process. Defenders of the image of the happy, carefree, preinvasion Tibet point out, not unreasonably, that the clumsiness of the eye gouging shows it to have been an exception; its detractors cite it as proof of a tyrannical regime and an uncivilized culture. But what is important here is not the choice, nor even the brutality, of the punishment. It is the fact that the need for it arose at all. A city that had to punish its political reformers may or may not have been brutal, but it cannot have been totally unified, and it cannot be accurately portrayed in terms of collective sentiment. Neither can its members have been wedded uncritically to the continuance of tradition. The Lungshar episode is significant not for the horror of his experience but because, in a state where there were only 200 or so lay governmental officials of rank, perhaps half as many of the elite were involved, even as late as the 1930s, in the process of designing innovative forms of governance and representation in a conscious process of political reconstruction and improvement.

The civil war that followed Retring's attempt to reclaim the regency in 1947 was more baroque in character. Retring had served as regent until 1941, when he had handed the position over to an older monk of similar rank. Like his fellow *hutuktu*, Demo, fifty years before, he came to regret the loss of power and seems to have allowed his retinue to conspire by various means to assassinate his successor, the regent Taktra. The last attempt was allegedly the dispatching of a primed hand grenade concealed in a parcel marked for the regent's personal attention. According to the official account, only the servant who opened the parcel was injured, and Retring, identified and arrested as the chief conspirator, died of natural causes a few days later in a dungeon in the bowels of the Potala Palace. Unofficial versions of these events say the hand grenade, which was displayed outside the Lhasa courthouse as evidence of the plot, showed no signs of having exploded, and insist that Retring must have been murdered. To be more specific, they allege that he was killed by those intent on avenging the humiliation of Lungshar fifteen years earlier. It is widely believed, without much evidence, that the killer did the deed by binding or beating the lama's testicles until the pain was so excruciating that Retring died.

The Japanese spy-explorer Hisao Kimura was living in Lhasa at the time, disguised as a Mongolian monk, and was himself briefly arrested on suspicion of involvement in the attempted coup. "Most Lhasans just felt that this was a rather foolish ploy in a struggle between rival nobles that would, in the normal run of things, continue behind the scenes without affecting everyday life," he told his biographer some four decades later. Retring must, however, have had wider support than just a group of nobles, because the monks of Sera Je took the opportunity to rise up in revolt and were defeated only after a week of fighting. According to the most recent autobiography of the fourteenth Dalai Lama, who describes having heard the sound of gunfire from his rooms in the Potala as a young boy, a "considerable number" of the Sera monks died in the aftermath of the abortive coup; the actual number was at least 200. "All in all the whole affair was very silly," he adds, another case where the tradition of exile writing for the benefit of foreigners falls short of complexity. There were some 20,000 monks in the capital alone, and the views of monks were never an insignificant factor in political decision making in the state. Kimura points out that the Sera monks, if they had not trusted so much in the power of amulets to deflect bullets, might very well have overthrown the government. Not quite such a silly affair after all, perhaps.

Retring and the Sera monks may not have had a modern ideology to fuel their intrigues, or a mission to improve Tibetan governance such as that attributed to Lungshar, or a moral wish to crusade against the decadence of established hierarchy—Tibetans and historians are still arguing about whether the government under Taktra was even more corrupt and incompetent than it had been under Retring, when it had unquestionably been so. Retring, like Demo one of the highest and in theory most spiritually elevated lamas in the country, appears to have had a simpler motive: he wanted power, and felt betrayed by the successor regent for not having yielded it to him. But this compelled him to seek practical, if, to Westerners, curious alliances, and he had written to the Chinese government for help of a distinctly modern kind, suggesting unsuccessfully that they send airplanes to scatter leaflets threatening to bomb Lhasa if he were opposed.

As for the Sera monks, they distrusted the slight inclinations toward modernization that they detected in such plans as the re-equipping of the Tibetan army, the setting up of schools to teach English, and the sending of aristocrats' children to India for higher education. Modernization, like the British, seemed to represent a threat to their traditions and their authority. Their assessment was by no means uninformed: they were well aware that Western theories of government rejected the paramount place granted to religion in the Tibetan political system, and they certainly knew that Western governments had little hesitation in imposing their views on weaker nations. Neither was their decision to support a partly religious conception of governance merely the unquestioned inheritance of tradition: it was part of a deliberate ideology, the exceptionality of which they took great pride in. When officials of the Tibetan government wrote to Gilbert Murray in the 1920s about his proposal that Tibet apply to join the League of Nations, they gave just such reasons for rejecting his approach.

But what is perhaps most intriguing to the Western observer is that, like Retring, the Sera monks had no qualms about turning for support to China, since it was the one nation they knew to be reliably opposed to Britain. "Better an enemy who is close at hand than a friend who is far," argued the *kalön*, or cabinet minister, Kabshöpa in opposing his more anglophilic colleagues, just as he had earlier denounced Lungshar for his attempts at alien innovation. Kabshöpa's apothegm, rich with the sinuousness of political compromise, evokes the complexities of Tibetan politics more eloquently than most historical texts; so does the sad irony that, fifty years later, his son, seeking refuge from the Chinese occupation, would flee to England. We might think that we can perceive now as errors, through the lens of hindsight, the judgments of Kabshöpa, or that by implication we can recognize what appears to be their converse, the long-standing ardency of Tibetan nationalism. But we would do well to recall the complexities of such events, not least the fact that it was the most conservative of the Lhasan elite who at that time encouraged the Chinese to intervene in the running of their state, and, in some cases, to overthrow it.

The police station was now in flames from where the crowd had torched the door to force entrance to the building. The plainclothesmen lurking in the crowd had long since been kicked and beaten and thrown out, and the monk-demonstrators arrested earlier that day were escaping through the smoke-filled windows. Even the Chinese with the Betacam had been forced by the hail of stones to run away. He was cleverer than the police, young boys who had dropped their guns before they fled. When he ran, he kept hold of his camera and within it the film that would later identify the protestors who at that time rejoiced.

At the far end of the Barkor Square I could see truckloads of troops waiting for orders to advance. There was no attempt by the demonstrators to force the police farther away than the edge of the square; people were busy reveling in the reclaiming of the Sungchöra. It seemed they were dancing on the grave of history, of three decades of submission that they had just buried. It didn't seem to be of concern to them that the dance would shortly end.

Knowing little of the history unfolding before us, we Westerners worried instead about how bad the end was going to be. We could see men in green moving on the flat rooftops behind the police station, beyond the range of stones. It was nearly ten o'clock: an hour had passed, long enough for a decision to be reached in some dank room within the Party offices. Among the Western travelers an arcane debate began. Some said we should mingle with the crowd to deter the police from shooting. I argued that we should watch and witness from the margins, lest we be filmed as evidence of foreign subversives in the crowd.

I had a better reason for preferring the sidelines that I did not confess, and that reason was fear. It was because of this that when the officer in the dark glasses stepped to the front edge of the roof and lifted his right hand slowly toward the crowd, I was standing to one side of his arc of fire.

It had not occurred to me before that you can't see bullets flying through the air. You can know them only from their aftermath, like a virus recognized by the scars left on a face. In the low-walled open square there was little resonance, and the reports sounded not much louder or more distinct than the firecrackers I had heard almost every day since reaching Guangdong on the coast of China three months earlier. The bricks spat out the truth in little spurts of dust as the first rounds nestled into the front wall of the Jokhang, six feet or so above the crowd.

I didn't stop to watch. I ran from the Shingra alcove across the southern Barkor to the doorway of the primary school on the far side of the police station. I don't know why I ran in that direction. As I reached the school wall, I saw the old monk Champa Tenzin from the Jokhang being carried on the

shoulders of the crowd, the hero of the moment for having led the rescue of the
prisoners from the flaming police station.

They placed him on a window ledge beside me for all the crowd to hail
and festoon with greeting scarves. The scarves showered down on him, arcing
through the air above our heads, a sort of slow-motion opposite to the bullets. I
could see the deep-pink patches of flesh, like open lips beaming in celebration,
where the fresh burns had peeled away the skin on his upper arms. He waved
the scarves. People cheered.

Dark Glasses was aiming down now, and people began to fall over: he
was shooting at their feet. Now two others had joined him, with long-bar-
reled guns, and they were less discriminating. Monks were being shot as they
escaped from the station windows and ran toward the crowd. Down a side
street, troops were moving forward. Someone was throwing furniture from the
windows of the school, trying to hit the policemen on the station roof. There
were no longer puffs from the brickwork above our heads; instead, people in the
crowd fell over. Suddenly others began to run. The Chinese had returned.

Behind the power struggles and state intrigues of pre–1950 Lhasa there
were other, less obvious forms of political diversity: the day-to-day dissemination of foreign and of heterodox opinions. In part this was a consequence of technology and its incursions: as the British troops had
made their way to Lhasa in the first years of the century, the telegraph
wire had followed. Even then, news took three hours to reach the invasion force from London, at least when it was still camped not so far
from the Indian border. The telegraph line reached the town of Gyantse,
halfway to Lhasa, within a year of the invasion and in 1921, at Tibetan
request, the British extended it to the capital. In the 1940s the Dalai
Lama had his own telephone, not to mention an American Dodge and
a Baby Austin with the license plate TIBET 1. By 1936, the British diplomat Spencer Chapman was able to report that he could hear in Lhasa
radio reports broadcast from London, and that many wealthy Lhasans,
of whom a significant number were fluent in English, had their own
radio sets.

There was also a measure of internationalism to the city's population
and its connections. The legation of the British was at Dekyi Lingka, and
that of the Nepalese at their residency just to the south of Shatra; the
Bhutanese had a consulate in the Barkor, and there was a consul representing the Ladakhi Muslims who had lived in the city for centuries.

Chinese too were once again allowed to take up residence and to set up a governmental office (and a radio transmitter) in the city after 1935, twenty-three years after their expulsion. Ideas flowed as much through trade as through diplomacy, and probably the most potent source of foreign thought was the hill resort in northeast India to which many traders and aristocrats repaired to procure wealth through commerce: the Indian town of Kalimpong. Like Paris to nineteenth-century Americans or to early Chinese Communists, it was where one went to acquire an education, to see the world, to become *urbane*. Again like Paris, it was a hotbed of radical ideas, where Tibetans from distant Kham and Amdo—the marchlands of eastern Tibet, closer to the influence of both Chinese Nationalists and early Chinese Communists, areas through which the latter had passed on the Long March in 1934–35—gathered to plan revolution, where the great Tibetan *émigré* scholar and radical nationalist Gendun Chöphel had written and studied, and where, later, Tibetan aristocrats would meet to plan guerrilla warfare with the CIA. It was there that children of most aspiring Lhasa families with wealth had been sent to acquire knowledge of English, and it was there that the Christian convert, Tharchin *Babu*, gathered Tibetan intellectuals together for over thirty years to write each week for the *Melong*, the only newspaper in Tibetan. Even the former dancer Tashi Tsering, who in 1964 became the first Tibetan exile in the West to return to Lhasa, had moved there from Chinese-occupied Lhasa in 1957 in his eagerness to acquire modern education and ideas.

But Kalimpong was not the only foreign source of divergent thought, and certainly not the one that would make the most lasting impact on the city. Kimura, the Japanese spy sent in disguise to check, needlessly, if anyone was using Tibetan routes to supply arms to Chiang Kai-shek's forces in Chongqing, recalled that on his return to Lhasa in 1948 he found a small, dissident group of Tibetans who met discreetly to discuss progressive ideas. The group included members of the highest aristocratic families in Lhasa. But unlike the coterie Lungshar had gathered around him some twelve years earlier, the orientation of its leaders was not toward ideas associated with the British in the south, but toward the east. By the 1940s China had already become the source of inspiration for the most energetic modernizers in Tibet.

At the center of this group of Chinese-inspired radicals was *Baba* Phuntsog Wanggyal. Through the good offices of Dorje Yuthok's husband, then residing with a different lover in Chamdo as its governor, the young revolutionary Phuntsog Wanggyal had been able to get permission to travel to Lhasa from his home in Bathang in the Kham area of eastern Tibet, arriving in the capital not long before Kimura. The governor knew of his protégé's progressive inclinations, but by 1943 Phuntsog Wanggyal was able to gain entrance to the Tibetan capital. Later to emerge as the leading Tibetan communist, he would become the main intermediary of the Chinese in their attempt to create an alliance with the Lhasa leadership after the invasion. But at this time he was known simply as a progressive, an intellectual secular radical from the east who had the advantage of fluent Chinese and of a modern education, gained partly from American missionaries in his hometown, partly from the Chinese nationalists who had educated him in Chongqing, and partly—though he may have been discreet about this at the time—from illicit copies of writings by Marx and other Western authors translated into Chinese by early Communists.

At the house of Phuntsog Wanggyal's friends in Lhasa, other Tibetans eager for contact with the outside, Chinese and modern worlds would gather. Among them were Phuntsog Tashi Takla, a childhood friend of the Dalai Lama's elder brother Gyalo Thondup and later a brother-in-law to the Dalai Lama as well as a participant in the 1951 and 1984 negotiations in Beijing. Both Phuntsog Tashi and Gyalo Thondup were from the east, fluent in Chinese, and partly educated by the Chinese Nationalists in pre-Communist days in Nanjing. Changngöpa, one of the more progressive aristocrats, was there too, as was Tomjor Tethong, three of whose sons were later to become ministers in the exile Tibetan government; it was in the Tethong family mansion in Lhasa that the young activists formed a group called the "Tibetan People's Unified Alliance."

Phuntsog Wanggyal already had an introduction to Dorje Yuthok from her estranged husband in Chamdo, and she arranged for him to meet with her brother, *Kalön* Surkhang. The twenty-one-year-old radical told the minister of their plan for reforming Tibetan politics and society, and their intention to stage an armed uprising against the Chinese in the eastern areas, to lead to the whole of the Tibetan plateau becoming a "combined regime." On the first visit, Phuntsog Wanggyal recited a song he had composed to call for the creation of a single Tibetan state— "Rise up, Rise up, Rise up, Tibetan Brothers." He sang it to the tune of "Marching Through Georgia" while his comrade Ngawang Kesang, also weaned by Christian missionaries, accompanied him on the organ. They moved Surkhang to tears, but to no result: the Tibetan government believed that the Japanese would defeat China and save them from the Chinese threat, and so saw no need to support a rebellion.

Among the would-be progressives of Lhasa who gathered in that house in the Barkor, few realized at that time that Phuntsog Wanggyal was a communist, or that the modernization they discussed would come so soon. Neither did they know that it would be not them but two of the aristocrats from that group—Takla and Tethong—who, having fled from their Chinese rulers, would live the rest of their lives in relative freedom. Phuntsog Wanggyal, neither an aristocrat nor an opponent of the Chinese modernists, would remain in Lhasa and, purged in the antirightist campaign of 1958, spend most of the following twenty years in prison.

Before Phuntsog Wanggyal gathered his group around him, two other houses had been centers of Chinese influence. In the eighteenth century the *ambans*—the commissioners sent by the Manchu emperors to represent them in Tibet—had lived in the Tromsikhang, the great mansion on the northern side of the Jokhang, built by the Sixth Dalai Lama and used by the Mongol ruler Lhazang Khan as his Lhasa residence until 1717. In 1751 two of these *ambans* had been killed in their rooms in the Tromsikhang by a Tibetan crowd after one of the commissioners had stabbed the then Chief Minister of Tibet to death. The assassination of the two Manchu officials, which the emperors seem to have failed to avenge at the time, was recorded on six stone tablets embedded in the front wall of the Tromsikhang. In the summer of 1997 most of the building was torn down as part of a wave of architectural transformation that characterized that decade. The stone tablets were taken away, "for reasons of safety," and only the frontage remained.

When Colonel Younghusband and the British Expeditionary Force arrived in Lhasa in 1904, they found that the *ambans*, and with them the center of Chinese influence in Lhasa, had moved to a different building. It was known as the Yamen, and was situated in a compound just within the Lingkor, to the southwest of the main city of Lhasa, in an area later known as Lubu. The British, greatly disconcerted by the discovery that the thirteenth Dalai Lama had fled to Mongolia just prior to their arrival, were desperate to find a person of rank worthy to sign a surrender agreement and to submit the Tibetan government to their demands, and so sought advice from China's representative, who in more propitious circumstances had claimed authority over the Tibetans. It was in the Yamen that Younghusband and the *Amban* Youtai had drunk tea while they planned the formal humiliation of the Tibetans whose soldiers the British officer had recently massacred in battle. The English visitors were struck by the fact that the *amban* offered them Huntley and Palmers biscuits, produced in the town of Reading, just to the west of London; the company still advertises this event as a highlight of its global history. But even the visitors noticed that the fate of the conquered was not dispensed with the same graciousness as the tea. The Imperial Commissioner "presented a never-failing front of sympathy and apparent good-feeling" toward the British, one of them wrote later, adding that Youtai "never made a speech or wrote a letter without referring to the pig-headed stupidity of the people entrusted to his care." It was for the former of these attitudes, certainly not the latter, that the *amban* was later dismissed by the emperor.

Eight years later, the Tibetans were given an opportunity by the collapse of the Qing dynasty to take revenge for his condescension and ordered his successors to leave Lhasa and Tibet for good, along with all Chinese troops and officials in the region. Later, history turned full circle yet again, and after 1959 the site once occupied by the Yamen came to be dwarfed by a compound to the south that comprised the new *junqu* or Chinese Military Headquarters in Lhasa, on what had been parkland along the riverside. Stretching half a mile from end to end, it is ten to twenty times larger than the Yamen ever was. It is only one of a dozen or more similar establishments within or bordering modern Lhasa, and not by any means the largest.

In 1934 a Chinese mission, sent to offer condolences on the death of the Great Thirteenth, was allowed to visit Lhasa, the first such officials to have been granted entry since the expulsion of 1912. It was at this time that a Chinese office, later to be termed the Tibet Office of the Commission for Mongolian and Tibetan Affairs, was once again set up in Lhasa. It was housed in the Kyitöpa, a building on the southwest corner of the Barkor, diagonally opposite the Sungchöra, the courtyard on the south side of the Jokhang used traditionally for debating. Later, after the Chinese Communists took over Tibet and the Chinese officials working at the Kyitöpa had fled to India and onward to Taiwan, the office was turned into a shop, and the building adjoining it became the Barkor Primary School. From its windows, in

October 1987, desks were dropped on Chinese policemen in an effort to stop their shooting from the police station roof, which it overlooked. Shortly after that incident, the Kyitöpa was rebuilt to house tourists and named the Mandala Hotel, in its time the only such establishment on the Lhasa Barkor.

From 1947, Phuntsog Wanggyal worked at the Kyitöpa teaching Chinese songs to the offspring of the more forward-thinking aristocrats and of some local Chinese and Tibetan Muslims, one of whom became his wife. He had somewhat untraditional tastes in music, and taught his students the "Internationale," the "March of the Volunteers," the "Ode to Yan'an," "The Yellow River Cantata," the "March of the Motherland," and "The Song of Wind" (the last two were Russian). "We moved slowly at first," he told his biographers, "trying to influence the thinking of students by teaching them revolutionary songs and talking about the issues and subjects the songs raised."

The Kyitöpa must have been a busy place, because it not only had the Chinese government office with its radio set on the top floor and the schoolchildren reciting revolutionary songs on the second floor, but also was the center for the many spies and spymasters who worked for Beijing under various guises. Lhasa had become a place of strategic importance, and four separate Chinese agencies had sent competing teams of agents and recruiters there with the officials from Beijing to collect information. There were the network run by China's Ministry of Defense, the system operated by the *junshe* or military investigation bureau of the Military Affairs Committee in Beijing, the *zhongtong* outfit working for the Nationalist Party, and the *xibeixitong* or northwest group organized by the regional administration, based in the Chinese city of Xi'an. The members of each were largely unknown to the others and rivalry was intense. The seniormost Chinese official in the Kyitöpa later wrote implying that he had not known which of his staff or community were spies working for someone else, and it was rumored that a Chinese man found murdered in the Barkor one night in 1949 had been a spy in the *junshe* punished by his handler for insubordination. Kimura had at least two Japanese agents working with him in the city, disguised as Mongolians, and, if Chinese accounts are correct, the British had their own spy network too, so efficient (it is claimed) that in 1949 they provided the Tibetan government with the identity of every crypto-Communist in Lhasa.

Among the most senior in this shadowy community was a Tibetan called Jiang Xinxi, a one-star general in the Chinese army whose official designation was "Liaison Officer to the Tibet garrison." He also held a secret position at the highest level of the Defense Ministry espionage operation in Tibet; at the same time he ran a restaurant in Lhasa called the Doshirnimba, probably as much to supplement his income as to add to his sources of information (the restaurant failed because everyone assumed its purpose was the latter). He was the uncle of Phuntsog Wanggyal and, despite their apparently opposite ideologies, the source of his protection in the city; he had written to the Nationalist government in Nanjing vouching that his nephew was not a Communist while knowing full well that he was. Later, after the Communists came to power, it was probably the nephew who protected the uncle, since General Jiang, then imprisoned in Chongqing, survived the vicious purges of 1952 and in his old age in the 1980s returned to the Tibetan capital where he had once been so prominent in the underground.

By the time Kimura began visiting Phuntsog Wanggyal and his friends in Lhasa, the house had become a center for Chinese study and for the whispering of modern, egalitarian ideas. Similar notions had been floated in the Lhasa air several times, such as at the short-lived English school at Gyantse in 1923, within Lungshar's group in 1933, and in the circle around Gendun Chöphel before his exile to India in 1939. But those currents of radicalism were influenced by British and Indian intellectuals; politically, they were in essence alien. The group that Kimura discovered was largely nourished by a neighboring culture, which had educated many of its members to the highest levels and which was rooted in the same solid history that the three buildings of the Tromsikhang, the Yamen, and the Kyitöpa embodied: centuries of Chinese influence in Tibet.

These gatherings were part of the daily comings and goings in the streets of Lhasa in the years before the invasion; they barely merit a mention in the pages of history. The events that do find a place in state narrative—such as the torture of Lungshar, the death of Retring, and the siege of Sera Je—are used by political factions as evidence to support whatever is their chosen moral assessment of Tibetan society. Some use such incidents to demonstrate the monasteries' resistance to modernity; others cite them as proof that the Lhasa establishment suppressed attempts to reunite Tibet with China; some deploy them to accuse Khampas or eastern Tibetans of wanting to unseat the central Tibetans' hold on power; others see the hand of British imperialism behind these groups.

Our endeavor here, however, is not to judge would-be Tibetan politicians and their associates but to describe the layered character of their capital, and to follow the web of meanings and historicities that constitute its nature. For archaeologists of the urban soul, these incidents and buildings are shards found among the substrata of the city that indicate the weaving of its moral structure and the complications of its narrative. They are threads of an experience more richly textured than the depictions of collective sentiment admit, each one adding, if we can but read them, to the intricacies of the city's fabric.

I stopped in the alleyway that leads south from the Barkor toward the Shatra, where two English people were said to have rooms. I leaned against a wall and took a breath. The gunfire from the police station roof had been aimed downward, and I had run directly away from the station. That meant I had run into and through the line of fire. So much for education. So much for literacy and intelligence.

Back on the Barkor, the street from which I had just come, a posse of men, still within firing range of the soldiers now advancing, were running into a shop. They were carrying a man awkwardly draped among them. Seconds later the group backed clumsily out of the shop door, still with their burden. There was a red cross painted on a sign above the door. I understood: the man was injured; the shop was a clinic.

The little group stumbled with their human burden down the alleyway and stopped beside me. Why me? What could I do? They lifted the ripped cloth around his leg to show the hole. I panicked. I had never seen a bullet wound before. I tried to look knowledgeable, but I couldn't pretend. "Hospital," I said, "hospital. Menkhang, menkhang." I pushed them away. I had already delayed them in getting him to a doctor.

A hospital? A brain cell stirred. I had already seen them go into the clinic in the Barkor and reemerge seconds later; no one could have treated him that fast. The staff had refused to treat him. If it was forbidden for the roadside clinic to help, it followed that if he went to a hospital, he would be arrested. That was why they had run to me.

In the strange world in which I now found myself, it was unimportant that bullets wound people. What mattered was that the wounds branded them as protestors, criminals. So they would die not from bullets but from lack of medical treatment.

The group half carried, half dragged their friend along the alleyway and disappeared into the maze of tiny streets that is the old city of Lhasa. From the Barkor the sound of shooting continued, muffled to a thin crackle by the thick, mud-packed stone walls of the old Tibetan houses, as if their ancient fabric could alone absorb the rifle fire.

FOREIGN VISITORS, OSCILLATIONS,
AND EXTREMES

The writings of Western visitors to Lhasa have their own tradition. "This city of gigantic palace and golden roof," wrote Perceval Landon, the correspondent for *The Times* of London who accompanied the British expedition in the Tibetan capital in the 1903–04 invasion; it was he who noticed the *amban*'s choice of biscuits. His description of the city's glittering rooftops was typical of Westerners' accounts of Lhasa at this time. Such observations were to be found in the recollections of exiled aristocrats and other travelers as well: "glistening in the sun were the golden roofs," wrote the Khampa lady Jamyang Sakya of her first view of Lhasa in 1951; "the golden roofs of its temples glittering," recalled Kimura no less poetically of the moment he had first seen the city some six years earlier.

Views of this kind in the writings of Western and exiled Tibetan writers typically invoke a notion of splendor and of unity. In the case of Western visitors, however, this perception was organized within a dualistic frame, where the gleaming images of religious dedication and architectural magnificence served to contrast with some contradictory, more earthy, impression. Thus their descriptions oscillate between two extremes, and their readings of Lhasa are suspended between two opposing nodes of moral value. It is as if Tibetans were to be permitted praise to offset the condemnation that it must accompany, or as if to indicate that wonders can be found even among the natural and the less civilized. Spencer Chapman, for example, the British diplomat who had listened to the news from London on his radio in Lhasa in 1936, saw the Potala Palace as representing "the very essence of the Tibetan people" in its mixture of splendor and ruggedness: "underneath this beauty [and] the exquisite workmanship of many of the smallest details," he wrote, "there is a lurking grimness."

For many of these Westerners, the two poles of their Tibetan experience were sanctity on the one hand and dirt on the other. The sanctity was perceived most often in the sight of the sun glinting on the gilded temple roofs or in the burgundy-colored robes of myriad monks, usually viewed from afar and often—perhaps to distance the writer from their beliefs—said to have looked like ants at work. The dirt was described most commonly in terms of smell. For those who entered Tibet by the shortest route from India, the odor was especially prominent in their minds, because in Phari, the first town after the border crossing, one could only walk on rooftops: all the roads and spaces between houses had for generations been filled several feet high with refuse and detritus. "Appallingly foul and dirty, possibly the dirtiest and foulest town on earth," announced Austine Waddell when he arrived there with the British troops in 1903 as Younghusband's medical officer: "a vast barrow in a muck-heap, with an all-pervading foul stench everywhere." He renamed the town "Phari-the-Foul." Not shy about honoring the Victorian tradition of branding a people according to the attributes of their landscape, he declared its inhabitants "to be in thorough keeping with the squalor and filth amongst which they live."

On reaching Lhasa itself, however, the more attentive of these visitors from the south sometimes noted that conditions were relatively clean, and it was with some surprise that Waddell recorded that 720 pounds of soap and 6,694 towels had been imported into Tibet from India in the first three months of 1899. He also observed that nearly every Tibetan soldier killed by the British troops in the massacre at Gyantse had been found—the British seem to have pillaged the corpses—to have had a bar of soap in his pack. Nevertheless, the initial impact of Phari or some similar experience generally overrode subsequent evidence of any Tibetan familiarity with hygiene.

Even Fosco Maraini, the photographer who accompanied the Italian Tibetologist Giuseppe Tucci in 1948 and perhaps the most refined of all the Western writers on Tibet, could not but express revulsion at the dirtiness of the Tibetans. Indeed, he reveled in the excessiveness of the filth he found: "the dirt is ancient, stupendous and three-dimensional," he wrote. He even christened it with the pseudo-scientific name of *foetor tibeticus*. Maraini, a brilliant observer of the finer details of human behavior that he encountered on his travels, not least when they allowed him to scrutinize feminine beauty, had written a famous paean to the elegance with which the Maharajah of Sikkim ate his peas—"the last pea, defeated and impaled on the fork, was raised to the royal lips, which opened delicately to receive it, as if about to give, or to receive, a kiss." The peas were in large part a device, the reader might suspect, to lead the writer to a more important matter, namely the transcendent beauty of the Maharajah's daughter.

This lady was a princess of Tibetan extraction, like all of the Sikkimese royal family, by the name of Pemá Chöki, who painted her toenails red and who came to represent to Maraini—in her beauty and intelligence, her liveliness of thought, her familiarity with modernity, and her mischievous attachment to what he saw as superstition—his deeply conflictual response to the Tibetan condition. The art historian Bernard Berenson read Maraini's account of this contrast as a revelation of the universal conformity that can be found beneath the sensually offensive and exotic, and described the reading of the book as if it had constituted an actual meeting with Tibetans:

Disgusted with smells, nauseated with food, [with] their gorgeous raiment, their dirt, their eyes, their bad smell, I encountered [in Maraini's descriptions of Tibet] fellow men singularly like ourselves...folk as good and true and intelligent as without questioning we assume that we are.

But Maraini, exalted by his long conversations with the princess who came to represent the core insight of his experience in Tibet, had sought to express a more nuanced sensitivity toward the aesthetic and moral discontinuities he believed he had encountered:

The association of Pemá Chöki with a *gön-khang* [a temple dedicated to wrathful deities] struck me as a criminal offence. It was impossible to imagine anything lovelier than the princess at that moment, with her colour, her jewels, and her youth, and impossible to imagine anything more revolting than a gön-khang, a dark, dusty pocket of stale air, stinking of rancid butter, containing skinless, greasy carcasses, with terrifying gods painted on the walls, riding monsters, wearing diadems of skulls and necklaces of human heads, and holding blood-filled skulls in their hands as cups.

The princess once more raised the transparent glass to her lips, sipped, smiled and continued, "But you don't even know what a gön-khang is!" She then gave me a full description. She spoke of bones and dances, of *dri-dug*, the sacred knife, of *dorje*, the thunderbolt, of garlands of skulls, of sceptres of impaled men. In her was Tibet, the secret and untranslated Tibet; Tibet, the land of exaltation, beauty, and horror, the land of open sky and stony wastes and foetid gön-khangs, of lofty peaks sparkling in the sun and of places where dead bodies are hacked to pieces to provide meals for the vultures; land of simplicity and cruelty, of purity and orgy....

How reconcile the divine purity and serenity of these mountains, the infinite sweetness of sky and space, with the stinking, blood-thirsty horror of the lamaist phantasmagoria? Yet both were Tibet. How reconcile those monstrous tutelary deities with the grace of Pemá Chöki? Perhaps the mystery of Pemá Chöki was to some extent the mystery of Tibet, and perhaps she could give me the clue to its solution.

The Italian scholar-traveler was not alone among foreigners in finding a difficult dislocation in the art of Tibet and the statuary of its temples, much as visitors to Phari had found in the dirt of its streets and the stench of its inhabitants. For many, the paintings of wrathful deities in particular were a sign of evil, or evidence of what one called "the diseased and sinister Tibetan imagination which revels in bones, blood and death, [and] delights in the revolting." For others of a more moralistic bent, it was not the symbolism of their art but the Tibetan form of Buddhism itself—Landon described it as the "living type of bigotry, cruelty and slavery"—that represented the negative pole of their experience of Tibet.

But these writers were pulled by deeply contradictory emotions. The lyricism of Landon's prose suggests that he was as much in love with that which he declared abhorrent as Maraini was with the daughter of the pea-eating prince. "Under the fierce sun of that day and the white gauze of the almost unclouded sky of Lhasa, it was not easy to find fault with the creed, however narrow and merciless, which built the Potala Palace and laid out the green spaces at its foot," enthused the man from *The Times*. "Lamaism has inspired the stones and gold of Lhasa, and nothing but Lamaism could have done this thing."

Landon was not the only European to see the religion as more than a curse or source of fear. The nineteenth-century German philosopher Hensoldt considered Tibetan Buddhism to be cultured and peaceful, and the great Swedish explorer Sven Hedin described Tibet as endowed with "the light of holiness." The moral polarity by which Western perceptions were structured allowed a vertiginous switching between the two extremes, as if lofty admiration propelled a guilt-ridden yearning for the previous object of condemnation. This metamorphosis of foreign invaders from a position of superior revulsion to one of intense flirtation found its apogee in the life of Colonel Younghusband himself.

The aristocrat, described by one biographer as the last great imperial adventurer, had driven 3,000 troops and twice as many retainers across the Himalayas in a needless exercise to project British imperial influence beyond India's northern perimeter. To obtain the support of his government, he had fomented a fear that Russian weapons were being imported into Tibet, presaging an attack on British India. There were, however, no Russians in Tibet, and only three Russian rifles and a few cartridges subsequently came to light; as in later wars of similar construction, the absence of weaponry required another *casus belli* to be produced. In this case it was the enforcement of the British right, as then perceived, to enter into correspondence with Lhasa over their claim to monopolize access to trans-Himalayan trade.

Since Younghusband had been instructed by London to take his troops only as far as was necessary to get the Tibetans to negotiate, he rejected each delegation sent to discuss terms with him on the grounds of their lack of seniority. This allowed him to push all the way to Lhasa, a project in which he deployed Maxim guns against Tibetans armed with flintlocks, many of whom he famously gunned down as they walked away in retreat, or, in one case, after they had been persuaded or cajoled to give up their defensive positions under the pretext of negotiating. His motivation is said by some to have been a simple fascination with the fabled city of golden rooftops and a desire to acquire fame as the first Westerner in modern times openly to enter it. He thus became the first man since the Dzungar Mongols in 1717 to have successfully invaded Tibet and taken its capital by force, and the person most responsible for the chain of Chinese invasions that beset Tibet in the following half century.

This was not how Younghusband saw his role. In September 1904, six months after having overseen what he described privately to his father as "a pure massacre" of Tibetan troops at Chumik Shenko (he blamed it entirely on the Tibetans) and four weeks after having forced the Tibetans to sign the surrender agreement in Lhasa, Younghusband returned with his troops to India, having lost only 34 of them in battle. The mind with which he left was the opposite of that with which he had arrived, at least in terms of what he chose to recollect: the military adventurer reconstructed himself as a spiritual pioneer. He wrote later of his experience at the moment of his departure, as he looked down from a high mountain pass:

> I went off alone to the mountainside and gave myself up to all the emotions of this eventful time....Bathed in the insinuating influences of the dreamy autumn evening, I was insensibly suffused with an almost intoxicating sense of elation and good-will. This exhilaration of the moment grew and grew till it thrilled through me with overpowering intensity. Never again could I think evil or again be at enmity with any man. All nature and all humanity were bathed in a rosy glowing radiancy; and life for the future seemed not but buoyancy and light.... That single hour on leaving Lhasa was worth all the rest of a lifetime.

His rebirth is not to be explained by guilt, of which there is no trace in his writings, or by doubt about the morality of his political excursions. Maybe the spiritual simply offered a new and, to his mind, uncharted territory to conquer; more likely, all great empires and their protagonists veer at moments of triumph between attraction to the truly vicious and to the apparently sublime. It was an experience that profoundly changed his life. Whatever the reasons for Younghusband's apparent shift in what is aptly called orientation in his perceptions of the East, the history of many foreign travelers in Tibet, not excluding some Chinese, is in part a story of foreigners becoming engrossed and entranced by that which initially repelled them.

It was already dark by the time I returned to the alleyway where a Tibetan had asked me to bring medicine. The streets of the old city were silent and deserted: there was no sign of police. Maybe they were celebrating somewhere. Maybe they knew that it was only necessary for them to wait.

The great wooden doors of the compound he had pointed out were closed: when I had promised I would return, I had forgotten that the doors might be shut. I pounded on them till someone came. Everyone in the neighborhood must have heard it. After some time, someone inside realized that it was a foreigner knocking and unbolted the giant door.

She led me and my acquaintance Steve to the right, along the side of the courtyard and down a short flight of steps. In the room at the bottom, someone was weeping. It sounded like an older woman. Another person stood up as we came in, but it was too dark to see more. I was steered toward the wooden pallet that was the bed. The woman lifted up the cloth to show where the bullet had gone in. I could see the hole, just above the ankle. It hadn't come out the other side.

The bleeding had already stopped, so there wasn't much to do. I cleaned the entry wound and poured on the powder I had bought in Hong Kong. I had seen it on television, on a show about an aid worker saved from infection after an accident in the Philippines. It wasn't the first time I had used it: in Golmud the week before, I had used some to treat a truck driver, injured in one of the regular street fights between drunken Tibetans and off-duty Chinese troops. They slashed one another with their belts, and the buckles scored deep scars in their faces. I had talked him into driving me south to Lhasa on the strength of that powder, so it had to be quite good.

It was now ten hours or more since the shooting; everything depended on how much blood he had lost. If it was a lot, he had to be taken to the hospital straightaway; otherwise they had maybe two days before the powder would be used up and infection would set in. Then they would have to take him to a doctor anyway.

Someone there spoke a little English and translated.

At the other end of the bed I could see the man's face. It convulsed from time to time with unknown thoughts. Deep brown wrinkles moved slightly across the cheekbones and sometimes caught the gleam from the flashlight Steve was shining on his leg. The wrinkles glistened with sweat. He wasn't young—perhaps forty—but he looked fifty or more, slightly undernourished, aging early. Probably born just before the Chinese arrived. He might even have taken part in the uprising of 1959, the last time that Lhasa had been convulsed by revolt. He had survived all that and the Cultural Revolution to be shot one blue-skied morning in October 1987, at the height of China's opening up.

It was clear that he understood the choices. His face contorted silently with the pain, either of the wound or of making decisions: he would die if he didn't get treatment, and if he did seek treatment, he would be arrested. The foreigners had a flashlight, a camera, and a powder that might help for a few days. These would only delay the choices. Otherwise the foreigners were useless.

Steve took a photograph of the leg. The incandescence of the flash injected our civilization momentarily into the dark space of the room, and for a brief, Goya-esque moment, the faces around the bed were bathed in a cruel white light. The photo was a vain attempt to make a memorial out of this man's pain, to make it look like we had done something. But we knew from the disasters of that morning, when photographs taken by foreigners had been confiscated by the police, that we could not dare to record his face. And we knew that photos without faces do not get published in the West.

We were led out into the night and hurried back to the hotel along deserted alleyways, despondent. Medically we could do little except warn of the consequences of avoiding treatment. It was only later that we recognized what we had achieved: we had banged on the door of their compound and had certainly led people to that room. What we had done had been in the great tradition of all foreign intervention, however well intentioned: probably more harm than good.

Not all outsiders were or are attracted by the contrasts they find within their experience of Tibet: some have viewed the place with unadulterated disgust. These have tended to be people with monolithic views of the world; ironically, they have also often been the people most convinced of their own sophistication and of the benefit they bring to the Tibetan people. Within this category we can include Chinese ideologues convinced of the horrors of prerevolutionary life in Tibet, for some of whom a more nuanced view has been, in some periods, professionally or morally inconvenient. We can also include modern Western missionaries, judging by a recruiting leaflet issued by one such organization in 1990:

> Is there no light that cuts through the demonic darkness in Tibet, a nation long steeped in demonism and Tibetan Buddhism called Lamaism?...Satan has enslaved the people to a lifetime pre-occupation with right words and works. "*Om mani padme hum*" and other phrases are chanted repeatedly to false gods.

Both Chinese propagandists and Christian fundamentalists have a unitary view of Tibet, one of undifferentiated awfulness. The Communists, in their sterner phases, have an endless fascination with what they believe to have been the cruelty of master-serf relations in traditional society, and the contemporary Protestant missionaries are convinced that the culture is satanic. Their views are the mirror image of the aristocratic myths of collective happiness. They constitute more than a mere attitude: the ideological stance they represent creates a web of concepts, some of which have potent consequences. It was a Chinese idea of this kind that led to the attempt to eliminate Tibetan ethnic identity during the 1960s and 1970s, as well as to similar efforts at purging traditional culture throughout China. Christian fundamentalists have damaged many of the cultures they have sought to enlighten, as has been shown in other cases. We might expect that in the process of transformation and discussion by which such views mutate into engines of persecution, the most crucial area of intellectual assertion is in the domains of racial superiority, religion, or social relations, matters on which their proponents claim unassailable authority. But in fact the driving force of these views is in large part the effort to reclaim history.

For absolutists have a perception of history that differs from that of other people. They see life as a historical process defined by a particular moment of redemption; before that moment everything is bad, and after it everything is good. If we might describe the writing of the imperial adventurers as vertical and organized around experience, that of the ideologues is lateral and temporal: they divide up the flat expanse of time into the incomplete and the fulfilled, rather than measure the heights and depths of sensual, coterminous, and contradictory experience. For the Chinese Communists the democratic reforms of 1959 thus reversed the awfulness of traditional Tibet to its mirror opposite, an equally indivisible happiness. For the Christian fundamentalists in 1990, everything was much the same as it was when Landon and Waddell arrived in 1903, because the Tibetans were still not redeemed as true believers: in their view, the moment of historical transformation will come only when the Tibetans are converted. This scheme, once established, absorbs and reorders all experience. For the missionaries, even the aroma of local foodstuffs can be fitted into this chronology as a marker of the absence of redemption: "They use rancid-smelling yak butter for just about everything—as a skin protector, as a tea drink or as an offering to idols," the contemporary missionaries' recruiting leaflet says of the Tibetans. At least the most dogmatic Western visitors of the 1990s were complaining about Tibetans' cooking instead of their appearance.

Chinese propagandists have a more complex task than complaining about the cuisine: they have to change the Tibetan view of history, and they do not have the words of any God to help them, a disadvantage that contemporary Chinese intellectuals have sometimes specifically lamented. Every inch of inroad into the massive hinterlands of pre-Communist thought has to be constructed laboriously. Textbooks have to be rewritten, the shape of the calendar has to be altered, the measurement of time has to be reordered, words must be invented to describe the claims of the new state, the great buildings and thoroughfares have to be given new names, and new stories have to be disseminated in the effort to construct a uniform, consistent account of the integration of Tibet within the Chinese motherland.

The project was and is highly fraught, because the effort to create the appearance of unity is ongoing: almost everything that can be seen in Tibet that is not specifically Tibetan is effectively a signboard saying INTEGRATION WORK IN PROGRESS. If Tibet had been a part of China before the arrival of the People's Liberation Army at its inner borders in October 1950, there was little to show for it. The few Chinese and their camp followers who had lived in Lhasa had been expelled by the Tibetan government in 1912 and again in 1949, but despite the recourse they had offered to anti-British conservatives and the intellectual stimulus they had brought through the likes of Phuntsog Wanggyal to progressives and radicals, they seem not to have made any impact on the infrastructure or material conditions of the country. Given that China was an empire until the time it was evicted from Tibet, and that empires do not act like nation-states in their endless effort to reproduce themselves in all particulars throughout the breadth of their domains, the lack of Chinese presence in the Tibetan landscape should not perhaps surprise us: there was nothing modern or statelike about the Tibet–China relationship before the twentieth century. There was, certainly, extensive influence on food, clothes, fashion, art, administrative terms, and the like, though strictly speaking, many of these were Mongol or Manchu rather than Chinese. But in any case, the absence of Chineseness is striking in one overriding particular: there was little translation of works from Chinese in all the spectacular vastness of Tibetan literature, even though that literature was founded on the translation of foreign writings. China, when it emerged as a nation-state a hundred years ago, slapped rudely out of inertia toward its western flank by Younghusband's quest for adventure, thus had centuries of deficit to make up for in its effort to render Tibet visibly an extension of the motherland.

From the late 1950s the work of integration, founded chiefly on military assertion and the administrative reordering of space, moved rapidly to include a rewriting of history. Part of that effort involved presenting incidents in which traditional Tibetan potentates appear to have acknowledged China's sovereignty over them—usually the acceptance of an honorific title or a seal of office from an emperor. Another, partly contradictory, effort involved presenting Tibet before the Chinese invasion as immersed in suffering and barbarity. New Tibetan printing presses produced works that showed earlier linkages between Tibet and China, most of which were administrative or titular rather than intellectual, while a separate literature, often dominated by grisly illustrations, was produced to record the depravities of preliberation Tibetan society, with maimed peasants, chained felons, and servants carrying aristocrats on their backs. The impact and logic of these presentations depended on an innovative and irrefutable division of time into a morally inflected past and present. A separate but more persuasive and significant literature appeared in the 1980s, presenting historical accounts that included substantial extracts from Tibetan and Chinese governmental correspondence, some of which indeed suggests a close and unequal administrative relationship in the era before the fall of the Qing in 1912.

The point in these surgical slicings of the past at which history was seen to pivot, the instant at which the traditional was transmuted into

the modern, was rigidly asserted, shaping a view of history and of meaning merely by its evocation. But that point was not the moment highlighted by the historical documents—the collapse of the Qing and the
unilateral declaration of independence by the thirteenth Dalai Lama.
Rather, it was the victory of the Chinese Communist forces on the central
Tibetan borders in 1950. The point of transition changed slightly over
time: later, for a while, it was the arrival of the People's Liberation Army
in the Tibetan capital one year later; for nearly a decade in the 1950s and
again in the early 1990s, it was the moment in May 1951 when the Tibetans signed the surrender agreement that acknowledged Chinese sovereignty. It was only after that agreement collapsed and the fourteenth Dalai
Lama fled to India that the pivotal point became March 1959, when the
Chinese implemented direct rule or, as they term it, *minzhu gaige*, democratic reform. Whichever of these dates is used, everything before it is
seen as backward, and since then history has moved inexorably forward.

The amputation of chronology seems crude when viewed retrospectively as an act of polemical rewriting, but it is part of any effort at national construction and is not particular to China. When Deng Xiaoping
replaced Mao as the paramount leader of the People's Republic after
1978, he had, like all new leaders, to distance the new regime from the
failed policies of its predecessors. For some years, Chinese publications
recalled the date in December 1978 ("the Third Plenary of the 11th Congress") as the moment dividing the good from the bad, when Deng had
the Party pass a ruling that practice, rather than Mao's dictums, should
be the "sole criterion of truth." But after the policy of "liberalization and
opening up" yielded dramatic achievements in terms of boosting the
rural economy (it had ended the commune system and allowed peasants
to farm their own land), almost all official documents began to use an
unspecified moment in 1980 as the instant of transition.

For Tibetans particularly, the effect was that the Cultural Revolution was supposed to be seen as the past, and everything after 1980 as
the present. Most Chinese statistics and descriptions of Tibet now use
that date to mark the beginning of Chinese modernization in Tibet,
much as if modern China had not been in control for the previous
thirty years. Tibetans, like everyone in China, were asked, in effect,
to forget the past (although in Tibet, alone among China's provinces
and regions, Tibetan leaders appointed during the Cultural Revolution
remained in their positions until the turn of the next century). This

would be academic, except that it is this device that allows outsiders to see Chinese governance as a benefit: had the previous decades not been excised from the Chinese calculations, the overall achievement in Tibet, at least, might have seemed marginal. Periodization allows us usefully to measure a certain kind of progress and improvement, but the calculation of net benefit is best left to participants, whose memories are more likely to be ordered by experience than by historical convention.

The Western writers of the imperial tradition did not see their arrival in Tibet as an end to history, probably because they had no intention to remain and reconstruct the place as part of a modern state. The British wanted Tibet to reject Russian or Chinese dominance, but they had no interest in lifting Tibetans out of their perceived misery or imposing an outside conception of civilization upon them. There is, however, one attribute that the Communist and Christian missionaries shared with the more elegant foreign writers: both of their views imply, though the ideologues and missionaries are loath to state it, that in some way Tibetans themselves considered their own lifestyle as positive. Both views therefore suggest that explanations other than those offered by visitors must be sought in order to explain the apparent anomalies and contradictions in outsiders' perceptions of Tibet. And, in the case of the visitors who seem to have been attracted by this world even while deploring what they saw as its revolting character, something more complex must have occurred in their experience of Tibet than is acknowledged in their descriptions.

3

THE SQUARE VIEW AND THE
OUTSTRETCHED DEMONESS

 To attempt to reach the complexity of visitors' experience, we must return to the Tibetans themselves. They
too have highly moral ideas about their country, but
these are expressed in a shape and style more complex
and more capable of variety than the ideas of foreigners
or the translated recollections of exiles. Tibetans' views include, for example, the square, the demoness, the concentric, and the multilayered.

R. A. Stein, one of the most distinguished Western Tibetologists,
suggested that Tibetans in early medieval times conceived their *locus
mundi* not only as a place encircled but also as a place *encadré*. That is,
they imagined themselves as surrounded by other lands, all in some
way more powerful than theirs. This conception of a four-sided arrangement around their country suggests a square, although they themselves
did not use that term. In classical Tibetan chronicles and writings, the
arrangement was described in terms of the four kings of the four directions, each possessing a different form of knowledge and capacity:

To the east, in China, is the king of divination;
In the south, in India, is the king of religion;

To the west, in Persia, is the king of wealth;
In the north is Gesar, the king of soldiers and war.

There was a peculiar aspect to this notion: one of self-displacement. Tibetans seem to have come to regard the moral heart of the square view as lying not in its geographic center but in the south, in India. This configuration, Stein says, was ordered according to moral or religious principles, with the northern part of the square constituting the least moral and most irreligious area. In this respect it seems that Tibetans saw their nation as having moved within this arrangement at certain times, so that it was at one time in the center and later at its periphery.

The arrangement reflected the physical realities of Tibet: the *chang-thang*—literally, the northern plain, stretching across the upper areas of northern and western Tibet—is a vast expanse that is largely uninhabitable, even by nomads and certainly by farmers or city dwellers. The south (and more especially the southeast), being at a lower elevation, is cultivable, more densely populated, and often lush in vegetation and edible produce; it includes the Yarlung valley, the reputed source of the Tibetan kingdom, as well as Samye, the earliest seat of what became the state religion. Lhasa lies in a valley at about 12,000 feet between the higher plateau and the river-fed areas to its south. A similar construction can be formed in miniature out of the geography of Lhasa, as was done in Tibetan and Chinese geomancy: to the south is the "wriggling turquoise dragon" that is the Kyichu River, and to the north are the marshlands behind Lhalu, to this day still for the most part uninhabited, and beyond them the "crawling tortoise" and the "tiger" mountains. The roads to Lhasa run east and west, but little more than mule tracks run to the north. All around the city, mountains tower, reaching to the sky.

At the point where the pilgrim leaves the Barkor Square to enter the north side of the circuit, the alley narrows and the crowd of hawkers, devotees, pilgrims from the east, and shopkeepers is thrust more closely one upon the other. At that point, just past the shops owned by the Panchen Lama and near the yogurt sellers' lane, I heard a voice whisper behind my left shoulder. "Amchi, amchi." The Tibetan word for doctor. Someone needed medicine. I stopped and turned around.

I felt the people around me stiffen as I became an obstruction to the wave of human traffic. Ancient mothers with their prayer wheels skirted me as they hobbled past. Khampas with braided hair strode by, looking for some new trade in turquoise of suspect origin. Among the faces of the crowd there was no expression of recognition or appeal. All eyes looked down or forward, and everyone continued past me; no one stopped or gestured. A middle-aged man, rather lean and tired in his stance, who might have been closest at my shoulder, pushed past me on his way around the temple, hurrying slightly, not looking back. I never saw his face.

I stood in the crowd and cursed. The movement of my head would have signaled to any watcher that I had been spoken to, and by whom. The whisperer must have thought I would know to follow him or her until we were out of sight of any observer before turning my head. I had misread the message.

The thin man, if it was he who had spoken, had already turned the next curve of the Barkor, past the corner where the carpets are laid out, beside the lane that leads to the Tromsikhang. If anyone had been watching, they would not have had time to follow him: he was safe. But someone who needed medicine was not.

It was the second time. Two days earlier, someone else had spoken to me as I was standing in front of the Jokhang, in the square itself. He had said to bring a doctor at three that afternoon, and gestured toward a small door set within the temple porch. I had found an American in the Banakshöl Hotel who had just finished medical school, who said he was a doctor. He was six feet tall and so dangerously conspicuous, but he would know how to treat the wounded. The two of us had waited an hour or more that afternoon, watching the doorway from across the square. No one came. The door stayed locked. Perhaps someone in the crowd was watching, but we were too conspicuous. We couldn't be approached.

At the dawn of the kingdom, Tibetans apparently saw themselves as situated in the center of their country's quadrangular arrangement. In the old documents from the imperial or dynastic era when Tibet was a military power, from the seventh to the ninth centuries, an oft-quoted poem had described Tibet as "the heart of the continent, the source of all rivers," and the area around Lhasa had been known as Ü, or the center. That term has never ceased to be used by Tibetans. But, perhaps around the end of the eleventh century, as Buddhism became prevalent for a second time, their perception of themselves was reordered according to a notion of morality within which they saw themselves as belonging to the northern, barren region—"as savages living in the north of the world," as Stein puts it.

It was a piece of self-deprecation that shows the Tibetans as very different in their modeling of space from their Chinese neighbors, who placed themselves in the *Zhongguo*, the Central Kingdom, residing unequivocally at the center of their world, representing the height of culture and power within their moral scheme. The Chinese view may seem arrogant to others, but it is perhaps only a variation of the nineteenth-century image of the British empire as a roseate suffusion on a map, as if nature itself intended pink ink to fill up available spaces in atlases.

Tibetan writers in the fourteenth century accentuated their peripherality in the eyes of others. "Not one single person is fond of the Tibetans, they say that Tibet is the kingdom of the hungry ghosts," records one chronicle, citing the words of a Chinese courtesan to a Tibetan minister who visited the Tang court in about 640. It goes on to describe the reaction of the Emperor Taizong and his court to the message delivered by the minister, mGar Tongtsen:

> The emperor looked at mGar with piercing eyes, [and then] the emperor and retinue burst into a roaring and unbecoming laughter. The emperor then proclaimed: "This impossible story is most wondrous! I am a descendant in unbroken line, up until the present, of the emperor of all China. The Tibetan king of yours cannot cope with my prowess and might. Go and ask whether your king is capable of enacting a secular law based upon the ten virtues!... Your Tibetan king is a great swaggerer. Does he or does he not hold the power to erect temples in that Tibetan country of yours?... In your country do you possess the riches that will enable you to take comfort in the five sensual pleasures?"

The texts revel in these insults to the Tibetan nation, because in response to each of the emperor's questions, mGar hands over a letter already written by the Tibetan king, answering each in turn. The emperor responds to the letter with yet more demands, and twice more is given prewritten replies that mGar has brought from Lhasa. For this feat mGar is permitted to enter a competition with the ministers of four other realms, whom he outwits, thus winning a Chinese princess for his king. The prejudices of power, this seems to say, are predictable to those who are less powerful but more insightful. The Tibetan view, at least in the eleventh century and probably much earlier, thus appears not to have been Tibetocentric or imperial, since it had come to regard power and high culture as emanating from elsewhere. This was not necessarily a result of modesty or lack of pride, for it had a function: it gave later rulers the grounds to claim not only a kind of inverted pride in their intellectual resourcefulness and skill but also a moral authority that stemmed from somewhere more civilized than their local competitors. The Tibetan rulers who wished to portray themselves as Buddhist thus asserted that the source of their standing and their claim to moral dominance was India, since it supplied the Buddhist teaching.

This explanation meant that Tibetan history was rewritten to present the arrival of Buddhism and the ascendancy of its protector-kings as a second point of transition, when the northern, barbaric Tibet imported the qualities of a central, civilized land. Tibetan historians writing within this scheme identify that point first with the ascendancy of the monarch Srongtsen Gampo in the seventh century—he would be revered subsequently as a *chögyal* or *dharmaraja*, a "religious king," not necessarily entirely accurately—and second after a 200-year "dark" period during which Buddhism was largely absent, with the arrival in Tibet of Indian scholar-monks such as Atisha around the year 1042. It is not a view wholly supported by historical detail, since some scholars argue that a thriving, earlier Tibetan culture had existed before either of these points of transition, and since many of Tibet's influences came from other parts of the square—from the Arabs, the Persians, the Uighurs, the Chinese, and the Mongolians. Medieval writing recalled the divinatory abilities introduced from China while emphasizing the religious inspiration coming from the south, but increasingly the latter came to be the prevalent way of recalling history in Tibet.

In resorting to this strategy of Buddhist legitimation, Tibetans have therefore not drawn much upon the earlier history of Tibet, when it was a great and expanding empire of its own in the seventh and eighth centuries. That achievement of conquest and expansiveness does not seem to have been seen as a source of authority and legitimacy, even though the Tibetans had conquered much of western China, even entering the great Chinese city of Xi'an in 763 and briefly appointing a puppet emperor there. In the later Tibetan, specifically Buddhist, view of the state, authority was to be derived from the excellence of one's cultural and religious inheritance or, literally, the *import*ance of foreign knowledge rather than military supremacy.

The modern Chinese state too seeks to avoid claiming authority by the act of conquest. As a communist regime, it hinges its self-image on notions of egalitarianism and social improvement and so, not unlike Tibet, has preferred to define a moral source for its legitimacy rather than rely on rights acquired through force or empire-building. In this respect the difference between the Chinese and the Tibetans is that in practice the Chinese Communists have not been able to dispense with visible reliance on force to sustain their claim, while the Tibetans before 1959 had successfully presented religion as the fount and practical expression of their legitimacy. That is at least how Tibetan politicians and some of their historians present it.

So the notion of the square was in fact more complex than at first appears. It was a shifting idea in which one seems to denigrate oneself, only to acquire the prestige of imported foreign attributes. Thus the square migrated to wherever the current moral heartland could be claimed to have arisen. As we shall see, part of what made Tibetan rulers feel that they had inherited moral or religious worth from the southern lands was architectural: the construction of temples and the creation of a city were key indicators that a morally valid civilization could be relocated in Tibet, and that Tibet could gradually become a center in its world.

The third time it happened, I was in the Barkor. I was on the north side, by the entrance to Murunyingpa, when someone nudged me again. They touched me gently as they passed, and I knew this time that I should just follow. He was shorter, older than the man I had seen before. From behind he seemed more confident, relaxed.

He took the alley that leads from the northeast darchen, the prayer-flag pole, toward the Kirey, and then turned down another passage toward the mosque. There he stopped and turned around, waiting for me to reach him. The street seemed deserted, but we were clearly visible; it was no place to talk. I had an idea: I would lead him to the Shatra mansion, where my friend B. stayed, and there we would be safe.

I passed him without speaking, motioning slightly, and he began to follow. I made my way back to the Barkor and rejoined it at the southeast corner, mingling with the crowd until the turning by the primary school. There I turned left, just before the site where workers were clearing the remains of the burned police station so that rebuilding could begin. I passed the long building that said it was a cinema but was probably only a damp room with half a dozen wooden benches, and turned the corner that led toward the Shatra.

There were fewer people in the back streets; I had to be careful to look relaxed. At the corner a young man was tied, hands behind his back, to a telegraph pole. I stopped for a few moments. He had that blank expression of despondency mixed with total hatred that I had sometimes seen on the face of a Tibetan who was deeply humiliated or insulted. A small group of onlookers read a sign that denounced him for some petty crime. They did nothing to add to his indignity other than stare. I couldn't tell what they thought of the methods of late revolutionary justice; I imagined it in this case not very different from prerevolutionary justice.

The great, ornamented porch of the former aristocratic mansion of Shatra was only a few yards away. Thirty years before, the doorway must have marked it as the house of a great family. I stopped briefly in front of it to check that my companion could see me enter, then turned into the courtyard. Around it on two sides ran a wooden balcony, and before me were the great south-facing dormer windows that marked the former day rooms of the nobles, designed to catch as much as possible of the Himalayan sun. Those rooms would have been handed to servants after the owners fled at the time of the uprising; now each room or pair of rooms was rented to a different family, and the place, like everywhere in the Old City, had fallen into disrepair.

I lingered in the courtyard, where a woman was washing clothes at the single pump, long enough so the man could see me take the staircase to the right. I waited at its top until he joined me.

There was, in fact, a more multivalent scheme in Tibetan historiography, which Stein himself noted was related to the view of the surrounding world as four-sided: the perception of nesting or concentric squares, embedded within the notion of the supine demoness. This famous image is a form of geomantic modeling of space, a technology the highest forms of which the Tibetans, as we have seen, associated with China. In particular, Tibetan history attributes a geomantic contribution made to their nation-building project by Wencheng, the Chinese princess given in 641 by the Emperor Taizong to the Tibetan king Srongtsen Gampo: it was this lady whose hand the minister mGar had requested at the imperial court, eliciting such mockery. To Chinese historians, the marriage came to be part of a process that we might call the continuous back-writing of history, which seeks ever older evidence that Tibet had in one or another sense long been part of the Chinese domain. But the marriage of Wencheng represented more than that: for the Chinese it symbolized the acquisition of civilization by the Tibetans, and not from the south, but from the east.

Elsewhere in the vast Tang domain, civilisation was reaching its apex, with the economy expanding and flourishing and the arts and all fields of culture attaining resplendent heights. An admirer of Tang civilisation, Songcain Gambo [Srongtsen Gampo] made several matrimonial approaches and finally brought himself to ask the emperor for the hand of one of the imperial daughters.

Thus a current Chinese handbook on Tibet, published in Beijing under the title *Tibet Today and Yesterday*. The book presents Wencheng as the person who introduced technology, music, and Chinese influence into Tibet. Protagonists of this view like to praise her, in particular, for having persuaded Tibetans to stop painting their faces red, which they supposedly had done until then to make themselves look more frightening in battle.

The perception of Wencheng as a civilizer is directly relevant to our study of Lhasa, for it shows that the idea of civilization was linked, in Chinese as in Roman thinking, to the idea of the city: she is seen as having made people into *civitates*, inhabitants of a city. For it was at the time of Srongtsen Gampo that the capital of Tibet moved from Yarlung to the banks of the Kyichu. He was the founder of Lhasa, and Wencheng was, in some presentations of this history, the source of his inspiration. Whether these accounts are accurate or not, she is seen as the main diviner siting the temples that would give the new city its prestige and its name—*Lha sa*, the place of the gods.

Tibetan writers do not generally credit her with the city's founding as such. The legend of its origin is picturesquely described by the contemporary Tibetan folklorist Tiley Chodag:

On one auspicious day, at the height of summer, the ambitious prince happened to be bathing in the limpid waters of the Kyichu river [which ran past his birthplace in Gyama Trikhang, some 40 miles upstream of Lhasa]. As he raised his head and looked into the distance, his attention was aroused by the abundance of water and grass and the beauty of the valley in the centre of which rose the prominent features of the Red Hill (Marpori) and Chagpori Hill. Geographically the place was of great strategic importance. Moreover, the spot was traditionally held to be a holy place, as Srongtsen Gampo's ancestor Lhato Thori Nyantsen, who was an incarnation of a heavenly god, had gone into meditation in seclusion on the high and solitary Red Hill as an example to later generations. Srongtsen Gampo resolved forthwith to shift the capital.

Chodag goes on to present the move as also the result of pragmatic logic—it provided, he says, the strategic base for Srongtsen Gampo's epic military expansion to the south and west, and for his expeditions east into western China. It was the early success of these expeditions that led to the requests sent to both the Nepalese king and the Chinese emperor for a princess as a bride; both, after some persuasion, complied. Srongtsen Gampo is thus always shown by earlier Tibetan artists, as the four-sided view would prefer, with one wife from the south and one from the east; his four or five Tibetan wives do not appear in the picture. Some of these accounts say that Srongtsen Gampo had moved his capital to the banks of the Kyichu in 633, eight years before Wencheng reached his country. If these are correct, it could be said that it was the move to Lhasa that brought Wencheng to Tibet rather than the other way around.

Shortly after the seat of the future Tibetan emperor was moved to the site that became known as Lhasa, the first step was taken, we are told, in constructing the great symbol of Tibetan urbanity that was later to become the Potala. We do not know if this was inspired by the Chinese princess—Tiley Chodag, writing from within Tibet, says ambiguously that her arrival at Lhasa "marked its transformation from a deserted swamp into a prosperous, thriving city," a form of words that suggests that she was able to bring assistance or funding for the work of draining marshlands and restraining floods, a modern interpretation of the many texts concerning temple construction in her time that dealt primarily with the challenges posed by *nāgas* or water demons and other forces. In these accounts Wencheng is always credited by Tibetan writers as the source of Srongtsen Gampo's magical success in outwitting the *nāgas* in the project of building the temples that were to be the heart of the new city.

Before we consider that magical dimension, we should first look more closely at the official Chinese view of Wencheng. Chinese records say that she and her escort introduced not only wine making, flour milling, paper making, and silk and ink making, but also the practice of agriculture. This echoes the Roman analogy, where the getting of civilization involves the suppression of nature and the building of cities: agriculture is, of course, putting the earth to the plow, and so is often seen as the most thorough form of the vanquishing of nature; the sexual implications of this view have been pursued by Michel Tournier in his writings. We will see later an analogy to this erotic conception of the conquering of natural forces in the perception of Lhasa credited to Wencheng.

If we accept the view that the Tang princess brought plowing as well as ink making to Tibet, her mission would seem a rational, pragmatic endeavor, rather than the mystical version preferred by the Tibetans. So it is for Chinese economists and dialecticians, for whom the arrival of Wencheng marked the moment when Tibetan society evolved from the level of pastoralists to that of cultivators. This meshes with the official view of China's "minority nationalities," which sees all peoples as occupying various levels in the predetermined process of social evolution— that is, the progression from the barbarism of hunting and gathering to the higher levels of industrialization, commerce, maximal exploitation of natural resources, and eventually socialism, or, in other words, modern Chinese society. Thus, if Wencheng marks this crucial stage in the civilizing of Tibetans, it can be argued that China, not India, played the crucial role in Tibetans' early evolution. By an unclear logic of inference, this is seen as supporting China's official view today, which is that Tibetans cannot evolve without the leadership of the Communist Party.

This depiction of Wencheng has therefore been incorporated into Chinese orthodoxy concerning Tibetan history. That agriculture is at the cloudy center of this view can be seen from the fact that it became dangerous to dispute its position in the Wencheng story: in the 1980s one Tibetan scholar, Chab-gag Dorje Tsering, is said to have been stripped of his post at the China Tibetology Institute in Beijing for having written that it was not Wencheng who had introduced farming to Tibet, although it is clear that the arrival of agriculture long preceded her, apart from, according to medieval histories, "the cultivation of radishes and turnips." The official view has anyway become since 1980 an industry of its own, with a stream of films, books, plays, and television series presenting the tale of the "wise and pretty princess" and her journey to Lhasa, used to depict the bringing of civilization from China to Tibet as a feminine form of state beneficence rather than a masculine resort to force.

That this involves some liberties with Tibetan history can be detected from the fact that some Tibetan sources (which also claim that the Chinese emperor was forced or tricked rather than begged by Srongtsen

Gampo to yield up a princess for marriage) say she was anything but pretty—one account claims that the Tibetan minister mGar was able to recognize her from among 300 women in the court by her lack of beauty, since he reasoned that an unattractive woman other than a princess would not have been presented to him. This account seems not to have deterred the same minister from getting her with child on the long journey to Lhasa, according to some later histories, which also imply that it was some years before Srongtsen got around even to meeting her once she had arrived. These versions are not found in all accounts, which may be why they have not affected the judgment of casting directors for the various state-sponsored films and television dramas that have been made in China about the princess, who always appears as ravishingly attractive.

Until the mid–1980s it had been argued that Wencheng's marriage was legal justification for China's invasion or reclamation of Tibet in 1950. This claim is nowadays replaced by a more sustainable argument, according to which China's formal right to ownership stems from a voluntary submission by the leaders of the Sakya clan—the predecessors of the squabbling lamas described by Jamyang Sakya in her autobiography—to the Yuan or Mongol leaders of China in the thirteenth century. Thus Wencheng's marriage to the Tibetan emperor has been described by official writers since the 1980s as having brought the two peoples into something "more than close friendship." But it represents far more than that: this marriage is a battle site in the struggle between Tibetan and Chinese writers over linear and square-based views of history, and an illustration of the perilous ambiguity of the latter, in which Tibetans had taken pride in denying their centrality and crediting the outside as the source of their legitimacy, thus making themselves vulnerable to the imposition of alternate histories and authority.

The enduring Tibetan perception of Wencheng's contribution does not center on the introduction of agriculture or other material benefits to Tibet, despite the acknowledgment of the turnips. It focuses not on economic inputs but on the mystical insight and sacred architecture that she contributed: she is seen as a visionary whose geomantic expertise enabled the great temples of Lhasa to be constructed on the most auspicious sites. She was thus either the source or a beneficiary of the Tibetan vision of the four-sided configuration, which attributed to the East exceptional ability in divination. For it is clear that in Tibetan tradition religious and divinatory ability were two different forms of cultural and intellectual excellence, to be found in and imported from different corners of the world. Western scholarship and history of Tibet has focused almost entirely on the first form and marginalized the second, just as Chinese historians have focused on what they see as civilizational attributes. But the ability to read the physical shape of the present for signs of the future is a form of knowledge highly valued in Tibetan culture and experience and central to the story of the founding of Lhasa.

B. was effusive, hospitable as ever. She showed scarcely a moment's surprise to see me arrive with a stranger even in such tense times, though ordinary Tibetans rarely dared to enter a foreign teacher's apartment or a tourist's hotel room. Her instinct anyway was to be open and convivial. Even if she had warned me then, it was too late.

She made tea and talked about nothing to put our visitor at ease; he sat in the kitchen beside the door. He would not enter the second, larger room. Some form of etiquette, I presumed. Someone was knocking repeatedly at the door. He shouted from the corridor that he needed to talk to B. about her keys. The caretaker. I unbolted the door and saw again one of those Tibetan expressions that lacks the smile or joviality or serenity of which foreign photographers are enamored. His face was nervous, intent, determined. Whatever the issue was, it had nothing to do with a key or with B.: once the door was open, he spoke a few brief words to my visitor, then left. B. never even saw him.

The visitor said little while we pressed tea upon him. He made his excuses and left soon afterward. Whatever had made him stop me in the Barkor now seemed less urgent. He had said something about his brother being ill, but had not asked for any medicine. His English was good—he had been educated in Nepal—and he said he would find us in a few days if he needed anything.

There must have been some kind of appointment, because I remember thinking it strange that two weeks later, neither of us had heard from him again. When Nick, another Western tourist, came to me and said he had met him in the street, I was not totally surprised to hear that he'd said he had been delayed for a week. He had been coming back from Shigatse, he said, and had been held up by all the police checks on the road. Everything had become tense in those days, and traveling was difficult again.

Nick was more concerned with something else. Our friend had asked to know my name. No one asked names in those times. Nick said it meant he was an informer. I said it couldn't be.

A few days later, I came across him myself. This time he said I had to meet him two days hence in a certain shop in the Barkor Square. I knew the place: it was just behind the new police station, the one opened two weeks before, which had previously been unmarked. It didn't seem the safest place to meet.

He said I must bring my friend Nick as well. The two of us had to be there.

My mouth felt dry. I felt the skin across my neck stretch with tension. There could be only one reason he wanted us both there. It was a chapter that had to be closed; I had read it wrong again.

I never saw him after that. I knew it was time to go.

By the time the buses were running to the border again and all of us could leave, another Tibetan quietly explained to me. The brother had not been ill; he was in prison. The police had visited my friend a few days after our meeting in the Shatra, and told him to get the names of the Westerners who had given medicine to those who had been shot. He now worked for them. There hadn't been a week-long trip to Shigatse. There had just been a week-long process of reminding him what might happen to his brother if he failed to cooperate.

Later I realized how he had been trapped. All Tibetan houses are built around a courtyard to which there is only one entrance. To see who comes and goes for each of the fifty or more families living within, you only need one person watching that one entrance. I had led my friend from the alleyway in Kirey to the great porch of the Shatra, across the courtyard, past the caretaker, and up the wooden staircase on the right. I had even opened the door so the caretaker would have a full view of him.

It was time to leave Tibet.

Even as she entered for the first time the valley that would become known as Lhasa, Wencheng is said in the Tibetan histories to have encountered problems that indicated the presence of antagonistic *nāgas* in the area: the cart carrying her gift of a Buddhist statue to the Tibetan king became stuck in the sand and could not be moved. At the same time, the Tibetans and the Nepalese, already concerned by the local spirits' thwarting of their efforts to construct a temple, rushed to the Chinese princess for advice about how to deal with these forces. Wencheng is then said to have performed a divination that enabled her to identify the geomantic character of the mountains and the river surrounding the Lhasa valley:

The eastern mountain peaks rise in waves,
Like angry tigers about to leap;
The two mountains to the west press into the gorge,
Like the outstretched wings of an eagle;
In the south the Kyichu River winds by,
Like a wriggling turquoise dragon;
The northern peaks rise in gentle folds,
Like a tortoise crawling on all fours.

This recognition of the qualities of the terrain completed only part of the process. She also had to identify the *sa dra* or "land enemies," the points of antagonism in the landscape that had to be ritually subdued. This became the source of the Tibetan view of the nested or concentric squares. The divination for which she is most famously remembered is her recognition of an outstretched *srinmo* or demoness lying on her back, with her head toward the northeast and her arms and legs spread-eagled across the country. The limbs of the demoness covered several hundred miles, reaching present-day Bhutan in the south and Kongpo, near the Indian border, in the east. At her center, though, the *srinmo* was much smaller: her breasts were marked by the two low hills that sit on the western side of the Lhasa valley—the Marpori, or Red Hill, on which the Potala now stands, and, immediately beside it, the Chagpori, the Iron Hill, on which the Tibetan Medical College would later be established. A few hundred yards to the west of Chagpori, the hill of Bemari, which now has on its peak the temple of King Gesar, marked the *mons veneris* of the demoness. Midway between these hills lay the Kyishöd Ö-tso, the Lake of Milk, which was her heart, or, some would say, her belly.

The technology of landscape divination required that each of the nodal points of the demoness who lay across the country be capped. The Tibetans, thus advised, set out to pin her to the ground by constructing temples on the key junctures of her anatomy, apparently to protect their emerging state from the threat that she might turn over or stand up. These temple stakes were laid out, at least in theory, in a series of nesting squares: an inner square of four temples, called the *Ru-nön* or "Suppression of the Horns," each between 60 and 200 miles from Lhasa, marked her hips and her shoulders; a middle square, called the *Thandul* or "Border Subduing" temples, held down the elbows and the knees. An outer square, formed by the four *Yangdul* or "Subduing Beyond the Borders" temples, pinned down her hands and feet. Above all, in order for the she-demon to be stilled, her belly, the Lake of Milk, had to be drained and filled in, and a temple constructed on that spot.

The notion of the three nested squares of the Ru-nön, the Thandul, and the Yangdul may have had in its time more than a merely spiritual function, as it was related to the organizing principle of the four *ru* or "horns," used to describe the areas under the administration of the Tibetan kings and to organize the raising of military forces. But what they tell us about the idea of Lhasa is our main interest here. However we interpret these explanations, they suggest that the city of Lhasa, and the state of Tibet as then depicted, was seen as taming and overcoming elemental forces. In addition, the model of concentric squares has a clearly defined center—it constructs Tibet as a physical and spiritual entity of which Lhasa is the hub. The model also defines the center of Lhasa: it is the temple that was built on the Lake of Milk, the Jokhang, the most sacred of all Tibetan religious monuments. Originally the name Lhasa, the place of the gods, referred to it alone. It is still the religious heart of Tibet and of the Tibetan cultural world.

The demoness view of Tibet indicates other concerns as well. First, it reflects the persistent problem of water in the history of Lhasa: throughout the centuries, the Kyichu River has had to be constantly contained by dikes, and construction has always been restricted by the difficulty of draining the Plain of Milk (the flat land north of the Kyichu), much of which was marshland. "The plain around the capital is almost without exception a water-sodden morass on which it is nearly impossible to travel for a hundred yards without encountering a quagmire," wrote Perceval Landon of the British march on Lhasa some 1,200 years after Wencheng had tried to staunch the Lake of Milk. "The road by which one approaches the capital is a causeway built four or five feet up from the surface of the marsh...the waving rushes of the plain conceal a treacherous depth of slime," he noted. It had long been prophesied that flooding would one day destroy the Lhasa temples, and every spring from 1562 until the 1940s the monks of Drepung renewed the city dikes. The water-sodden pastureland to the northeast of the Potala has resisted the encroachment of the city, and today remains largely free of buildings.

The use of temples simultaneously to contain the demoness and to define the nation's territory also suggests that the idea of the nation is linked to the belief that architecture and construction should triumph over nature. In that sense the idea of the nation is, in this system, similar to the idea of the city, which is the most complex expression of architectural achievement. This is, at least, the view implicitly ascribed to Wencheng and her Chinese astrologers since the eleventh century. The pre-nation state is perceived as a female with her sexuality dominant, and the construction of both the city and the state are achieved by the suppression of these sexual energies. On such a basis is Lhasa built.

In essence this is the standard, Roman model of expanding societies. But the Tibetan description of city and nation building was transformed over the centuries, partly because much of the population remained nomadic and partly because it chose to incorporate a monastic paradigm within its social organization. We have little knowledge of the physical structure of the city between its founding and the seventeenth century, other than that its main buildings were the temple of the Jokhang, sited according to Wencheng's divinations, and the temple of Ramoche, constructed by Wencheng herself in the sand where her cart had been stuck. During much of this time Lhasa was not the political capital or administrative center of the country, as it had been from the seventh to the ninth centuries, but a famous center of pilgrimage and devotion focused on the Jokhang. But by the time the Buddhist scholar and reformer Tsongkhapa died there in 1419, having established the great monasteries that surround the city and having founded what came to be the *Gelugpa*, the ruling school of Tibetan Buddhism, Lhasa had been reinvented: it now housed monasteries that attracted thousands of men committed to a life of celibacy, from whose ranks the future leaders of Tibet would be drawn.

Somehow, Lhasa had redefined itself. Instead of being dedicated to vanquishing nature, many of its people were now involved in the pursuit of higher goals through the restraint of their own natures. When the British arrived 500 years after the great monasteries of Ganden, Drepung, and Sera had been founded, they considered the city to be almost totally devoid of men: they accepted the Nepalese consul's calculation that of the 7,000 Tibetans living there, 5,500 were women and the remainder either Chinese or living in the monasteries. Chinese and later British sources say that there were 40,000 monks in Lhasa at the time.

From this description one could believe that the demoness had extracted her revenge for having been pinned down by Srongtsen Gampo and his second wife more than a millennium before.

The Thandul and the Yangdul temples have long since disappeared as major sites, overshadowed by the great institutional monasteries and their subsidiary houses that emerged largely at the inspiration of Tsong-khapa and that still form one of several vast networks of monasteries stretching from Ladakh to Mongolia, defining the physical space within which Tibetan culture and political life is practiced. The area contained within the modern, post-fourteenth-century network of monasteries stretches twice as far as the Yangdul did, yet it was linked to a worldview that in theory avoided external contact, exploitation of resources, and industrialization. The demoness divined by imported eastern technology, the nested squares of temple stakes, the religious resources brought from the south, the use of architectural exuberance to stand for civilized progress, the network of nature-subduing monasteries: these are the conceptual foundations on which the city of Lhasa has been built.

4

THE CITY, THE CIRCLE

Even before its construction was completed at the end of the seventeenth century, the Potala Palace dominated the experience of travelers to Lhasa. Situated on the summit of Marpori, the Red Hill, it is the natural focus of the Lhasa valley; as the seat of the ruler and a military stronghold, as well as the former residence of the imperial ancestors, it might have been expected to be the center of the new capital. But throughout history, the Potala has been regarded by Tibetans as outside the city. It is the Jokhang temple, low and physically unprepossessing, on the flat land near the river, that is the heart of Lhasa.

The Tibetan capital is a densely packed warren of streets built between two concentric circles that have the Jokhang at their center: the *Barkor*, the "middle circuit," which runs around the walls of the Jokhang temple complex, and the *Lingkor*, or outer circuit. Like all such pilgrimage routes in Tibet, the Lingkor was defined by mystical, not human, geography: it had to encompass the major sites of spiritual rather than architectural significance in the locality, including intervening areas of countryside or wilderness. So the Lhasa Lingkor travels for more than a mile beyond the edge of the traditional conurbation, beside the river Kyichu, so that it can include in the western curve of its ellipse the two hills of Chagpori and Marpori. That the Potala lies within the Lhasa Lingkor thus does not mean it was within the traditional city. It did not stand alone—below it was a village known as Shöl, whose residents the present Dalai Lama describes observing from his window as a child; it had been of considerable importance since the seventeenth century as the site of government offices and the official dungeons, as well as brothels. But Shöl was regarded as a separate village outside the city. The Potala thus was like the sun in the Ptolemaic view: the life of the city basked in its light but revolved around the temple of the Jokhang.

Four other buildings define the spiritual geography of Lhasa. About a mile west of the Potala lies the Summer Palace of the Dalai Lama, the Norbulingka, also a site of pilgrimage, though not of geomantic significance. Beyond these two palaces is a third circle. It is formed by the *densasum*, the three monastic seats that Tsongkhapa and his disciples founded in the early fifteenth century: the monastery of Drepung to the west, on the southern flank of the mountain of Gamphel Ri that Wencheng recognized as one wing of the eagle pressing down; Sera monastery to the north, where the flat land meets the slopes of Gyaltsen Ri, probably one leg of the crawling tortoise; and, some 20 miles to the east, near the birthplace of Srongtsen Gampo, the monastery of Ganden, remote but crucial to Lhasans' later perception of their city.

We found N. near his room; luckily this time we did not have to enter. There were still a few tourists around, so it didn't look too bad. We told him quickly what question we needed to ask his superior before we left the country, and, whatever he thought about it, he agreed to take us to meet him.

He led us to the foot of a steep flight of steps cut into the mountainside, and signaled that we should wait there a while. He climbed up and disappeared through a small door at the top of the stairs. We waited and tried to look innocuous, but we were already higher up the mountain than any tourists ever go.

N. reemerged and beckoned us up the stairway. Beyond the door was a small anteroom, and then a curtained doorway. We kicked our shoes off, even though it took more time. After all, this was the deputy director, so we had to show respect.

He was sitting with his back to the window on a hard bed covered with a patterned yellow cloth. The afternoon sun behind him made it hard to see his face, but he was old, very old, very wrinkled.

He wasn't prepossessing and showed no sign of confidence, let alone charisma. He was a thin, anxious, aged man burdened by a high position. The school had been shut down for nearly two decades, and when they had reopened it in 1981, there had been almost no survivors left who remembered the teachings and who had not been forced to take up other professions in the interim. So probably he had been obliged by circumstance to take the job.

He offered us each a boiled sweet from a wicker basket that sat on a low table in front of him. I asked my question: Did he give permission for us to tell people in the outside world the names of his staff members who had been imprisoned? "Yes," he said. It wouldn't bring them any worse suffering than they had already undergone.

And then he talked. We hadn't asked him to. And he didn't talk about what we should do; he talked about the college. There had been an election for the post of director, he said, and for the deputies as well, and it had been fixed. The Chinese had decided who should be nominated, and there was no one else to vote for.

I had got it wrong: it wasn't because he was the last one left that he was the deputy director; it was because the Chinese had told him to be the deputy director. That meant they considered him an ally. I guessed that was why he looked so worn and sorrowful.

The staff had all wanted their most learned teacher to have the post, he continued, but the Chinese had said no. The election had been a fabrication.

And then he cried. Real tears came out of his eyes. The deputy director was weeping. I didn't understand. The tears looked as though they would fall into the wicker basket full of boiled sweets. There was something much more grievous about the staged nomination of the director than I could understand, more serious even than the imprisonment of the staff. Whatever it was, it meant a lot to this old man.

There was not much time—we had to return to the city before we were noticed—and I didn't know what to say. So I asked my other question, my big question. It was meant to sound like an act of generosity, to show that I cared about what he thought and to suggest that I had real influence. "What," I asked, "should we tell our government when we get back?" Was there any message he wished to have passed on?

"Which government is that?" he asked.

"The British," I explained.

He wasn't crying anymore, and he seemed composed. He thought a little and then, almost imperceptibly, he shook his head. And then he said, "The British betrayed us in the past and will betray us in the future."

There was no message to deliver.

The city thus revolves around a temple in the shadow of three hills. From one of them a sacred palace looks down, while a second, more recent palace marks the western entrance to the valley just beyond the cluster of the hills. These are in turn encircled by a ring of great monasteries on the slopes of surrounding mountains, of which sometimes four and sometimes eight constituted, in a much earlier perception, the outermost in a series of propitious rings around the capital.

Just as the four-sided view of the Tibetan world had once located its moral center in Buddhist India while depending on earlier Chinese divination skills to facilitate the importation of those resources, the circular view of Lhasa was also defined initially by magical and later by religious considerations. But the fact that its heart was the Jokhang and its focus and justification became the centrality of Buddhism, or that after the fourteenth century it redefined itself in terms of monasteries, did not mean that the city or its people were necessarily kind or good or moral. That is quite another issue.

The Western idea of sanctity, for example, suggests that places centered on religion should be calm, serene, and tranquil; this is a fundamental aspect of our concept of the sacred. There is a sense of a special space where noise, appearance, even air and light, are more refined in quality; this is exemplified by the architecture, and especially the height, of our temples and our churches. This idea of sanctity as tranquility is associated with religious specialists in Tibet as well—the term *gönpa* or monastery in Tibetan originally meant "deserted place"—and can be found in the writings of some of the exiled aristocrats, where it probably reflects the instinct felt by any nobleman who wants to escape the turmoil of interaction with the lower classes and so looks to religious buildings to offer such a haven. But, just as religious buildings in Tibet did not usually aspire to height, lay religious practice did not always entail quietude or calm.

"Tranquility" was probably not a term that often characterized the city of Lhasa. The great monastic institutions of Sera, Drepung, and

Ganden, each at their prime having between 5,000 and 10,000 monks, could not have been oases of serenity with such numbers crowded into dormitories with few comforts and fewer distractions. There were *dob-dobs*, or police monks, in each monastery to maintain order, and other police in the city, but on some occasions fighting broke out on a scale that threatened the stability of the state, as in the revolt of the monks of Sera Je in 1947. The physical power and threat of such large groups of men must have been quite daunting to individuals as well as to the government. Tashi Tsering, for example, who as a child in 1942 was enrolled by force in the Dalai Lama's dance troupe, describes in his autobiography the constant risk of being kidnapped by senior monks in search of attractive young men to keep as sexual partners. However holy its conceptual orientation, the city of Lhasa was not in every way an otherworldly place.

The Barkor likewise may have been a site of pilgrimage, but it was also a marketplace, since the best place to sell goods to devotees was where they gathered daily to perform their primary ritual, the circum-ambulation of the Jokhang; there was no sense of contradiction between commerce and religion. If we look more carefully at the accounts of Tibetans and even foreign visitors, the excitement of Lhasa was as much about shopping as about prayer, or their combination: "there is nothing one cannot buy, or at least order," wrote Heinrich Harrer of his time there in the 1940s. "One even finds the Elizabeth Arden specialties, and there is a keen demand for them. American overshoes, dating from the last war, are displayed between joints of yak's meat and chunks of butter. You can order, too, sewing-machines, radio sets and gramophones and hit up Bing Crosby's latest records for your next party," he added.

Kimura gave an even longer list of what could be obtained in the Barkor, including American, British, and Japanese guns, ammunition, and hand grenades. Tibetan and Western visitors alike rejoiced at the prospect of shopping in preinvasion Lhasa. But the pleasures of con-sumerism came to an abrupt end when the Chinese arrived and closed the border with India. "One of the biggest changes in the city itself was the absence of the lively central market," wrote the former dancer Tashi Tsering of his return to Lhasa in 1966, after ten years abroad:

There was nothing for sale on the streets anymore. Gone were the cramped booths heaped full of wares, the voices of salesmen and customers laughing and haggling, and the many tea and beer shops I used to frequent. In their place were a few poorly stocked government stores. It soon became clear that the people weren't very well fed, either. Food was rationed, and there was almost no meat or butter or potatoes. I had lived in the old Lhasa for many years and was under no illusions about its shortcomings. However, there had always been a lot of food, and if you had any money to spend at all you had quite a bit of freedom and choice. Now the food was rationed at low levels.

It is one of the great tragicomic ironies of the Chinese presence that since the new transition point of 1980, Beijing's main claim to legitimacy in Tibet has been the fact that it has brought consumer commodities to Tibet: until the Chinese arrived, the shops of Lhasa had been full of them.

It was not only the shopping that struck Western visitors to preinvasion Lhasa, once they had recovered from the splendor of the Potala. Although their writings dwell on the exotic and mystical aspects of Tibetan culture, what appears to have imparted an aura of beauty and excellence to the city had nothing to do with religion: it was its parks and gardens. Landon is one of the few foreigners to give full credit to their impact:

> This city of gigantic palace and golden roof, these wild stretches of woodland, these acres of close-cropped grazing land and marshy grass, ringed and delimited by high trees or lazy streamlets of brown transparent water over which the branches almost meet.... Between the palace on our left and the town a mile away in front of us there is this arcadian luxuriance interposing a mile-wide belt of green...with trees numerous [enough] in themselves to give Lhasa a reputation as a garden city. In this stretch of green unspoiled by house or temple, and roadless save for one diverging highway, Lhasa has a feature which no other town on earth can rival. Between and over the glades and woodlands of the city of Lhasa itself peeps an adobe stretch of narrow streets and flat-topped houses crowned here and there with a blaze of golden roofs or gilded cupolas.

Zasak Taring's map of 1959 shows a circle of twenty-two *lingkas* or parks, each with its own name, surrounding the city, especially along the north bank of the Kyichu River and beyond Chagpori, most of them half a mile or more in breadth. They were in general not carefully manicured exercises in horticulture, as are public parks in Europe or China, but open areas largely left to nature. Written history may tell us that the culture of Lhasa revolved around religious festivals, but oral tradition suggests that, as with the week-long parties described by Dorje Yuthok, the Lhasa year focused just as much on the days when everyone went to picnic in the lingkas. Today, except for the Dalai Lama's Summer Palace, a small part of the Shugtri Lingka (now renamed the People's Park), and the Lukhang, those parks have disappeared. They lie beneath the offices, dormitory blocks, and barracks that make up the modern city.

And although Lhasans see their home as a city of temples surrounded by monasteries, its detailed layout was not shaped by its religious edifices. Unlike the Potala and the three great monastic seats that, by virtue of their siting on hilltops or on mountain slopes, dominate the city, the temples within Lhasa proper had no architectural dominance, as far as we can tell: they have no spire, as on Christian edifices, to mark them; no pagoda, as with temples in China; no dome, as on the mosques of Mughal India; and no grand squares, *durbars*, or gardens to emphasize their importance. Even the Ramoche, built by Wencheng at the same time as the Jokhang, has little physical presence compared to the great monasteries draped on mountainsides across Tibet. Although the *lhakhang*—the temples or houses of the gods—are of great significance to practitioners in Lhasa, it had not been felt necessary to amplify the prominence of these buildings by their design or location. The focus of the city is its role as a place of pilgrimage, but if we study the layout of the alleyways and houses of traditional Lhasa, beyond the purview of the Jokhang, we see that it is the market squares and the mansions of the aristocrats that have shaped the street plan of the city. With this in mind, we turn to the picture today.

"He is an important monk," someone had once told me. But this was never said publicly. To those outside that tiny cell of underground activists, he was a young man who went to discos and got drunk and lived with his father (only he wasn't his father) in a tiny set of rooms on the west side of Lhasa. I was shown his letter, but it said nothing about religion, and no one had ever seen this monk near a temple. Still, he had never written in his own hand before, and his friends insisted that whatever he said was important.

Seven years had passed since I had been in Tibet. I had cried when we had finally reached Nepal, after long days walking through snowdrifts and over the remains of houses tossed aside by avalanches. And my tears had not been so much in sorrow as in relief. Still, as I looked back at the mountains looming over the town of Dram-mo and the Friendship Bridge, Tibet had seemed magnificent and statuesque, and the town perched on the distant slopes had looked so much sturdier and more modern than the shacks and hovels of Nepal.

After the letter arrived, I came to think of him privately as the Maybe Monk, but he, like the mountains, dominated the little world around him. I had heard that it was from him that people in Lhasa found out who was in prison, which of them were in solitary confinement, who had been beaten, and who had staged a protest against conditions there; for those were the days when even in the prisons, Tibetans staged demonstrations. And for years there was a story that the Maybe Monk had smuggled food into the prison, so that the captives would have a better chance to keep their bodies strong. He had a friend or a cousin in the military, it was said, and that was how he could do so much.

The letter said he needed money, a small amount, to buy clothing to send to the prisoners. There was even a kind of budget, with so many prisoners requiring so many pairs of running shoes. I had seen these sorts of things before.

Later I heard that one of his relatives had also received a letter; they had sent the money. It had also been for running shoes, but a lot of running shoes. He had wanted to set up a shop, he had said, and use the profits to pay back the loan and fund the purchase of shoes for the prisoners. But the shop never opened and the loan was not repaid.

The final letter, I heard, came in 1993. One thing had changed by then: the Chinese had announced a plan to make Lhasa into a special economic zone. That meant lower taxes, higher profits, and lots of incentives to set up businesses. And there were special rewards for anyone who could bring in foreign money. Suddenly Tibetans had the chance to get rich, especially if they were good at talking.

I knew that another of the monk's friends abroad had received a message saying watches were needed, a particular brand. The correspondents were distantly related and questions were not asked. Anyway, the monk was a pa-wo, a hero of the underground. Three expensive watches were bought and sent to him by hand. He must have needed them as bribes to win over officials in the prisons or on the police force, his friends reasoned.

In the final letter, the Maybe Monk had described a new and better way to help raise money to clothe the prisoners: he had been offered the chance to invest in a new company that would make carpets with modern designs. After all, the carpets from Tibet are among the best in the world, that's what the magazines in China say. He wanted $30,000.

Not even his relatives answered that request.

The opening up of private enterprise hadn't been the only change in 1993: the Chinese had also crushed the underground. In April a man from Tromsikhang had been detained. People said he had given names; that meant he had been tortured. Other members of his cell had talked, and at least one of them had connections with another cell. By the end of the summer half a dozen groups, all with names like the Young Tiger Cubs or the Youth of the Three Regions or the Lion Youth for Freedom, were gone.

In one raid the police had found a typewriter in the room of a man whom they knew to be illiterate. So they had found a neighbor who had books, and among the books a letter, and within the letter a note about conditions in the prisons. The letter writer was known to be a quiet sort of person, but of an evening he had the habit of visiting the small set of rooms in the west of Lhasa where the Maybe Monk lived with the man who was not in fact his father. That was how they got the Maybe Monk. Unless, that is, they knew him already.

Nobody now speaks about the Maybe Monk. Even the relative abroad was vague about a call from Beijing a year later suggesting an urgent meeting there to discuss his latest proposition. No one ever says that anything has changed, but they don't talk about his spiritual lineage much these days, or about how, since 1993, he makes his living. Or about his daily meetings with his policeman friend.

So I don't know how he gets by now. Maybe one of his investments paid off, or maybe someone else believed the talk about the running shoes. I really couldn't say. But when I last heard, eight years ago, the payment for information was 400 yuan a story, two months' income at the time. At least, that's what I heard. I suspect he doesn't do too badly nowadays.

5

MONUMENTAL STATEMENTS AND
STREET PLANS

There never was a single Lhasa, though in the past there had been a shared language in the vocabulary of its construction. Today, as always, there are many Lhasas. But their languages are in conflict: the vernaculars of the city are multiple and mutually incoherent and its overall legibility has been impaired. About eight of these architectural languages can be easily discerned, as can, to some extent, the world-views that inspired them.

The discordance of those languages became more apparent with the abrupt expansion of the city in the 1980s. In 1984, eight years after the death of Chairman Mao, it was announced that Beijing would invest in forty-three capital construction projects in Tibet. A series of grand build-ings appeared on the outskirts of Lhasa, including the Lhasa Hotel, the Mass Art House, the People's Hospital, and a bus terminal. Tourism had been declared a principal part of the economy, and one year later the tide of new construction reached into the heart of the old town: the buildings on the western side of the Jokhang temple, not far from where the gates of Lhasa had stood when the British troops marched in, were demolished. Some say it was done against the wishes of the inhabitants of the area, but there are no public records of local views at the time. The old houses in front of the temple were replaced by a pedestrian plaza surrounded by modern shops and with small, low-walled flower beds at its center. Known as the Barkor Square, it became the touristic heart of the city, and indeed of Tibet: it is where the buses and official sedans first line up to disgorge audiences arriving in Lhasa to admire the remnants of traditional Tibetan life and architecture.

The rest of the old town remained a densely packed warren of streets around the Barkor, focused on the selling of goods and acts of pilgrimage and circumambulation centered on the Jokhang. A few of the noble mansions like the Shatra remained intact, but since the 1960s almost all the traditional houses, now under government or absentee ownership, had been allowed to deteriorate to a condition where demolition had seemed to both the government and the occupants the only conceivable resolution. Each spring, after the New Year, a wave of destruction would recommence and another 40 or so of the 600 traditional buildings that had constituted Lhasa in the 1950s would be demolished.

The great houses of the nobility, each known by the family name of its former owners, had been the landmarks of these streets beyond the Barkor. The alleyways of the traditional area of Lhasa, now the Tibetan quarter, had threaded erratically between them and the smaller temples constructed in their midst. As the mansions fell into disrepair and the streets were widened, the former were no longer shaping forces in the city plan. Those that were renovated as offices, shops, or modern housing blocks lost the traces of their distinctive histories, and their names and memories became less prominent. In their place the dominant sites in the layout of the Tibetan quarter, besides the Jokhang at its center, were the remaining market areas, primarily the Barkor, still crowded with shops and street stalls, and the Tromsikhang, where in 1993 an orange-colored concrete building had been constructed with 1,800 stalls, the largest purpose-built shopping center in Tibet.

The frenzy of construction in the late 1980s marked the final enclosure of what had been the original city within the newly superimposed, expanding urban grid. Abruptly, after nearly forty years, the isolated settlements and clustered structures scattered across the valley floor had been connected and extended into an unbroken swathe of urban construction, within which the old city was a small, poetic counterpoint. The Norbulingka was no longer a park that lay beyond the fields and woods surrounding Lhasa, which the Dalai Lama would cross when he sought to evade the summer heat. The open land that had separated the middle circuit of the Barkor from the outer circuit of the Lingkor, and the city from the Potala, had disappeared. All became part of a single conurbation that stretched for several miles beyond them.

By the late 1980s what was once the city of Lhasa had become the Tibetan quarter. No longer an entity in itself, it had become a fraction of the city that stretched on either side of it seamlessly from the western face of the Jokhang toward Tölung on the western outskirts, and from the mosque at the eastern edge of the quarter out toward Karma Gönsar on the road to Drak Yerpa. The city that even in the 1970s remained between the Barkor and the Lingkor, and then only in that area closest to the Jokhang, now lay between the Barkor and the outer ring formed by the great monasteries of Drepung and Sera. The conurbation reached the foot of the mountains on which the two monasteries stand. So far nothing else has been built on the mountain slopes, but wherever the marshes have been drained the valley floor is filling up.

We do not know what place this greater Lhasa has in the mind of the traditional Tibetan Buddhist, for whom the center of the city presumably remains the Jokhang. But we can guess that the Lhasa experienced by the Chinese administrator or the modern Tibetan businessman is ordered according to some different scheme. Perhaps its center is the Party headquarters in the former Shugtri Lingka, or perhaps it is the Friendship Store on People's Road; probably it depends on who these people are and where they work. But their ideas of the city are most likely organized by the concept that underlies the design of the new city's streets: the grid. Long thoroughfares, straight as Roman roads, running from east to west and from north to south, divide the buildings of New Lhasa. The two arteries of Beijing Lu and Jinzhu Lu, each some five miles or more in length, at their eastern extremities cut through the Tibetan quarter, so that it looks like a blot of ink dropped on the otherwise tidy map of the metropolis. The new city of Lhasa may, to the Chinese visitor or the modern businessman, appear—except for the inkblot of the Barkor—not unlike a square: ordered, precise, and regular.

The plan to reconstruct Lhasa along such lines formed slowly in the minds of the new Chinese rulers. Although entire quarters of cities in the Chinese hinterland were bulldozed to make way for parade grounds and factories, after their arrival in Tibet in 1951, the new administrators proceeded slowly, avoiding grand gestures and careful not to overstretch their resources, which could only be imported with great difficulty since there was then no road connecting the two domains. In the first years after the suppression of the uprising in 1959, there was therefore little attempt at urban expansion in Lhasa; it was cheaper to move into existing houses bought during the early 1950s from noble families, who used the money to build new Tibetan-style houses for themselves in the suburbs, as had been fashionable for some twenty years. After the uprising, the new state appropriated the houses of those who had fled to India or been sent to prison and used them for offices and staff dormitories, often without any change to their appearance or much upkeep of their structure. There were not many outward signs of the new regime. The Communist Party had been more or less invisible in the 1950s, housed in the mansion of the Yuthok family, on the very edge of the original city beside what had once been the city gate; it had not proclaimed its presence at that time by erecting its own buildings. Only in the mid–1960s did it construct new headquarters in the Shugtri Lingka, the former park below the Potala Palace, just outside what was still then the boundary of the city.

The new administration did build temporary structures on the outskirts of the town, at some distance from the city; even in 1982 Henrich Harrer, returning to Lhasa as a tourist after thirty years, was struck by the maze of tin roofs on the new buildings he could see from the Potala. Many of the permanent dormitories and offices put up before the mid–1980s were also sited beyond the urban area; it was cheaper and more convenient to build around the traditional city rather than to rebuild it. Sewers, infrastructure, and roads could be put in easily in the former farmland, and with less risk of upsetting the inhabitants. These new settlements—office compounds called in Chinese *danwei* or governmental work units—seem to have been regarded as satellite conurbations, outside rather than part of Lhasa. They must have functioned in some way like a military cantonment in British India, a parallel town beside the indigenous city, with a separate life and character.

Now the garrison settlement and its clusters around Lhasa expanded to become the larger part of a new city. In 1988, when the Harvard-trained sociologist Ma Rong went to Lhasa, he was struck by the contrast between the new areas and the remnants of the historical city. For largely pragmatic reasons, and to save money, he wrote, "the main body of the unit households [his term for the governmental work units] are located in the 'middle zone' between the old urban district and the suburbs." He described the result of this phenomenon:

> Three groups live in separate zones. Most of the unit households [the work units] consist of a large yard surrounded by walls or fences, and the majority of [government] employees and their families live and work within this area. Therefore they have limited chances (especially the Hans) to contact native Tibetans, who mainly live in the old urban district or in the suburbs. For this reason, the Han (who work in governmental units and live in the yard of their unit) are, to a certain extent, actually separated from native Tibetans in Lhasa. Construction materials and styles are different in the separate zones.... Because of these differences in their appearance, visitors to Lhasa can easily distinguish them.

For Ma, this was the opposite of healthy urban growth, and a cause of continued misunderstanding between the Tibetans and the Han. Indeed, it seems strange that a government committed to the unity of nationalities had constructed a city where after four decades the lines of ethnic cleavage were unmistakable even in the architecture. It was more or less by chance that the old town had not been demolished and rebuilt in the previous 40 years to enable a fuller commingling of the peoples, as Ma noted admiringly existed in Inner Mongolia, where, he pointed out, 81 percent of the population were Han by 1990. It was almost as if the *nāgas* and the ancient spirits had interfered with the dreams of Lhasa city builders yet again.

The buildings of the new Chinese city of Lhasa erected before the late 1980s were large, symmetrical, and regular; they were architectural statements of the solidity and purposiveness of the new regime. They were not magnificent or ceremonial, as were the grand constructions by European powers in their colonies. They were, in general, square, utilitarian blocks without decoration or adornment, each inside a square, walled compound of its own. The horizontal squares that were now marked by the grid of new streets on the city map thus existed in the vertical plane as well.

These new roads and buildings of the late 1970s and the early 1980s were named after the claimed achievements and aspirations of the Chinese state—the People's Cultural Palace, the Friendship Store, People's Street, Happiness Street, Beijing Street, Liberation Street, Education Street. In retrospect the choice of names appears unfortunate, for declaring their goals in stone and on signboards seems to imply some doubt about whether the Chinese authorities had achieved or could achieve them. This was not the first time that foreign rulers sought to make a statement by reshaping the streets of another nation's capital. In 1767, to take one case, fifty years after the annexation of Scotland, the Hanoverian kings of England began a building program on land to the north of Edinburgh. The elegant squares and townhouses of the new development were laid out in a series of grid-shaped rectangles and thoroughfares to one side of what is now called the Old City. Today that grid dominates the city and is its center and defining style. "The building of the new town contained many messages," writes one Scottish geographer:

> The urban form of straight lines and rectangular squares, a counterpoint to the organic density of the old town, was a solid metaphor for an enlightened society...a rational, ordered universe susceptible to human understanding and control.

Unlike the Chinese Communists, the Hanoverians did not use the new streets to recite their achievements or to repeat the sources of their authority. Instead they simply named them after the members and titles of their family: Frederick Street, Hanover Street, Queen Street, George Street, Princess Street, and Charlotte Square. But in other ways Lhasa's situation was not unlike that of Edinburgh. It was, for one thing, also the capital of a mountain territory with a strong and traditional religious culture scorned by the new rulers; it had also been annexed, through a claimed but disputed legal process, by a neighboring state. In both cases the new rulers belonged to an aspirant dynasty that had foreign, protestant, progressivist, and puritanical ideas. Both dynasties were capable of immense feats of organization, rapid technological advancement, and inordinate cruelty. Like the Chinese Communists, the Hanoverians, in the suppression of the Catholic Uprising of 1745, eventually waged a campaign of extreme savagery against opponents of the annexation. In both cases, the rulers waited two or more decades after putting down rebellions before investing the large amounts of capital required to re- · construct the former capitals in a style that would communicate in stone the pacification and reordering of the alien city, along with the world-view of the new regime.

By the mid–1980s, as the Chinese economy began to benefit from the surge produced by the successes of liberalization, the first signs emerged that the new plans for Lhasa might go beyond the bleakness of Stalinist utilitarianism, the style that until 1984 had dominated new construction. It was announced that trees would be planted along the new thoroughfares, and in the official city plan of 1980 they were defined as one of the three criteria by which Lhasa could be recognized as a "modern socialist city":

> Lhasa must therefore be built up in a gradual and rational way conforming to the following criteria: well-structured, full of nationality characteristics, with lots of trees to provide a congenial environment and so on, to create a city that is relatively perfect, beneficial for production, convenient for daily life, rich, civilized and clean.

It was an attempt to convey, in those halcyon days of relative Chinese liberalism, a certain individualized and local character in the city design then being planned. Parks had once been, as we have seen, a dominant feature of traditional Lhasa, and to Chinese officialdom they probably suggested a divergence from the bleak, utilitarian era of Maoism that had just come to an end—they signaled the hope that central planning could encourage a leisure society and commercial achievement, as it had tried unsuccessfully to do through collective enterprise. The Chinese vision in the 1980s was not, however, of untrained or wild parks, as in the old Lhasa, but of ordered roadside greenery: what the planners had in mind was the tree-lined boulevard.

This was in itself a recrudescence. In 1905 one of the last *ambans* had given 1,000 *taels* of silver for workers to plant trees along the road from Lhasa to Gyantse, without effect since no plan had been made to care for the trees once they had been planted. In the 1950s, before the uprising and the flight of the Dalai Lama, when Beijing's policies toward central Tibet were still relatively relaxed, the Chinese authorities had again encouraged the creation of such boulevards in Lhasa. The newly planted trees were among the first things Jamyang Sakya noticed when she returned to Lhasa in 1959, and that Tashi Tsering noted when he came back in 1966:

> A decade had passed since I left Lhasa for India, and a great deal had changed. As I initially looked around, I was struck by the many new houses, buildings, and roads. The size and scope of Lhasa had increased dramatically. I was particularly impressed with the many trees lining the highways, and thought this was a wonderful addition. However, I quickly learned that physical changes weren't the whole story.

It was not that the Lhasa aristocrats had ever been averse to the ordered arrangement of flowers or parks—indeed, many houses had had window boxes, which much impressed the British when they first arrived; forty years later, Heinrich Harrer too expressed his delight at seeing these flowers in the streets of Lhasa. The British had in turn been admired for the carefully cultivated flower and vegetable gardens of the British residency at Dekyi Lingka, "the Park of Happiness," just beside the Norbulingka. It was Hugh Richardson, the most famous of the British residents in Lhasa, who in the 1940s introduced geraniums to Tibet; they are still among the most popular houseplants in the Tibetan capital. Even before his time, the garden at Dekyi Lingka, had been turned by the British into a statement of Hanoverian elegance and grandeur in miniature: like the costume that the British diplomats wore for state ceremonies in Lhasa—a tight waistcoat and breeches, almost unchanged from eighteenth-century court dress, quite the opposite of the voluminous, loose-fitting robes of Tibetan dignitaries—it reflected the British sense of imperial refinement and of the control they exercised over nature. Perhaps the tree-lined avenues planned by the Chinese were intended to express similar ideas.

Great empires usually do more than simply replace the winding streets of their colonies with geometric avenues. At some point in their arc of confidence they seek to build great monuments to themselves and their philosophies. Trafalgar Square in London, the Champs-Elysées in Paris, and Tiananmen Square in Beijing all reflect the celebration in the home capitals of imperial strength and confidence, expressed in the construction of linear, planned, large-scale, and repetitive statements in stone. Such statements were also made in the capitals of the colonies, creating sharp contrasts within cities that had until then grown organically, evolving over a long period for a multitude of functional and religious reasons into a form particular to the culture and place. In Delhi, for example, the vast network of spacious lawns and driveways created by Lutyens around the Lok Sabha sits awkwardly beside the anarchic alleyways of Chandni Chowk that cluster around the Jammu Masjid. One can imagine how in the colonial era such impositions must have been part of a deeply politicized and divided discourse.

That kind of architecture came to Lhasa on such a scale only in September 1995, when the authorities decided to mark in lavish style the granting of autonomy to the central Tibetan areas thirty years before. What they really must have wished to celebrate was the reemergence of the Chinese, and thus the Tibetan, economy after decades of socialist experimentation; perhaps they also recognized that after nearly seven years of almost constant protests in the streets, the energies of Tibetan dissidents were more or less exhausted. Sixty-two construction projects were announced as a sort of birthday present to the region. As in the previous such plan in 1984, these included hotels, government offices, power stations, and telecommunications links. "Their great importance lies in improving Tibet's backward infrastructure," wrote the officials. Not all the new investment was directed at improving the economy: two of the projects, which the officials did not mention in their publicity, were new headquarters buildings for the Party.

It was time to go back to Lhasa. It had been many years, I was only a few days' journey away, and I had not heard of any demonstrations in the Barkor or of armed police watching from the rooftops. I'd read that the People's Cultural Palace had become a disco, and that there were brothels all along the road outside the military camp. There was said to be a giant painted billboard of the Dutch soccer star Ruud Gullit, advertising Adidas shoes. And the Rambo bar, the shack that used to face the People's Park, had been replaced by a proper building that sold parts for Peugeot motorcars.

The hotels were better too, I'd heard, and so many taxis and private cars crowded the streets that there were traffic jams in Beijing Lu. Lots of big new hotels and a leisure village beyond Tölung had gone up, together with an entertainment complex on Thieves' Island that was to include a casino.

I was a little worried that my name might appear on some official computer, but that was probably merely paranoia. Each hotel has a computer now, but they don't always work—a few months earlier the computer had failed at the Kyichu, the new hotel on Dekyi Shar Lam. That had led to the whole place being ordered to close for three months, because it had failed to register some visitors. Not that it mattered much to the locals, more concerned that the hotel didn't even have a decent discotheque. Actually, the employees had registered the visitors, but had not sent the information by modem to the foreign affairs police. That's what the computers are for, after all. It was bad luck that, unbeknown to the staff, one of the guests that week had been an American politician visiting incognito. So the hotel had been closed down as a punishment.

When I arrived at the border post at Dram-mo, the computers were not working there either. That suited me fine. The policeman checked my name in a big book to see if I was banned. The text was in Chinese, of course, but the banned names stood out in large, clear English letters. I could make out one name upside down, that of an English journalist I knew well who had made some films about Tibet. Alongside I could just make out a list of all her pseudonyms. I felt a twinge of jealousy. Then I remembered I felt relieved to be unknown.

The state hotel where I had stayed ten years earlier looked even dowdier than before. The roads were far worse, so that everyone had to jump from stone to stone to avoid the mud. But the signs of urban renewal were also there: the small shops, many of them operated by Tibetans, the lavish archway saying WELCOME TO THE PEOPLE'S REPUBLIC *under construction at the entrance to town, and the satellite dishes on the rooftops.*

In the doorway of a Chinese teashop, a farmer from the hills stood in a ragged chupa, watching images on the television screen, till he was shooed away by the owner's family. There was a megaphone on the roof, and the soundtrack from the film reverberated through the town in a language that neither the farmer nor I could understand, but that he and his fellow farmers could hear on mountain slopes far across the valley anyway.

On the wall of the teashop was a color photograph of a boa constrictor draped around the private parts of a naked Western woman. "Natassia Kinski and the Serpent" said the caption, printed in bold letters below her body. The photographer's name appeared in bold, publicity-minded lettering across

the bottom of the poster: Richard Avedon. Sweet irony: Avedon's son was fa-
mous in the West as the author of the first popular history criticizing China's
policies in Tibet.

On the other wall was a drawing of an unsmiling policeman, saluting as
he looked out from the notice board. The captions were written beside him in
all three languages, Chinese, Tibetan, English: "Police Advice," it said, "Keep
the National Unity Consciously."

By the beginning of September 1995 the construction teams, acting on
orders from leaders in Beijing, had created at the foot of the Potala a
vast military parade ground called the New Potala Palace Square, with a
flagpole at its center and an ornamental fountain on the backs of Chinese dragons carved out of stone. It was a space of magnificent redun-
dancy, regarded widely as a sort of replica of Tiananmen Square in the
national capital. Both are designed to host lavish ceremonies, parades,
and mass meetings, events where the message is imparted not by the
speeches but by the number of people present in one place, arranged in
unbroken lines and facing in one direction. Previously such assemblies
had been held in the People's Sports Stadium, which its audiences must
have often noticed was not primarily designed for the political meetings
or sentencing rallies they attended there. Lhasa was thus given a formal
space in which grand statements could be delivered by its rulers in the
appropriate manner.

The design of urban spaces is more than an exercise in architectural
aesthetics. It is the silent sending of a set of messages, the meaning of
which emerges when, like all hypotheses, they are tested by their oppo-
sites. Some of the villagers of Shöl, the last significant section of traditional Tibetan housing outside the Barkor area, whose homes had to be
demolished to make way for the square, were a manageable antithesis;
they were given compensation and moved to the north side of the city.
In August 1999 a part-time builder called Tashi Tsering produced the
meaning of the square by offering an explicit contradiction: he climbed
the flagpole at its center and pulled down the Chinese flag. He took his
own life in prison six months later. His friend who ran the orphanage
near Lhalu where he sometimes worked was given a life sentence. The
orphanage director's wife received a ten-year sentence; the cook, the ac-
countant, the math teacher, and the children's nannies spent one, two,
or three years in prison after the flagpole incident. The reasons for these

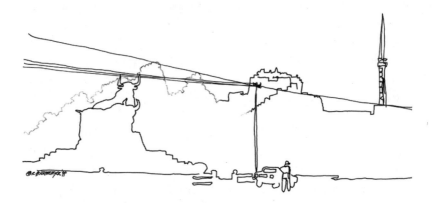

detentions are obscure, except that they were some form of collective punishment for the gesture the part-time builder had made in the New Potala Palace Square.

The square generated other kinds of stories that tell its meanings through what it does not tolerate. These are of a whispered, lighter kind. Like Romans in World War II Italy who changed the name of the Vittorio Emmanuele II monument to the Wedding Cake, Tibetans renamed their local replica of Tiananmen: in teahouses and in bars they called it the Kalachakra Square, because it provides enough space for Tibetans to gather in thousands when the ceremony of that name is next performed. This is probably not the purpose that the design team were told to think of when they planned the square, because in modern times only the Dalai Lama performs the Kalachakra. So the new square will not be likely to justify its second name in the lifetime of the current Chinese system.

Across the city other, smaller statements were made in the monumental style, and other murmured stories hovered around them, pecking at their official meanings. The Golden Yaks, a giant statue of two such beasts painted gold, was erected by the city's leaders at a crossroads just beyond the western end of the Potala Square, part of a series of new, gargantuan sculptures in rock or gold placed at city junctions. THE TREASURE OF THE PLATEAU, reads the inscription at its base. It seems to have been intended, like many efforts at civic activity in Tibet, to counter the prominence of religion in the organization of the calendar and the city by reminding Tibetans of the material basis of their prosperity. Some Lhasans, however, viewed the two yaks differently: as statues of the two most prominent Tibetans in the Vichy government. The pair are credited with an imaginary conversation that, as is usual in Tibetan political humor, mocks Tibetans for their credulity. One yak is Pasang, the highest Tibetan woman in the Communist Party in Tibet, looking upward and saying that things are horrible and the sky is going to fall on her head. The other yak is Ragti, the highest Tibetan male in the Party: he is telling Pasang, "It doesn't matter, we can increase the price of fuel yet again."

Within a year or so, the popular account of the two yaks' conversation changed. The humor became more bleak and self-deprecating, as if recalling the medieval stories told of Minister mGar's reception at the court of the Chinese emperor in the seventh century. Ragti, looking ahead along Beijing Road toward the new Potala Square and beyond it to the Chinese capital, is asking Pasang if the Tibetan masses are still following behind. She is looking back along the road leading west and replying, "Yes, the masses are still with us."

In a later version, the yak Ragti tells Pasang not to worry about the masses, because Beijing is anyway sending trucks with more and better beer.

The meaning is clear enough: Tibetan leaders are domesticated beasts, and, much like them, the Tibetan people can be relied upon to accept whatever their rulers demand or offer. But, these street tales also seem to say, just like mGar a millennium before, Tibetans also can predict what the next demands or offers are going to be.

6

FROM CONCRETE TO BLUE GLASS

 Architecturally the New Potala Palace Square, as Lhasa's version of Tiananmen is called officially, is a prominent but not entirely typical feature of the city's landscape. It is a gesture of bravura in concrete intended to exude confidence and conviction, made just one year after the collapse of Washington's threat to impose trade restrictions on China for its human rights abuses, at a time when China had exposed such threats from the West as effectively empty bluster. This air of confidence was a new phenomenon, however, and it was rapidly superseded by another mode of architectural self-assertion that soon replaced the monumental style: the use of glass and chrome to offset concrete structures.

Concrete. During the decades following the arrival of the Chinese army, the main form of industrial production had been cement; even the minor construction before the 1980s could not have taken place without the factories that produced it. Though glorified in publicity brochures produced by the state at the time they were built, they were an ugly addition to the city. Tibetans who worked in those factories during the Cultural Revolution are said to be dying now from cancers initiated by the dust clouds that still hang over their precincts. Walking to Sera monastery one day in 2001 by a little-known back route leading from

Dode across the foot of the mountains, just below the sky burial site, I discovered why locals rarely use that mile-long path: the prevailing breeze carries the dust from the smokestacks of one of the city's cement factories and deposits piles of fine, white powder across acres of largely unused and abandoned land just below the mountains and the famous monastery for as far as one can see. Long before I had reached Sera, every part of my body and my clothes was coated in white residue. Only garbage pickers and the destitute lived there, searching for resaleable items in what had become a vast, polluted city dump.

Building primarily in cement offered the advantage that fewer trees would need to be cut down in Tibet. This rationale was largely theoretical, because the Tibetan forests were anyway then being cleared to supply the market for timber in inland China. But these factories had symbolic resonance for the leaders in Tibet because almost no other large-scale industries had appeared in the region since the Chinese authorities had arrived. For many of those years, China was in Stalinist mode and committed to heavy industry as the key to its development, but cement remained probably the only significant industrial product in Tibet. In the year 2000 the government planned to produce nearly half a million tons of cement annually from its plants in Tibet, a quarter of it from Lhasa. Until the railway from China reaches Lhasa in 2006 and the roads are sufficiently improved to allow mines to operate profitably, construction is likely to remain Tibet's major form of heavy industry.

In the late 1990s concrete, which had built the countless dormitory blocks and government offices of the 1970s, the 43 projects of 1984, the 62 projects of 1994, and the New Potala Square, was abruptly displaced as the visible hallmark of urban construction: modernist architecture hit Lhasa. All over the city, buildings were erected with glass fronts and pyramidal shapes, towers, steel frames, and asymmetrical contours. The vertical rectangle had become outmoded, and geometric form had arrived. With it came multistory blocks and aesthetic flourishes, rhomboid roofs and triangulated profiles, individualism and architectural boldness. It was a leap in style, a quantum shift rather than an evolution, from the unindividuated character of the centrally planned city construction of the earlier era, though it too emanated from plans concocted in the Chinese capital. The 1980 urban schema, with its instructions for Lhasa to remain a city "full of nationality characteristics," slipped into the past and became for a while a footnote as the planners reveled in modernist experiment.

The new style was in effect an architectural hymn of praise to Deng Xiaoping, then the paramount leader of the People's Republic, after he came out of retirement in 1992 to make an excursion to the southeast coast of China, where its greatest cities were experimenting with more or less unfettered capitalism. The trip had been widely publicized in the official Chinese press as a signal of Deng's approval for high-speed marketization of the economy, and it was made clear that this should be pursued in every region of China. In practice the reform meant that what officials termed "nonpublic" businesses were to be promoted at any cost, and, less prominently, that the state would no longer guarantee the funding of education, health services, and social welfare. The drive to implement these reforms was called the Spring Tide, because it was intended to sweep across the country, including the western, "backward" areas.

In Lhasa, certain Tibetan leaders in the Party waged a fierce and unsuccessful battle against some aspects of the reforms. It was not that they objected to the market economy or that they retained any nostalgia for socialist economics, a notion that had long since faded from the Chinese and Tibetan political landscapes. But those within the upper reaches of the Party must have realized that in Tibet these reforms were being promoted by local Chinese leaders with different aims in mind: ending preferential economic and policy concessions for Tibetans, stalling the discussion of Tibetan-centered development, and promoting further Chinese migration to the area.

The moderates' attempt to resist the Spring Tide failed, and Deng's drive for instant marketization brought immediate and visible results to Lhasa, the consequence not of organic shifts but of central policy mandates. In April 1992 every government department was instructed to convert the ground-floor frontage of any property it owned on a main road into spaces that could be rented out as shops. These became the box-shaped, one-room shops that then proliferated on all the main streets of Lhasa, leased to a new breed of petty entrepreneurs, most of whom appeared to be Chinese. During 1993, 5,300 "individually run enterprises" were set up in Lhasa; 15 years earlier there had been 489 in the whole of the Tibet Autonomous Region. Wherever possible, new purpose-built premises were erected to house markets and department stores. The new concrete-block market building in the Tromsikhang was one of 23 constructed in Tibet that year as the Spring Tide swept across the country.

This, the architecture of petty commerce, was the first wave of the tide. Its face was unremarkable: small garagelike shops along every major thoroughfare, festooned with loud signs, or featureless rectangular market halls. The new buildings had, at least along more important streets, one aesthetic embellishment: the concrete frontages were usually clad with large white tiles that for Western visitors made the streets look like the interior of a giant toilet or a bathroom. The second wave came about a year later, as the market reforms began to attract serious investment. The style changed from small bars and cigarette stalls in boxlike buildings to large stores and hotels housed in blocks designed according to the principles of new Chinese modernism, featuring giant panes of blue glass, sweeping diagonals, and geometric designs. The Shanghai waterfront had arrived in Tibet with unexpected rapidity.

The food stores in Dram-mo had another new addition: phone booths. They were wooden cubicles installed at the shopkeeper's expense on the street beside the shop front, with a little bench on which to sit while you made your call. I discovered something had really changed: now you could telephone Europe directly. Telecommunications had reached this town even before the road was finished.

I had been back in Tibet about two hours by then, and I started to relax. The man who owned the phone booth sat beside me while I made my call; he wanted to practice his English. He had only a few words; one of them was "Dharamsala," the town in India where the Dalai Lama lived. I said I had heard of it. He registered no reaction. Business was all right, he said; the taxes were high but not too bad. He had come from the east with his brother to start a small boarding house. Then he dropped another phrase into the conversation, almost inconsequentially: "Dalai Lama."

I said yes, I knew of him; he seemed to be a good person, I said, keen to change the subject. He said he knew that the Dalai Lama had visited Taiwan earlier that year. We had been talking for maybe four minutes by then, and I was getting slightly nervous. I asked if it was all right for him to talk with me. He said yes, he could practice his English, as long as we did not speak—he switched back to Tibetan to say this—about politics. I relaxed. That seemed okay; I didn't want to talk about politics either. We didn't mention the Dalai Lama again, we talked about business instead.

I pulled out a pencil and a piece of paper to explain some question about how much a phone call costs. By then seven or eight minutes had passed. Then I saw the face of the phone man change: he was looking over my shoulder. I heard the torrent of Chinese from behind me. It was a younger man in an anorak, looking angry. Something was wrong, and it was evidently me. "You have to go away immediately," said the man who owned the phone.

I tried to leave unhurriedly, so as not to incriminate him further. I could not understand what the man in the anorak was saying, but it was clear that we should not have talked. There was no sign that the phone man was going to be taken away; this looked more like a public warning. After all, I told myself, it was only ten minutes, including my time on the phone. But I knew the encounter would go in his file—everyone in China has a file. I had seen some of them once, ten years before, the morning after they burned down the police station in the Barkor. People had whooped with joy as they found their files, waved them in the air, and then destroyed them in the embers of the building.

Maybe the pencil and paper had been the signal that attracted the plainclothes policeman, Party official, state security man, or man from the neighborhood committee—whichever one he was. But it was more likely something simpler: in Tibet it doesn't matter if you talk about politics, it matters if you look like you might be talking about politics.

A very basic error. I had only planned to be in town a few hours anyway, but it was better to leave immediately. Here where I had no history, and where the computers weren't plugged in, within three hours I had already gotten someone into trouble. Staying in Lhasa was out of the question.

It could not have been coincidence, this abrupt arrival of a style: something had changed to make it possible, and that something was cash. All the inland Chinese provinces had been instructed by the central authorities to spend large sums of money on new construction in Tibet, and major roads and shopping malls, often named after the places that had funded them, were appearing in Tibetan towns. Those provinces, eager to show their munificence toward their fellow citizens in the poorer parts of China, had also brought in their own architects to design the monuments to their donations, and thus had exported their eastern Chinese styles to those areas without recourse to early 1980s notions that had recognized some value in indigenous aesthetics.

Smaller entrepreneurs also received a boost from the new policies. The central government had apparently instructed banks to lend to businessmen who were interested in building larger commercial premises. Interest rates were set artificially low, and the entrepreneurs were, it is said, allowed or encouraged to speculate on the stock market with the cash during the planning stage of their project. This meant that more money could be made by investing in the Hong Kong stock exchange than by relying on the new venture, once it was completed, to generate income. The success of the venture thus became secondary to the speculation with the cash. The bigger the construction project, the greater the loan that could be sought and the profits that could be made trading stocks.

Under such conditions, by 1994 the most prolific kind of commercial project in Lhasa, and throughout Tibet, was the one that required the lowest operating costs but the highest startup funding. The answer appeared in neon lights along the streets of every town in the region: the karaoke bar and its relatives. Lhasa became a city of bars, nightclubs, and 24-hour hair salons of dubious purpose. In 1998 one Tibetan exile reported that on a return visit he had counted 238 dance halls or karaoke bars and 658 places that he deemed brothels along 18 of the main streets of the capital. The People's Cultural Palace, on the southern edge of what is now the Potala Square, was rechristened JJ's after the New York discotheque, and soon nightclubs with names like the Sunlight, the Dynasty, and Sun City were appearing in the new modernist style of architecture, bringing the total in the city to about 30. In August 1996 the official Party newspaper in Tibet published a letter from an unnamed reader:

Comrade Editor:

On a recent stroll through the streets of Lhasa, this writer discovered that the shop signs of several stores, restaurants, and karaoke dance halls showed extremely poor taste. Their display is strongly colored by feudal superstitions, low and vulgar, of mean style, with some even making indiscriminate use of foreign names. For example, "Rich and Powerful," "Imperial King," "Little Sister Awaits You," "Keep You Here at Night," "Cute Babes," "Forget Me Not," and so on. There are some that quite simply take New York and London and "move them in" to Lhasa.

The letter writer went on to demand that the authorities "purify Lha-sa's bad cultural appearance." But if the names above these premises changed, the construction did not. On Gumalingka or Thieves' Island, formerly the favored summer picnic ground of Lhasa Tibetans, an en-tertainment complex of neon-fronted bars and restaurants, planned to include a multistory hotel and to cover a square mile, was initiated by a Macao consortium in partnership with the Lhasa government. Beside the Potala the first seven-story building in the city center sprang up, a new telecommunications headquarters with sweeping curves and a blue glass front whose towers rival the palace on its hilltop. In less than four years after the completion of the New Potala Square, the Chinese state had found a new vocabulary to express its grand designs and ideas of power in the region. Glass and metallic office blocks, the language of modernity, entertainment, and wealth, had extended the limited lexicon of monumental parade grounds.

By 1997 the city of Lhasa covered 20 square miles, 17 times its area when the Chinese had arrived. The Tibetan quarter was down to about half its original size, and was shrinking fast. The central authorities, who had declared tourism one of Tibet's five "pillar industries" and had successfully petitioned UNESCO to include the Potala on its list of World Heritage sites (after the giant square had been completed), com-pensated for the new dominance of modern architecture by reinforcing rules from the early 1980s that restricted construction work in areas adjacent to a "national relic." Buildings in such locations could still be demolished without much difficulty, but new construction had to be in a style that blended with the monument. In Tibet these rules were applied to the area around the Jokhang, where, besides the temples and the handful of secular buildings protected as state monuments, about 150 of the old buildings were still standing by the turn of the millennium, many of them small and undistinguished, desperately in need of recon-struction or repair. The rapid demolition of the old houses around the Barkor could continue, but their replacements had to be aesthetically in keeping with the temple.

This led to the development of the hybrid or "New Tibetan" style, in which buildings in touristic areas of Lhasa began to be constructed. The street frontages of houses in this style look to the untrained eye some-what similar to the buildings they replaced: window frames picked out in black, blue-and-white striped awnings shielding the windows, stone block-like exteriors, and lightly corniced tops along a flat roof. But the structural details of Tibetan architecture are missing: the walls do not taper and do not have cavity insulation, the windows are rectangular and too large, the interior pillars are gone, and the main construction material is concrete. The exterior is cosmetic: the new Tibetan style is thus a concrete utilitarian dormitory block with a decorative façade.

The problem with these buildings was not so much aesthetic as practical. They looked muted and, to tourists, they seemed somewhat in character. But they suffered from the same defects as the dormitory blocks in the other parts of the town: their design was unsuited to the climate, damp in winter, too hot in summer. In the old buildings earth bricks in double rows had provided insulation against the cold and retained warmth; the low, timber-framed ceilings and smaller windows had also kept in heat. These qualities were lost in the switch to concrete, single-layer walls. Similarly, the protection offered against collapse in the event of earthquakes by the heavy, tapering walls of the old style cannot be matched by concrete blocks perched on thin crossbeams. The new buildings also lacked provision for any improvement in the supply of water or power to match the increase in the density of occupants, so that by 1997, still only 70 percent of the inhabitants of Lhasa had access to tap water. An attempt in 1992 to construct a sewage system in the Tibetan quarter had failed, but not before the city authorities had destroyed many of the city toilets built in the traditional twin-drop system used for generations in Tibetan settlements, replacing them with public toilets painted in lurid white and orange with a single drop system that never dries out and thus remains unsanitary. Late in the twentieth century the Tibetan quarter of Lhasa was thus a confusion of religiosity, decaying mansions, feverish construction, half-planned amenities, and demolition sites as it faced the onward rush of rapid modernization.

I walked back to the border, slowly, so as not to attract attention. I bought two Thermos bottles, some plastic toys, and small gifts from some Tibetan stall holders, haggling briefly for effect to make my impossibly short visit look plausible. By the time I reached the border post, it was closed at what seemed to me the middle of the afternoon: I had forgotten that the police, like all officials in Tibet, operated on Beijing time, set 2,000 km to the east, while the town, like neighboring Nepal, ran according to the sun, two and a quarter hours behind.

The police chief was Tibetan. He lay on a bed in his vest and trousers. He was busy cracking melon seeds and watching a film on television. Faded pictures of barely clad women had been torn from newspapers and stuck up on the wall beside the compulsory picture calendar. Three Chinese youths in uniforms sat on the other bed, watching the chief cracking melon seeds and watching the film on television. He didn't look at me. I asked if I could be allowed to pass through the border post en route to Nepal even though I was late and the post had officially just closed. He motioned me to a stool: I was to sit down. I knew I had a chance.

From somewhere in my memory I retrieved the laws of face: he could not easily make a concession, especially to a foreigner; it would be a sign of weakness. My best hope was to let him humiliate me. It had to be just a little, enough to impress the subordinates on the other bed but not so much as to make me of insufficient rank to merit the concession. I began to plead my case, slowly, without raising my voice. I tried not to become plaintive or exhibit desperation.

It took only twenty minutes to complete the ritual. Then, without a word or a glance to me, a man appeared with a suitcase. He laid it on the chief's bed, among the discarded casings of the melon seeds, got out his official paraphernalia, stamped my passport, and waved me through.

I was past the main checkpoint, but I had not yet left Chinese territory: there was a final police post at the Friendship Bridge, perhaps a thousand feet below. I began to walk down the winding mountain road. It was dark, very dark, and the walk would take two hours, unless I tried the short cuts. Last time I had met a Nepali smuggling a ghetto blaster across the border who had shown me the paths across the cliff face that cut off the corners of the winding road. This time I didn't dare take the short cuts in case I slipped. There was no moon, it was pitch black, and I wasn't as fit as I had been before.

Guard dogs howled as I passed the little barracks halfway between the border town and the bridge. I had read about this place: it's where Tibetans are held when they are caught trying to cross back into Tibet after going to study secretly in schools in Dharamsala, or after traveling illegally as pilgrims to see the Dalai Lama. There's a room with nothing in it except a barred window, and at night they are chained one to another in a line, the last one chained to the window bars so that only the people at the end of the line can lie down. The others sleep standing up.

I picked up stones from the untarred road in case the dogs were loose. Otherwise, there was nothing for me to fear. I was a foreigner, and the police never touch foreigners in China.

It was nearly an hour before I saw a vehicle on the road, a jeep. I couldn't expect a lift, because it was coming the wrong way, climbing up the mountain toward me. I saw it leave the police post on the Chinese side of the river far below and start to negotiate the rutted track toward the border town I had just left. I could see the beam of its headlights below me as it made the slow climb up from the bridge.

When it reached me I could see only the headlights, blinding me as the jeep approached; I moved to the outside edge of the road to let it past. I knew that in the dark I would look just like any local on his way to sell cheap Thermoses in the Nepali market across the border next morning. I swung my arms more widely from my body so the bottles I carried would show clearly in silhouette.

The jeep drove straight toward me, the headlights rushing directly into my face. Maybe I lifted up my hands and the Thermoses to shield my eyes; maybe that was why they did not see me clearly. I backed off rapidly to the side. The headlights swung toward me again. Again I moved sideways. Again the lights followed me. I had nowhere else to go; behind me the road curved abruptly, leaving a cliff edge to the side. To my right, six inches away, was a vertical drop of perhaps 100 or 200 feet. I moved onto the last inches of solid ground.

At the final moment the jeep swerved to avoid me and screeched to a halt; it had, of course, all been a little late-night entertainment for the occupants. A policeman rolled down the window, began to shout abuse in Chinese, and then realized I was a tourist. The reaction was stranger than the abuse: the policeman shouted at his driver and the jeep roared away as fast as possible into the night. It was as though a group of children had been caught misbehaving.

Standing in the pitch black of the mountainside, I tried to collect my thoughts. In the glare of the headlights, alone in the no-man's land at night, they had thought I was Tibetan or Nepali.

I hurried onward with my Thermos bottles toward the bridge below, and, beyond the bridge, Nepal. And Kathmandu, and an airplane back to London.

7

THE NEW FLAMBOYANCE AND THE
TIBETAN PALM TREE

With the new century, Lhasa changed.

For probably the first time in a hundred years, a new form of indigenous architecture emerged in the city: private houses built in a hybrid Tibetan style. In the early twentieth century the importation of steel gird-ers from India, used to reinforce the framework of new buildings, had made redundant the use of pillars in Tibetan homes, so an indigenous variation of traditional Tibetan architecture had thus developed in Lhasa in the construction of houses on the outskirts of the city. The last of these was probably built in the early 1950s, when *Kalön* Ngapö, having sold the family mansion in the Barkor to the new government, had a new home built in one of the former parks on the banks of the Kyichu. No major stylistic innovations in Tibetan building had appeared since then, and neither had anyone been allowed to own private property or leaseholds. But a new set of circumstances coalesced in the late 1990s.

Just as pillarless rooms had arrived in Lhasa as a result of the British forcing Tibetans to trade with them, the changes a century later were an architectural consequence of policies imposed by the state, an op-portunity turned to their advantage by those Tibetans in a position to do so. At some point in the mid–1990s, as the drive for marketization was gathering momentum, it must have become clear to the local leadership that the benefits represented by the plethora of new shops, arcades, bars, and office blocks lining every street might be offset in the minds of Tibetan residents by the increase in merchants, investors, hawkers, and work-seekers from inland China who accompanied them, as well as by the demise of guaranteed social services. The Party therefore implemented one of its most effective policies in the region and increased the wages of all government employees.

The class made up of Tibetans employed by the government in Lhasa and their families probably includes about half of the city's indigenous population, as well as the vast majority of those with education and with foreign access and connections. This class had already been defined by prohibitions—it was the same group that had been forbidden from 1994 to have images or photographs of the Dalai Lama, and that had been ordered two years later not to practice religion in any form. The ban on images of the Dalai Lama was extended the following year to everyone, but only these government employees and their families, notwithstanding the promises in the Chinese constitution, were prohibited from religious practice. So it is not unlikely that some compensatory policy for the cadre class was felt to be expedient.

Many of these government staff thus saw their incomes rise dramatically. Others were allowed to take early retirement with full pay, sometimes when only in their forties. And at the same time Beijing, anxious to cut the costs of running a welfare state, had ruled that officials were allowed to move out of the accommodations provided by their work units and encouraged to take out low-interest loans in order to lease land on which to construct their own homes. For a few years in the late 1990s, as Beijing sought to initiate a private property market without allowing ownership, the right to private use of plots of land, valid for fifty years, was sold at bargain prices.

In Lhasa, several hundred Tibetan officials and their families rapidly moved out of the concrete-block work units where they had been housed since soon after the arrival of the People's Liberation Army. By the early years of the new century scores of new homes were being built on the outskirts of the city, to the east in Karma Gönsar, where 400 years before the Gelugpas had torched the single Karma Kagyu monastery then remaining in the city, and to the north in Tuanjie xincun, a

Chinese-created suburb whose name means "New Unity Village." The new houses were almost all in a hybrid Tibetan style that had recently begun to be developed by Tibetan officials building homes for retirement. It is sometimes called the New *Simsha* style, after the houses of aristocrats and high lamas that it recalls: Tibetan in appearance, but modern in amenities. These new buildings used wood only for window frames and lintels, and preformed concrete blocks in place of hewn stone, but their shape and dimensions were reminiscent of traditional forms. They had small walled and gardened courtyards, often with ornamental doors and patios for flowers, sometimes with glass roofs over the terraces, and they always faced south to catch the winter sun. Inside, many had Western-style chandeliers hanging from the ceilings, giant television sets, and other modern conveniences, but the walls were often painted with a traditional Tibetan frieze. The larger ones had outbuildings in the yard for the kitchen and the dining room. Other traditional accoutrements of wealth and property came with the architecture and the cash: mastiffs chained beside the giant gateways to guard the premises, and domestic servants from the countryside working for miniscule wages. A new style of Tibetan housing, living, and class division had finally emerged.

Another return to indigenous aesthetics had also taken place: the Tibetanization of parks. For decades Chinese city planners had been creating traditional Chinese-style gardens in Lhasa for public use that looked nothing like the paintings of landscape artists or photographs from Suzhou, because the grass wasted away through lack of water, the pagodas became dilapidated, and the ornamental lakes stagnated. Few people went to these places for picnics. But in the mid–1990s, on the road between Lhasa and Pabongka, where the giant rock lies that Princess Wencheng had recognized as a tortoise, the old water mill at Nyangdren that once ground *tsampa* or barley flour for the Dalai Lama was renovated and the land around it laid out as rambling hillside parkland with streams, trees, and terraces, a re-creation of a *lingka*. The buildings at the site are modern blocks without Tibetan character, but that matters little to the Tibetans who, on summer weekends, revive there the picnic practices of their ancestors, setting up tents and playing cards and mahjong.

A second Tibetan-style park appeared in 2003, this one with Tibetan-style buildings: the *Xianzudao*—the Island of the Footprint of the Gods. The park, which is also referred to as the New Norbulingka,

lies within a giant, walled enclosure by the river where a replica of the Podrang Sarpa, the palace of the current Dalai Lama's family, has been built. Although the structural work is in concrete, the reproduction of its externalities is exact, and within the park other replicas of old Lhasa houses dot the gardens. These are for use as hotels, but it is the space around them, and the Tibetan context they provide, that on the weekends entices Tibetans to hold yet more picnic parties. This was not a policy move by the local authorities or a shift in governmental aesthetics, but a private venture by a rich Tibetan, gambling that a knowledge of Tibetan tastes and inclinations can yield profits for a bright investor.

Casual visitors to Lhasa are unlikely to see these expressions of Tibetan recrudescence. They are more likely to be struck by the scale of modernization, with all the hallmarks of the global metropolis. Hypermarkets as large as anything in Beijing or Paris have appeared along the outer ring roads of the city, and giant housing developments offer private homes in walled compounds with private parks for the very rich, to the south of Sera monastery. These housing colonies have their benefits, because it is probably due to them that the cement factory whose dust-spewing smokestacks turned the land around Sera white has been moved to the edge of the city.

The old Tibetan houses beside the Snowland hotel, on what is now the western edge of the Tibetan quarter, were replaced by blocks with Tibetan-style façades, and the Barkor was repaved again with giant slabs. All decorative frontages were removed from the Barkor shops (except, it seems, from the giant antiques arcades, whose owners, usually not Tibetan, were permitted to put up carved Tibetan door frames), so the alleyways have acquired a flat, regular, expansive surface, and what once seemed a cluttered skein of passages is now a broad, well-regulated set of pedestrian thoroughfares. The rough, tin-covered market stalls have been replaced by units of identical design and size, and along the former alleyways, elaborate lampposts have been erected with art deco frills, each sprouting a cluster of twenty separate lamps on ornamental metal branches.

Elsewhere in the city, streets have been rebuilt; each bears the name of the inland province that sponsored it. In 2001 Beijing Lu, the last main street with a significant number of Tibetan stores, was repaved to mark the visit of a Chinese leader to preside over another parade in the Potala Square commemorating Tibetan liberation. The development caused disruption at the time: most shops and hotels on Beijing Lu were unable to accept customers for some months because of the piles of mud and debris shifted to their front doors, where once there had been sidewalks. But by the time the new road was completed, the citizens were able to enjoy, at least on television, "a song and dance performance marking the 50th anniversary of the peaceful liberation of Tibet at the square in front of the Potala Palace and 'Holiday Night,' the fireworks show and performance [that] highlighted the great development in Tibet following the region's peaceful liberation."

The development style of the new century was crowned by architectural flourishes, odes to urban flamboyance. A 120-foot-high replica of a mountain, ultramodernist, angular, and concrete, was erected opposite the Potala Palace, across the new parade square, to mark the Everest-high achievement of half a century of Tibetan liberation. The first multistory block close to the traditional part of the city also went up that year, with the result that from the roof of the Jokhang temple you can no longer see the monastery of Sera on the slope north of the city. Thirteen stories high—ten floors higher than everything around it—with winglike flourishes on its roof, it stands some 300 yards from the Ramoche, the seventh-century temple built by Princess Wencheng on the site where the geomantic forces had made her cart get stuck just as she entered Lhasa. The tower block, a few feet outside the boundary of the official conservation zone within which buildings may not exceed four stories, is the new headquarters of the city's Public Security Bureau; the police, it was said, needed to be able to look down into surrounding courtyards and homes.

The site chosen by city planners as the centerpiece for architectural display was the main street popularly known as Yuthok Lam, the Street of the Turquoise Roof, after the blue roof tiles on the ornamental covered bridge that, some say, gave Dorje Yuthok's illustrious family its name. The bridge beside what had once been the gateway to the city had become just a building amid countless buildings, with nothing running beneath or over it, an ungrammatical memento of the watery forces that had bedeviled Srongtsen Gampo's city-building efforts a millennium earlier, and of the causeway cutting through the marshes along which the British troops and journalists had traveled as they crossed the empty land between the Potala and the city a hundred years before.

The street popularly known as Yuthok Lam had been renamed People's Road after liberation, since it connected the Jokhang temple at its eastern end with the new People's Government Headquarters at the western end, and in 1965 it had been the site of Lhasa's first official "market street." The bridge with the turquoise roof, now within the confines of the Lhasa customs office, had been scheduled for demolition at one time in the 1990s, but the planners decided to refurbish it as a monument. The other buildings on the street were reconstructed as modern stores selling fashionable clothes, flat-screen television sets, karaoke suites, and other goods. At its mid-point crossroads, video screens displaying advertising films were put up in the style of a miniature Times Square, and a stage has been set up outside the giant department store so that the salesgirls can demonstrate the virtues of fashionable commodities to passersby and persuade them through megaphones to enter the establishment.

At night along the length of the new Yuthok Lam, 20-foot-high decorative illuminated bollards flash different colors in sequence. Ornamental abstract Chinese sculptures in stainless steel, resembling curled-up dragons, mark the entrance to the thoroughfare. On the sidewalk, plastic mushrooms painted red with white spots, the size of a stone horse-mounting block or an upturned trash can, have been placed at regular intervals. When their wiring was still in working order, they played pop music every time a pedestrian walked by.

The most striking feature of the new flamboyance is horticultural: there are now palm trees on Yuthok Lam. These were imported from the inland areas, where they have become common sights at crossroads in major Chinese cities. One has appeared in front of the new leisure center at the university as well; two others have been placed beside the Golden Yaks. Their trunks are smooth and slender; each has between nine and twelve fronds at its peak, startling green, and at least five coconuts. At three or four points along Yuthok Lam they tower over the street in perpetual multicolored efflorescence.

The palm tree is not indigenous to Tibet, however, and these are made of plastic.

Western journalists and writers like myself found that our stories of five or ten years earlier had to be rewritten. Like our predecessors who had come with the British invasion a century before, we arrived prepared to write about the iniquities of the system and departed somewhat in awe of its achievements. This time the achievements were economic rather than spiritual, the system was Chinese rather than Tibetan, and the change was effected by major alterations in local policies more than by the exigencies of foreign outlook or temperament. Those who had created narratives after 1987 that focused on dissent, protest, and their suppression by the state found themselves wandering down streets where there were fewer police visible and far less crime than in the cities from which they had come. Those streets were now lined with arcades, malls, and shops advertising the same cornucopia of endlessly available commodity goods we were accustomed from our own histories to see as the goal of social progress.

Visiting writers struggled with the difficulty of reconciling the sudden and visible surge of material prosperity with remembered concerns about political abuse, of which they could no longer see or hear evidence. One Western writer, after visiting Tibet, wrote a book-length apology for having been an active campaigner for Tibetan dissidents in the fifteen years before. Some social scientists produced studies aiming to discredit claims by Tibetan exiles; one set out to prove that conditions of rule in Tibet could not be termed colonial and that the exile leader's statements could not be trusted. Other writers seemed offended at the tone of popular Western rhetoric about Tibet, from which they wished to separate themselves, or embarrassed by what they now saw as their own naïveté. For some, what they encountered in their visits to twenty-first-century Tibet seemed more prominent and meaningful than the disturbing events about which they had read a decade earlier.

The modern mechanisms of discreet control still abounded—video cameras to monitor the crowds, plainclothes policemen, informants, professional eavesdroppers, electronic surveillance, and so forth—but more had changed than policing methods: in the capital open demonstrations against the government had ceased. Some 200 protests had been reported from Tibet in the years after the one I experienced on my first visit, but, although there was news of incidents in other, often rural, areas, few had been heard of in Lhasa after 1996. The calculus of dissent had changed. Anyone who expressed open disapproval of state policy faced long years in prison, and it must have seemed that the public statement of such sentiments was not worth the costs it would necessarily entail to one's life and family. In any case, most of the Tibetans bold enough to risk taking to the streets either were in prison or had fled to India. I had by chance seen a sign of public dissent in the Tibetan capital when a miniature device of some sort exploded outside a courthouse in October 2000. Police rushed everywhere in a state of high anxiety to make sure no foreign tourist would realize what had occurred, but I was there long enough to observe that the only effect was a little streak of rubbish scattered across the pavement, not distinguishable from what was usually there before the sweeper ladies in their soiled blue work clothes arrived with their long brooms early every morning. Foreign writers were unlikely to see any such event, and, since they could speak to few people, they had to rely on what they saw more than on what they heard. The story that thus confronted them was not opposition but development.

This was not the only change in foreign writing about Tibet. At just the same time in the 1990s, Chinese writers and artists also found a new genre, one familiar in Western writing since at least the time when James Hilton wrote *Lost Horizon*: the eulogy for the beauty of Tibet's landscape, the grandeur of its traditional architecture, and the charm of its people and their "colorful" beliefs. Since 2003 a million tourists have visited Tibet each year, 20 times the number in 1987, and 90 percent of them have been Chinese citizens gazing with newly acquired interest, by no means always superficial, at the more exotic parts of their nation.

This gaze of the new Chinese middle classes toward the promise offered by their western hinterlands was linked to a movement that had been widespread in republican China in the decades before the Communists took over: the rediscovery of Tibet as a source of Buddhist teaching. Eighteen years before, I had seen Chinese tourists laughing publicly at the sight of Chinese Buddhist monks bravely trying to perform a simple ceremony in the temple atop the giant Buddha in Leshan, in the province of Sichuan. That same year, in the Gelugpa temple in Zorge in the eastern Tibetan borderlands, I had, unnoticed, watched a cadre in knee-high boots stride up and down a temple walkway screaming abuse at an assembly of several hundred monks who had been taking part in formal theological debate before an audience of nomads. In Lhasa in 1988, Chinese visitors, along with the Chinese troop patrols, had customarily walked the wrong way around the Jokhang in order to show a healthy distance from Tibetan notions of religious propriety.

But among the wave of Chinese visitors in the new millennium a substantial number, including cadres from the inland areas, were Buddhists who had come to see Tibet as the font of a recaptured spiritual tradition. Chinese visitors to the Jokhang would offer scarves and gifts to the statues of the Buddha, and sometimes bow before them. I met a Chinese businessmen who had traveled to Lhasa on his summer holiday from his office in Korea just to hear a Tibetan lama speak. I knew one Tibetan lama in Lhasa, a mid-ranking official whose colleagues did not know of his religious standing, in whose house at least three Chinese people had lived for several years, looking to outsiders like unobtrusive tenants but actually there as his disciples. Among my friends in the city were two Chinese students who had taken Tibetan names and learned the language. They had visited most of the major lamas remaining in Chinese territory, and were producing textbooks in Chinese for students of Buddhism. Not unlike Younghusband, though with far greater seriousness and learning, some of the Chinese whose parents had arrived in Tibet to liberate it from itself had become devotees of its culture and beliefs.

The increase in individual Chinese religiosity was particular to a certain sector and was not matched by greater tolerance of Tibetan Buddhism by the state. At the end of the 1990s an opposite trend had begun: stronger controls in monasteries, a general order forbidding officials and their families from engaging in any form of religious activity, and a ban on any schoolchildren or older students attending religious ceremonies.

With the century, I changed too. Instead of a reader of books about Tibet and an occasional visitor, I became for months at a time a foreign resident. Aspects of the city that had seemed before 2000 to be elements of fabled history or scars of modern encroachment became in time the normal drabness of my uninspiring, lived environment. As I became accustomed to the spread of urbanization, it lost the ability to shock and became simply normative.

I had a semiofficial position at the university, where each summer I would herd as best I could the students I brought with me from America and Europe, hounding them into the classrooms where they studied during the day and out of the nightclubs and bars that they frequented at night. They lived with me in a university building reserved for foreigners, into which we were locked each night at 11:30. There was little or no contact with other students on the campus, though we were not told of any explicit rule forbidding it. Those who visited us had to show their identity cards and sign their names, and few Tibetans came to see us. There were other foreign students and teachers in our dormitory who were vague about their aims in coming to Tibet to study one of the world's more difficult languages and who had a stream of local visitors, apparently unhindered by officialdom. These foreigners, it seemed, were Protestant missionaries, discreetly working to alter the history of Tibet in a more radical way than the Chinese Communists had managed. The Chinese ban on such endeavors was not enforced as long as their activities were private, and each Sunday our fellow students of unclear aim would go by bus to a local orphanage where no one spoke English and no one knew the meanings of the songs they taught the children. One day by chance I saw a student from Korea putting his hand on the heads of infants among the pilgrims in the Potala and whispering words that, when challenged, he declared to me were the real blessings these lost people yearn for. An American of similar persuasion counseled me more gently, explaining that Tibetan Buddhists are damned to hell. Later she returned to apologize for her omission in having failed to add that I am too.

We nonmissionaries mainly inferred the rules that limited us through a vague sense of recent history or from collective fears. These last were more effective than explicit prohibitions. We were not permitted more than a day's journey outside the city without a permit and an escort, but we were free to wander at will within the urban area, which was growing by the day. We were not told of many other regulations, although for some reason we were not allowed to travel by bus outside the city, even with an escort. Other limitations emerged osmotically, as when one afternoon after class a student brought a local friend, a nun, back to visit her in the dormitory, and I was summoned by an outraged official. I should already have known, she said, shocked at my ignorance, that such people had "old brains." That was the only way we discovered what no Westerner could have envisaged: without express permission, monks and nuns were forbidden to enter the university campus. I discovered later that this rule of separation applied to most official precincts in the city. Indigenous religiosity had come to be for the Chinese not unlike what personal hygiene had been for Younghusband and his crew.

My two narratives thus converged into one stream. There was no longer history on the one hand and experience on the other. There was no task more exacting than persuading teachers to assign homework for the classes, meeting local colleagues for lunch or dinner, having my students complete their coursework, or helping them avoid breaching known or unknown laws. For at least a portion of each year I became a part of the contents of buildings that I had until then viewed as an outsider. Their distinctiveness blurred, and the project of describing them became hard to maintain. As my life in Lhasa filled with the momentary excitements and quotidian despairs of work, relationships, food, and sleep, the streets I had studied became ways to get to a meeting or a meal, and buildings whose history I had once dreamed of understanding became permeable exteriors of which only the contents mattered: they became unnoticed extensions of the people I knew and the ways in which they lived, talked, and slept. Any clarity of vision that I had once thought I had upon arrival became obscured, and the lines that Italo Calvino had said were written in the corners of city streets and the gratings of windows became invisible. They could not be deciphered. They were no longer available as the distinct elements that the foreign writer wishes for, to control, describe, and play with according to his or her dreams.

But that was only true of the spaces in which I lived and moved—the university, the bookstores, the newly constructed Tibetan-style homes of my fellow teachers, the Muslim and Chinese restaurants I frequented, and the spaces in between. There was the photocopy shop run by a Chinese woman I had once briefly met in a train station in Qinghai, and the bicycle repair store, the last in Lhasa to be run by a Tibetan, where I bought endless nuts and bolts and inner tubes to encourage its survival. All of these places belonged to the new forms of architecture: white-tiled garage, Stalinist block, blue-fronted modernist, or *faux*-Tibetan concrete. But between these sites I had colonized with my familiarity were other buildings that remained unknown. Their visible, impenetrable exteriors resisted my gaze. They had contents and histories with which I had no acquaintance. Thus simplified, they remained lexical items with which I could weave stories. But, knowing both too little and too much, I could no longer claim the confidence to expound upon them.

I rarely dared to enter these unfamiliar places, not certain about the perimeters of safety for those living there. Especially I was nervous about entering any of the old houses still standing in the Barkor, the yet unbroken links to the Tibetan past. These still spoke of stories too dangerous for me to dally with, too close to the perils I had known ten or twenty years before. I didn't want to be reminded of the errors I had made then, or to repeat them now. Maybe the memories were ghosts that should long since have been expelled. On several occasions, other foreigners told me that they had made such visits without incident. My anxiety was probably the exaggeration of an overactive mind.

One day a Western scholar came to speak to my students at the university. He was a distinguished figure in Tibetan studies and had spent considerable time in Lhasa. He argued that any diffidence about entering Tibetan houses and talking to the locals amounted to needless paranoia. For years, he said, he had spoken to every Tibetan he met and entered their houses without constraint, and that as long as one avoided saying anything political, no harm could ensue.

I accepted the next invitations that came to me by chance, to see if the professor was correct. There were three, all unsolicited, and all from people who knew nothing of my past and whom I had never met before and never saw again.

The first came the next day. I was teaching at the university that term and met with my students each week in a teahouse, in a group; that was the only time I saw my Tibetan students outside the classroom. The Chinese students came often to visit me, or took me to their homes. There was no reticence with them, and no concern about official sanctions; one even suggested marriage. But with the Tibetans none of that had happened till that day, when I met one with a friend in the street. The friend invited me alone to his home nearby. It was one of the last old buildings in the Barkor, and I wandered around its courtyard and its sagging rooftops, played with the children, and took a picture of an ancient saddlebag hanging in the shrine room that technically he was not supposed to have. Then he took me to a room in another part of the building where an elderly man, nearly blind, sat alone in the dark. I asked no questions; I knew my visit had gone beyond playing with the children. The old man had not met a Tibetan-speaking foreigner since his youth, and told me, unasked, of twenty years he had spent in prison. He said the best part of his life had been destroyed. In the 1950s he had been a radical, eager to rebuild his country and its society with the tools of modern knowledge. But he had thought to do that in a Tibetan way,

and had paid the price. Maybe he was one of those who had met earlier with Phuntsog Wanggyal in the Kyitöpa, or had dreamed of going
to study in Kalimpong, as had the dancer Tashi Tsering. But reading
about such a history was much easier than encountering a person
who had lived one. I left the room as fast as decorum would allow in
case he was discovered speaking to me. I did not see him or my host
again. The following summer, when I returned to Lhasa, the house
had been demolished.

The second invitation came the next day, when I was buying something in my friend T.'s shop and a young Tibetan friend of hers came
in. He was also from the countryside, but he could read and write, and
he wanted to take me to his workplace next door to help him practice
English and to entertain his colleagues. We wouldn't be alone, and he
was unlikely to have any troubling memories such as I had heard about
the day before. So I went with him into a new, utilitarian factory where
Tibetans worked at machines and turned out assembly-line products.
Lots of people thronged the hallway, and everyone could hear the patter
of our anodyne remarks. Then I was taken around the factory offices to
greet the staff, and by chance found myself alone for a few minutes in
a small, sealed cubicle with a middle-aged woman from the stock order-
ing department. She told me that Tibet had been ruined by its new rulers, that the culture was being destroyed, and that she was waiting for
the Dalai Lama to return. Again I left as rapidly as possible.

The last time, I was with the Western scholar. He took me to visit a
Tibetan family he knew. After a while he left the room, and someone
told me we were all leaving to go somewhere else. I was bundled, along
with the family's children and the maid, into one of a fleet of taxis. I
thought the professor was coming too, but when we arrived somewhere
on the far side of the city, by now swathed in night, I realized that he had
not been brought with us; he must have still been in the other house,
drinking tea and not discussing politics.

Here, on the outskirts of the metropolis, I didn't get the chance
to discuss anything: I was told. An important official described how
his superiors had just shut down a major project he was involved in,
related to Tibetan culture. He had spent several years checking the
project documents with his colleagues and superiors to make sure
there were no ambiguities, but it had been closed down anyway for
some political transgression, and he was awaiting a decision on his

punishment. I couldn't follow all the details that had gotten him into trouble, except one that related to the provenance of some ancient Tibetan artifact that might or might not have had a Chinese origin, but I understood that his punishment would be either early retirement, being sacked without pension, or judicial sentencing. I think in the end it was the second, but I am not sure.

After that, I stopped accepting invitations.

8

MESTIZO:
TWO NARRATIVES CONVERGE

 In a teahouse opposite the university, I was talking with a student from Australia about her academic progress. We were in one of the countless rows along the new city streets of featureless, two-story, garage-type cavities constructed out of concrete since the 1990s. Four identical stores alongside it served the Tibetan population of the campus. The room was barely larger than a shack, with two low tables on either side, each with a pair of benches roughly hewn out of wood. A crude partition had been set up to ward off the fumes from the gas stove in the back, where the sister of my main Tibetan student worked daily until midnight preparing all the dishes on the menu. As in every Tibetan teahouse, these were sweet tea or butter tea, or, for those who wanted to eat, a meat broth, called *thupa,* or rice and potatoes with flecks of beef, called *sha 'mdre.*

Like her fellow teahouse workers, the sister was from the countryside and could not read or write. But her brother had married a city woman who, having obtained a clerical position in the office that manages Lhasa's monasteries, had been able to afford a business license. It was hanging on the wall, carefully framed. Near it was a picture of a yak's skull. It was draped with a white *khata* and so must have become a sacred emblem of Tibet, probably of recent origin. There were posters of football players and Chinese pop stars. Above the door hung a faded photograph of a leafless tree, an image whose significance, if it had any, I did not know.

The table was stained with the marks of countless cups and bowls, and among them a student of the English language had carved the words *I lvoe.* The imperfect spelling did not detract from the care with which each serif of each letter was engraved. I imagined the girl who inspired such graffiti giggling at its cosmopolitan daring.

The usual customers were male youths who in the evenings were most often, if they had the cash, the worse for wear from alcohol. But it was still afternoon and an older woman, rotund and extroverted, was sitting at the next table. Her son was studying at the university across the road; she herself had not had such an education. She was explaining to her friends why a certain lama deserved respect above all others in the city. There were few lamas left in Lhasa whom she knew of, and it sounded like she had never met one face to face; I realized I'd never heard a normal Tibetan in Lhasa talk openly about a spiritual master. Probably it was because, except for the great *Geshe* Lamrim, whom I had tried unsuccessfully to visit at Drepung on my first trip to Tibet, ten years before he died in 1997, none had received permission to give teachings to the public.

The lama she respected was one she had heard about but whose name she did not know. So she described his achievements to her friends, which were that he had restored two or three dilapidated Tibetan mansions in the Lhasa Barkor to their original condition. He knew the design and layout of all the old Tibetan buildings that had stood in the capital in the old days, she said, and could draw their plans from memory and recite the histories of their occupants.

I realized that she was referring to Minyak Chökyi Gyaltsen, whom Western scholars think of as a kind of scholar-architect, an autodidact, perhaps the only such Tibetan to have shared that kind of knowledge. He was brought out of decades of seclusion after 1990 partly through the efforts of a young German enthusiast, who for a short while had been allowed to bring in foreign funds for restoration work until he was expelled. But for the lady in the teahouse, Minyak Chökyi Gyaltsen was a *rinpoche*, a revered spiritual master, and his work on Lhasa's physical fabric a mark of exceptional learning and religiosity.

It was the first time I had heard an ordinary Tibetan lament the loss of Tibetan-style buildings. "I would never live in one of those buildings built by Chinese," she said. "I only feel comfortable in a Tibetan one." I recalled those Westerners who five years earlier had scoffed at the years of fund raising the German did to support renovation work by Tibetan craftsman, largely unemployed until he had arrived. Only bourgeois foreigners cared about old buildings, his critics had said, insisting that modern Tibetans preferred creature comforts and were indifferent to matters of aesthetics and tradition. If that had ever been so, it seemed that it was no longer the case.

My closest Chinese friend in Lhasa at that time owned an Internet shop opposite the side gate of the university. He had come to Tibet not by choice but because his wife taught piano in the music school, and it was easy for him to make good money on the side by hiring out computers by the hour. In his arcades young boys of all nationalities played war games all night, and girls sent messages to friends in inland China. The war games were voiced in American English. The computers wrote in English or Chinese.

He was a man of endless charm and sophistication and spoke perfect, unaccented English with a strong smattering of American slang, even though he had never been beyond his country's borders. We drove in a cab past the rows of flashing neon signs that illuminate the frontage of the new development on Thieves' Island, the former picnic site now turned into a maze of lush restaurants, stores, and brothels. He had just treated me to a meal of Sichuan hot-pot in a luxurious eatery on the western edge of town, where uniformed flunkies had helped us into our cab and where at least 200 Chinese and Tibetan customers were paying a month's official wages for a taste of inland cuisine and opulent milieu.

As we passed the beckoning signs of nightlife on Thieves' Island, I had asked my friend what he thought of the city. He was the only person I knew in Lhasa who would have been unafraid to criticize the government, had he wished to, and not only when its officers raided his arcades, ostensibly for some technical abuse of Internet regulations, in order to extract a bribe. "I do not like what we have done to this city," he said. I thrilled to find confirmation of my own unstated sentiments.

"We have not treated these Tibetans as well as they deserve," he continued. "The buildings are too low. What this place needs is tower blocks like we have in Chengdu."

I mumbled something, confused.

"Is that the religion women cannot practice?"

It was the third time we had met in the two rooms that made up her family's apartment. Since she was studying English, it was okay for me to visit her. Past the Potala, right at the fork, across the roundabout, and into the Chinese part of Lhasa. Left at the second alleyway after the Golden Yaks.

"Is that the what?" I said. It wasn't very good English, and I was only there on the pretext that I spoke English well. Once a week, Thursday nights. It had taken me a while to find my way. No one seemed to be watching and I always waited until nightfall, but tourists rarely visited this part of town, west of the Golden Yaks, so it made no difference: I was conspicuous anyway.

There was a door in the wall on the far side of the courtyard, across a sward of splinters left by the glass-cutters who worked there during the day. Probably Chinese, I thought viciously, who knew all about hard work and private enterprise but hadn't discovered the broom.

Beyond the door in the wall was a second, tiny courtyard leading to the two rooms cut out of a former outhouse. The first was lined with gilt knickknacks and kitschy calendars. What I could see of the second was lined with books.

"Youtai religion," she explained. The Chinese term for Jews and Judaism. "Women cannot practice."

There was only one place I knew where that statement had been formulated. She couldn't have seen it; they don't show that sort of film in Tibet. They show Hong Kong martial arts films and Hindi movies and dubbed action films featuring Sylvester Stallone. Nothing too troubling for the mind: mostly about violence, mostly about men, very little about love or sex, nothing about religion. And twenty-five-part television marathons about Tibetans' liberation from feudal overlords by fresh-faced youths dressed in the plain, faded green of the PLA uniform, which was now so popular that on Thieves' Island on the south side of the city you could rent a private room in a restaurant and be served by girls wearing the same 1950s uniforms, only newly creased and unfaded, and revolutionarily bright red lipstick.

And anyway all the cinemas in town except for two were closed, because some smart planner in the Party had worked out that wealthy people don't take part in demonstrations and tripled all the salaries. So everyone with a job had bought a VCR, even the Tibetans. But she still didn't have one, so she couldn't have seen it. And she clearly didn't know that the ban on Jewish women studying had passed from most of our communities fifty years ago. This was a one-source piece of knowledge, and that source could only be ...

"Yen-tel," she said. "Yen-tel."

She came back from the other room with A Collection of the World's 1,000 Best Films. At least I think it was called that, but I can't read Chinese. But there, under 1982 or 1983, it was: "Directed by Barbra Streisand, Produced by Barbra Streisand, Starring Barbra Streisand, Yentl, the story of the Jewish girl who won't accept that the study of religion is not allowed for her." The girl of whom Bashevis Singer had written in his wicked, impenetrable, and subversive way; the girl who had disguised herself as a boy in order to study and who, in her desperation to maintain the illusion, had ended up in a wholly fabricated marriage. And who after many years had been turned into the heroine of a sepia-toned Hollywood epic for which they hadn't given Babs even a copper yak, let alone an Oscar.

My Thursday evening pupil was not far from Barbra's age. Once, I had heard my pupil sing, a spiritual she had learned in its entirety from a Japanese film in which a "Negro," as she put it, had died after falling from a cliff for some reason I couldn't grasp, singing. She had sung divinely, evoking his suffering and that of his people, and I had sat there on her sofa among the nylon cushions and the plastic flowers and discreetly cried. But she didn't have a film star's looks. The horn-rimmed spectacles, the scraped-back hair, the asexual garb, the absence of adornment, severity of appearance. At first, three weeks before, in the Snowlands restaurant where she had asked if I would teach her, she had seemed more like an Asian Rosa Klebb. She embodied the Chinese puritan, the type who were already too committed to abandon woolen stockings for skin-tight polyester suits and nylons when the market had arrived, or, rather, had been pushed in. Or the ones who gambled that the state bureaucracy was a safer bet than the main street stores and nightclubs that they maybe had realized, even then, were sure as the spring tide to come.

She didn't only look like a stern-faced Chinese cadre: she was a Chinese cadre. A very high-up Chinese cadre. At the last lesson I finally dared to ask, "What do you do?"

"You would not understand," she said. "I have seen films. I know what Americans in offices do. Especially New York. They work, all the time. It's a different system here. We do nothing. We play mahjong and we do nothing. It's different here."

Her gamble had been right, of course: she did nothing all day and still got paid. Handsomely by local standards, 2,000 kuai a month, I'd bet. Of course she'd been right: the Party wouldn't yet break the iron rice bowl in Tibet, the lifelong social safety net. Tibet is one place where it doesn't mind paying for compliance, at least among officials. Anyway, she had hedged her bets both ways: she had long since told her husband to leave, and had bought part-ownership of a high-class nightclub, in which Sichuanese migrant girls in scanty outfits—Tibetan girls, she said, just don't know how to do it—served liquor to Chinese soldiers and office staff who were drinking up their altitude allowances and remoteness bonuses but still had plenty left to squander in brothels on their way back to their bare and lonely one-lightbulb rooms in China's western outpost.

That's a smart cadre. Play it both ways.

She served more tea. Chinese leaf tea, almost colorless, bitter but refreshing in the intense cold since the sun had gone down. I was still trying to exonerate my religion. It was just a custom in some communities, I stammered hopeful-ly, the ban on female learning has no written basis. "They were the ones who killed Yishu," *she declared. The Chinese word for Jesus. So now I knew where she had learned her English: it must have been from the officially sanctioned foreign English teachers, the same covert Protestant evangelists who had told me that all Tibetans were damned to hell. My forebears had killed Jesus, so I understood why I should go there; what the Tibetans had done, I wasn't sure. But the missionaries weren't there to explain these things to foreigners. They had more pressing work to do.*

She looked through the book and wrote some notes on films she found. Bullit. Star Wars. Vertigo. *Her pen was lavishly inlaid with fake lapis la-zuli, an excess of plastic opulence.* "Presented to Tibet's Cadres by the Central Authorities' Representative Delegation on the 30th Anniversary of Peaceful Liberation," *was faintly etched on it in Tibetan. It ran out of ink again. I lent her mine.*

"I was in it," *I said.* "The tailor. The apprentice tailor."

She took no notice; she was writing in her notebook. A long description of her father's life lay across its pages, written in a grotesque cursive that knew no horizontals, and she was copying my corrections to her homework from the week before. He had been a landless laborer in the Yunnanese southwest fifty years before, and had fled to join Maoist guerrillas in the hills after beating his landlord's donkey to death by mistake. But it wasn't his oppressed creden-tials that had brought him to high office under the new regime: it was the happenstance that he had learned Tibetan in his youth while driving animals to market across the mountains in northwest Yunnan. First he was a translator for the arriving army as it followed the passes he had so often crossed, then he had some years of education in the cadre school, and finally he became a county leader, or as she put it, a district magistrate. This woman ate foreign-language dictionaries for breakfast.

"She reads everything," the Tibetan girl from the Snowlands told me later. "All she does is read. None of us knows as much as her. She's read all of The Water Margin. *And not just the* Dream of the Red Chamber, *either. Other things too," she said. "She hardly goes out, she just reads."*

I remembered the Dostoevsky I had recognized among the rows of Chinese novels next to the photo of her taken as a student twenty years earlier at college, with the red neck scarf that marked her Party future. It was printed on the lightly plasticated paper used for posters at that time; too large for any private photograph, it had some caption printed underneath. She must have been a propaganda model whose image was distributed across the country. My God, she had been beautiful then. Joyous, gleaming, flush with the promise of revolution. Now rows and rows of bookshelves towered around the dusty memorabilia of a thrilling youth. There were cheap encyclopedias leaning against the empty fish tank, and picture books of other countries stacked beside the songbird's cage. And all across the glass-topped table were ornate cups and boxes filled with plastic flower stems and fountain pens whose reservoirs no longer would accept ink.

She passed me the next installment of her homework. This time it was not about her father. It was about her mother, who had been even poorer than her husband, and had become a much higher cadre than either him or their ever-so-accomplished daughter. Something really high, but this was not for telling, not even in the quest to acquire more vocabulary. All I knew was that the mother had been born of poor farmers in the hills just west of the Drichu, and had traveled to Lhasa behind the army for which her husband was then translating. Swept up in that great movement, she had ended up by the 1970s as a leader in Tibet.

That was when I realized. West of the Drichu lay the heartlands of Tibet. My pupil couldn't write Tibetan, she couldn't read it, she could only speak it with effort; she surely wore no chupa, and she didn't eat parched barley flour. But her mother was Tibetan. And on weekends and late at night, perhaps, or sometimes in her dreams, maybe, the daughter was Tibetan too.

The Tibetan language likes to play with unequal pairings and conflicting negatives: ra ma lug, lha ma yin—*neither beast nor bird, neither goat nor sheep, neither god nor human. Tibetans do not describe such people as "half this, half that," but as "gya ma bod": neither Chinese nor Tibetan. I watched her add more new words to her vocabulary list and wondered if I was looking into the mixed, the hybrid, the nondual, the undivided, the commingled, the neither-being-nor-not-being described in the Higher Sutras. Then I remembered I was looking at the Cadre Who Played It Both Ways, who was weaned on Marx and who had graduated on Bashevis Singer. The Tibetan* mestizo.

I wonder what my pupil is doing now. Whether she had to answer questions about the unofficial evening classes. Whether she kept her resolve to sell the nightclub holding. Whether she is still writing in her notebook, hoping for some Western teacher to come one day to check the endless pages of cursive confessional. Whether she dreams she is Tibetan. Whether she still thinks Jews are all misogynists. Why she never asked me who the assistant tailor was.

Bashevis Singer and Hollywood gave Yentl a glorious ending, by having her escape the misery of her homeland and the fiction of her marriage by taking a boat to America. Being great writers of fiction and crafters of dreams, they never told us if she was happy when she got there. Or if she retained the knowledge of her religion and her language after the first few years had passed. Or if the culture left behind survived. They didn't describe the Land of Individual Freedom where Barbra had been unhappy as a child, and where in Manhattan, men still survive by roaming the streets at night and pulling Coke cans out of garbage bins to turn in for maybe $15 a day. They just described the soaring ecstasy of a flight to somewhere else.

The half-goat, half-sheep grazes both the pastureland and the mountainsides; she doesn't run away to sea. The pure-breed lives only in the imagination, and finally migrates in pursuit of dreams; the hybrid buys shares in nightclubs, reads books in foreign languages, and adapts. The one enchants, the other discards outward charms. With her the future lies.

9

THE MULTILAYERED STREETS

The architectural styles to be seen along the city streets are words in a text through which one can infer the simultaneous existence of the many Lhasas that today crowd one another for space and dominance within the evolving city. There is the traditional mud-packed, stone-and-timber house in a winding alley, perhaps occupied by a practicing Buddhist who wishes to be near the Jokhang; there are the false-fronted houses of the New Tibetan style, inhabited by Tibetan tenants and by settlers from the Chinese plains, in the city's heart. There are the featureless rectangular blocks laid out along the grids imposed across the city, which are the most prolific type of building to be found in the capital, housing state offices and their Chinese and Tibetan employees. Garage-like teahouses owned by semi-indigent Tibetans mingle with the small-time bars of petty Chinese migrants from Sichuan. The great square and the smaller efforts at grand, colonial statuary are pointed out by leaders as signs of progress. The modernist nightclubs and multistory blocks mark the new, expanding commercial city and the opportunities for citizens with the urge or the wherewithal to spend their wealth. To them can be added the *Simsha* style of Tibetan retro buildings and picnic parks that hint at recollections of the past, and the official flamboyance of the new

street decorations, with their plastic palm trees and their singing mush-rooms planted along the showcase thoroughfares of Lhasa.

Of these eight styles, and the worldviews they represent, six were cre-ated by the new administrators of the region as expressions of one or another form of power or benevolence. These styles articulated the ad-ministration's role and purpose in Tibet, a constant oscillation between implanting civilization and the suppression of dissent. In this way China has not been dissimilar from other rulers in annexed lands. Where new China's contribution to Tibet stood out was in its early aesthetic choices. Unlike Western colonial architects, who sought to exhibit elegance as well as power, for some decades Chinese socialists demonstrated the determination and capability to build great cities, the hallmark of self-conscious civilizations, without including the display of refinement in their creations. Perhaps it was because China was then impoverished, or because within it lingered an ideological imperative, learned from the Soviets, to discard self-conscious artistry.

Or perhaps their idea of the city at that time involved an instinctual extirpation of energies that, like alleyways, tapered house frames, and decorated windows, seemed irrational and unnecessary. One can imag-ine that if the new administrators of Tibet had found a demoness stretched across the countryside, they would not have merely pinned her down as Princess Wencheng did, but would have tried to extinguish every trace of her existence in order to obliterate the untamed forces of female and premetropolitan nature. The Tibetans too had some regard, especially from the time Tsongkhapa established his three monasteries around Lhasa, for the taming of unruly passion, in that many men and women chose monastic professions and thus wore unvaried and non-gendered dress. But the Tibetans had not sought to eliminate the exis-tence of aesthetic sensibility, least of all in the vivacity of their architec-ture. The construction in Lhasa between 1959 and the 1990s thus spoke of a governmental instinct to suppress natural energies not only in the realm of ethics and social engineering but also in architecture and design.

Of the six styles that constitute the Chinese contribution to the ar-chitecture of new Tibet, two—the dormitory block and the garagelike shop—are statements of this antiaesthetic functionalism. The first still dominates the city: indistinguishable rectangular buildings made out of concrete, with few distinctive features and little use of color, arranged along straight roads dissecting the city, the older ones contained within a walled courtyard, giving one point of access and control and imparting a sense of fortification, as if the world outside might be a threat to the building and its inhabitants. They are a monument to a time that some wish to forget, before the 1980 turning point was inserted into Tibetan and Chinese history. The most recent styles—the New Tibetan, the monumental, the modernist, and the new flamboyance—also come from the East, the land of divination, but in a later form. They evince an urge to decorate as well as to construct. If they convey a message written by the state, it is of national success and aspiration, and is increasingly a call for the individual desire repressed earlier to triumph over ideology and memories of the past.

The indigenous styles, the traditional townhouse and the New *Simsha*, like the picnic grounds, are part of a conversation with the Tibetan past and a dream about the future that speak of the benefits that come with modernity, and of the memory of something important in the culture that the Chinese experiment in Tibet has sometimes sought to extirpate and at other times sought to reeducate. Within the walled and unwalled compounds of the city formed by these streets and buildings live people the archaeology of whose lives can scarcely be read from their exteriors, and whose present surroundings may speak nothing of their histories and desires. Those who were once aristocrats in pillared mansions with south-facing balconies may now reside in a corner of a crowded tenement. In the rain-stained offices of the government, a former yak herder works as a clerk. The general manager of the grand hotel, who is about to die, wonders if he would have been spared cancer had he remained a monk. The land on which his office stands was once a park where foreign visitors watched antlike monks thronging gold-roofed temples. The famous lama's new townhouse has been constructed in Tibetan style, financed by the sale of statues stolen from the Ramoche. A couple whispering words of love at night in a deserted parking lot forget they are standing on the roof beams of the hall of slumbering *nāgas*. In a concrete dormitory lives a woman from Gyantse; she never heard the Maxim guns as they mowed down her great-uncle. The pockmarked youth from the northern plateau selling CDs behind the blue-glass frontage of the department store belongs to the fifteenth generation of the offspring of King Gesar and has dreams of fighting men at night. The pop star singing Chinese songs under the spinning disco lights of what used to be the People's Cultural Palace thinks wistfully of her mother, who spoke a language she has forgotten now. The hawker from Sichuan selling turnips is unaware they are already growing at mGar's descendants' plot of land, where the straight new road cuts through the suburbs and becomes a track again on the sandy outskirts of the city.

These people and these streets contain within their memories one another's histories and futures, so that to the outsider—the foreigner, the visitor, and the conqueror—the square, the circle, the demoness, and the multilayered become confused and indistinguishable, as if in a story written, recited, and perhaps understood only by those who are in it.

The restaurant where I met him was not cheap, but it was near the office. Anyway, it was Chinese, so he would probably feel at home. The style was ultramodern and minimal, with square white pillars and metal chairs. Giant uncurtained windows stretched the full length of the building, so we could watch the London commuters struggling home against the rain. It didn't offer intimacy or comfort, but at least it looked expensive. And that is always an advantage.

He made a valiant effort to keep the conversation going. It wasn't like the banquets he described in Lhasa, when everyone drank till they were sick and then drank more. And there was no way I was going to sing or shout or dance, as I knew he would have done back home. But he made an effort to act as if he was enjoying himself.

We talked about work and how much there was to do, and about Christmas and how commercialized it was, and about his health and how it was getting better since he had arrived, since those early days when we had hidden him in attic rooms until asylum papers had been secured. He ordered another bottle of Kingfisher and we talked about how he couldn't sleep unless he drank a lot. I didn't ask, because I find tears so embarrassing, but obviously he was missing home. And then he told a joke.

It was an exceptional joke, because I had never understood any other joke he had told me, and he was always telling jokes that seemed more like proverbs, which I didn't understand and which didn't make me laugh. But this one seemed to be extraordinarily English. At least, it had an Englishman in it. Strange, because it was apparently quite true.

This Englishman had been bald and very tall. He must have been one of the diplomats stationed in Gyantse, in southern Tibet, before the war. I had been to Gyantse once, ten years before. I had seen the fort. So I could relate to this.

The Englishman had been invited to a dinner by Phala, the local lord of Gyantse. For the first course each guest was presented with a large pancake, steaming hot. Everyone waited for the Englishman to begin. But since there was no silverware, he was unsure what to do. So he waited to see what Phala would do with his pancake. Phala put it on his head. So the Englishman did too.

The joke was funny because Phala had lots of hair, braided and pinned up on his head, in the style of all Tibetan aristocrats, and the British man was bald, so the pancake must have burned his pate, a pain he no doubt had to hide. I could understand that. And my friend explained that it was Phala's lesson to the British, because the Tibetans who went to India had always been laughed at for not knowing what cutlery to use. So I thought I got it. It was all about the English being pompous and assuming they knew more than the Tibetans. I thought I got it.

So then he told another joke.

There were two men, one from Tsang in the south of Tibet and one from Lhasa. They met by chance one day at the top of the Gampa-la, the pass on the road south from the capital that leads toward Gyantse.

"Tell me," said the man from Tsang, "what is Lhasa like?"

"Do you mean," said the man from Lhasa, "that you have never been there?"

"No, I have never been there," said the man from Tsang.

"Then I could tell you anything I wanted," replied the man from Lhasa.

My friend the old Tibetan went red in the face with contentment and roared with laughter at his joke. I beamed approval conscientiously and muttered how hilarious it was.

The restaurant suddenly seemed rather cramped. I was acutely embarrassed. Why was it funny that the man from Tsang would believe anything he was told about Lhasa? I really didn't get it. I couldn't understand at all. The old Tibetan was still laughing. I couldn't understand at all.

PREFACE

Page xiii. **Foreign interpretations of Tibet:** The leading works on Western representations of Tibet are Peter Bishop's book, *The Myth of Shangri-La: Tibet, Travel Writing, and the Western Creation of Sacred Landscape* (Berkeley: University of California Press, 1989), and Donald C. Lopez's study, *Prisoners of Shangri-La: Tibetan Buddhism and the West* (Chicago: University of Chicago Press, 1998). A collection of scholarly essays on the same theme can be found in Thierry Dodin and Heinz Räther, eds., *Imagining Tibet: Perceptions, Projections, and Fantasies* (Boston: Wisdom, 2001). See also Peter Bishop's essay, "Reading the Potala," in Toni Huber, ed., *Sacred Spaces and Powerful Places in Tibetan Culture* (Dharamsala: Library of Tibetan Works and Archives, 1999). Martin Brauen has produced a valuable study of material representations of Tibet in his book *Dreamworld Tibet: Western Illusions* (New York and Tokyo: Weatherhill, 2004).

Page xiv. **Madame Blavatsky:** Helena Petrovna Blavatsky (1831–1891) explained the esoteric system that she called Theosophy in a number of books, including *Isis Unveiled: A Master Key to the Mysteries of Ancient and Modern Science and Theology* (New York: J. W. Bouton, 1877, 2 vols.) and *The Secret Doctrine: The Synthesis of Science, Religion, and Philosophy* (London: The Theosophical Publishing Company, 1888, 2 vols.). She claimed that her ideas were the result of mystical contact with an unidentified "master" in Tibet. For a discussion of her uses of the Tibet motif, see Poul Pedersen, "Tibet, Theosophy, and the Psychologization of Buddhism," in Thierry Dodin and Heinz Räther, eds., *Imagining Tibet*, 151–66.

Page xxi. **The British Invasion**: A detailed account of the expedition led by Colonel Francis Younghusband in 1903–4 is given in Charles Allen, *Duel in the Snows: The True Story of the Younghusband Mission to Lhasa* (London: John Murray, 2004). See also Peter Fleming, *Bayonets to Lhasa: The First Full Account of the British Invasion of Tibet in 1904* (London: R. Hart-Davis and New York: Harper, 1961) and Parshotam Mehra, *The Younghusband Mission: An Interpretation* (New York: Asia Publishing House, 1968). Younghusband's career is described in Patrick French's biography, *Younghusband: The Last Great Imperial Adventurer* (London: HarperCollins, 1994). The colonel's own account was published as *India and Tibet: a history of the relations which have subsisted between the two countries from the time of Warren Hastings to 1910; with a particular account of the Mission to Lhasa of 1904* (London: John Murray, 1910).

Page xxiii. **Luciano Petech:** Probably the most influential Western historian of Tibet, used the term "protectorate" to describe Tibet's status from the eighteenth century, in the title of his definitive study, *China and Tibet in the Early XVIIIth Century—History of the Establishment of the Chinese Protectorate in Tibet* (*Monographies du T'oung Pao*, Leiden: E. J. Brill, 1972).

Page xxvi. **Monasteries closed before the Cultural Revolution**: The number of monasteries closed down in central and western Tibet in the early 1960s is known from "The 70,000 Character Petition," written by the tenth Panchen Lama in China in 1962. The text remains secret within China but was published in translation in Robert Barnett, ed., *A Poisoned Arrow: The Secret Petition of the Tenth Panchen Lama* (London: Tibet Information Network, 1998). The Panchen Lama wrote that "before democratic reform [1959], there were more than 2,500 large, medium and small monasteries in Tibet. After democratic reform, only 70 or so monasteries were kept in existence by the government. This was a reduction of more than 97%" (52). The term "Tibet" would not have included the eastern Tibetan areas of Amdo or eastern Kham. At the time, the Panchen Lama was nominally in the position equivalent to Governor of Tibet, had just completed a lengthy inspection tour of conditions in many Tibetan areas, and had access to official statistics. The petition, which was submitted confidentially to the Chinese premier, Zhou Enlai, and then passed to Mao Zedong, also referred to thousands of arbitrary arrests and killings, and accused local officials of allowing famine to spread in many areas.

Page xxvii. **Ideas of democracy, freedom, and Tibetan nationhood**: The political conditions and concepts behind the 1987 demonstrations are discussed in detail in Ronald Schwartz, *The Circle of Protest: Political Ritual in the Tibetan Uprising, 1987–1992* (London: Christopher Hurst and New York: Columbia University Press, 1994). The study is based on research among Tibetans in Lhasa at the time. The only published photograph of the first protest in the series of demonstrations that began on September 27, 1987 was taken by Steve Lehman and is reproduced in *The Tibetans: Struggle to Survive* (New York: Umbrage Editions, 1998).

Page xxviii. **The concessions offered in the early 1980s**: A list of the concessional policies carried out by the Chinese authorities during the early 1980s is given in "Reflections on the Current State of Theoretical Policy in Tibet" (*Xizang Ribao* [the Chinese-language edition of the official party paper, *Tibet Daily*], August 7, 1989). The article, a polemical attack on those concessions was signed by "The Tibet Youth Association for Theory." "From June 1979 to November 1985," it argues, "though there were a great many speeches aimed at eliminating 'leftism,' among those hundreds of editorials and reviews there were only eight articles that stuck to the 'Four Cardinal Principles,' all of which were published during the campaign for 'the Elimination of Bourgeois Liberalization.' Over this long period, theoretical and ideological emphasis has been on a discussion of 'Re-understanding of Tibet' and 'Proceeding in All Cases from the Reality of Tibet.' Nationality theory and religion became the most popular subjects. Though many sociopolitical activities were in the name of Marxism and Maoism, in practice the Marxist and Maoist principles were lost." The Four Cardinal Principles, as promoted by Deng Xiaoping, were the supremacy of "the socialist road"; the supremacy of the Marxist-Leninist-Maoist system; the leadership of the Communist Party; and the democratic dictatorship of the proletariat. The last was later changed to "the democratic dictatorship of the people." I am grateful to the late Graham Clarke and to Jinchai Clarke for having drawn my attention to this important article. For critical accounts of policies in the Tibet Autonomous Region during the early 1980s, see Tsering Shakya, *The Dragon in the Land of Snows: A History of Modern Tibet Since 1947* (London: Pimlico and New York: Columbia University Press, 1999), 394–409; Tseten Wangchuk Sharlho, "China's Reforms in Tibet: Issues and Dilemmas," *Journal of Contemporary China* 1, no. 1 (Fall 1993): 34–60; and Warren Smith, *Tibetan Nation: A History of Tibetan Nationalism and Sino-Tibetan Relations* (Boulder: Westview, 1996), 563–96.

PREAMBLE

Page 1. **The Grove of Wild Roses**: This phrase is a translation of the name of Sera, a famous monastery founded in 1419 about two miles north of the center of Lhasa; the name is often mistranslated as "the place of hail." "The heap of rice" is the literal meaning of Drepung, the monastery five miles west of the capital, founded in 1416. The name is sometimes said to have arisen because of the appearance from afar of the white buildings on the slopes of Mount Gamphel Utse, but is more likely a reference to Dhanyakataka, the "string of grain," an early Buddhist monastery that flourished in Orissa in eastern India (see Sarat Chandra Das, *Tibetan-English Dictionary* [Calcutta: Bengal Secretariat Book Depot, 1902], 929); the site is now within Andhra Pradesh. "The place of bliss" is a loose translation of Ganden (literally, "having joy"), the Tibetan term for the Mahayana Buddhist paradise known in Sanskrit as Tushita. The name was given to the monastery that was founded in 1409 some 35 miles north-east of the city. These are the monasteries known in Tibetan as the *densasum*, or "the three seats." They were founded by the religious reformer Tsongkhapa (1357–1419) or his followers and led to the establishment of the Gelugpa school of Tibetan Buddhism—known in Chinese and some other sources as the "Yellow Hat" school—which became the dominant political force in Tibet after 1642 under its principal teachers, the Dalai Lamas. Before 1959 there are said to have been 5,000 monks in Sera, 10,000 in Drepung, and 7,000 in Ganden. The monasteries were unofficially reported in 2000 to have approximately 300, 700, and 200 monks respectively.

Page 1. **A city of some 200,000 people**: In the census carried out by the Chinese authorities in 1990 the population of the urban area of Lhasa was given as 163,000, and 29.5 percent of the inhabitants were identified as not Tibetans. This figure did not include temporary migrants, sometimes estimated in official documents at between 70,000 and 150,000 a year, or the military. Chinese official statistics concerning Lhasa are confusing because they usually relate to the larger area called in Chinese *Lasa shi,* literally the city or municipality of Lhasa. This term refers to a vast territory, equivalent in the Chinese administrative system to a *diqu* or prefecture, that includes hundreds of square miles of pasture and rural land, many towns, and seven other counties besides the actual city of Lhasa. The census in 2000 reported 141,500 Tibetans and some 75,000 Chinese, Hui (Chinese Muslims), and others as living in "city areas" of the TAR; the phrase probably refers to the built-up area at the center of the Lhasa conurbation, but could also include Shigatse, the second most important urban area in Tibet, which is sometimes also defined by the Chinese authorities as a city. The figures, probably underestimates, suggest that the official population for Lhasa and Shigatse was about 216,500. The latter town is sometimes estimated at having a population of 20,000 to 30,000. See "Overview of the Tibetan Population in the PRC from the 2000 Census," Tibet Information Network, September 30, 2003.

1. THE UNITARY VIEW

Page 5. **Dorje Yuthok's autobiography**: The autobiography of Dorje Yuthok, *House of the Turquoise Roof* (Ithaca, NY: Snow Lion, 1990), is one of several accounts of life in Lhasa produced in English in the late twentieth century by exiled Tibetan aristocrats or their biographers. Others include Rinchen Dolma Taring, *Daughter of Tibet* (London: John Murray, 1970); Jamyang Sakya and Julie Emery, *Princess in the Land of Snows: The Life of Jamyang Sakya in Tibet* (Boston: Shambhala, 1990); Jetsun Pema with Gilles Van Grasdorff, *Tibet: My Story: An Autobiography by the Sister of the Dalai Lama* (Shaftesbury, Dorset: Element, 1997); D. N. Tsarong, *In the Service of His Country: The Biography of Dasang Damdul Tsarong, Commander General of Tibet* (Ithaca, NY: Snow Lion,

2000); and Namgyal Lhamo Takla, *Born in Lhasa* (Ithaca, NY: Snow Lion, 2001). All of these except for the Tsarong volume are by women from noble families. The publication of English-language autobiographies by Tibetans in exile has been studied in Laurie Hovell McMillin, *English in Tibet, Tibet in English: Self-Presentation in Tibet and the Diaspora* (Basingstoke: Palgrave, 2001). A number of biographies and autobiographies of important lamas were also produced, such as those of the Dalai Lama, Chogyam Trungpa, and Khyongla Rato Rinpoche.

Page 6. **Rinchen Lhamo**: Rinchen Lhamo's book about the Tibetan people, which includes her comments on the attitudes of Londoners toward them, is the earliest English-language account by a Tibetan. It was published as *We Tibetans: An Intimate Picture, by a Woman of Tibet of an Interesting and Distinctive People* (London: Seeley Service and Co., 1926; reprint, New York: Potala Publications, 1995), 95–96. Rinchen Lhamo came from a wealthy family in Kham (eastern Tibet) and married Louis Macgrath King, an English diplomat who had been stationed in Dartsend (Tachienlu), and returned with him to London. The couple communicated in Chinese. She continues the remark cited here as follows: "Just before I came to Europe a high official connected with Tibetan politics said in my presence that the Tibetans were a simple people. This remark was so wide of the fact that I could not refrain from laughing. He was merely giving utterance to a conventional statement about us put into vogue by the travellers." The Dharamsala-based historian Tashi Tsering cites this quotation in his discussion of earlier Tibetan writings about Tibet and Tibetans, *How the Tibetans Have Regarded Themselves Through the Ages* (Dharamsala: Amnye Machen Institute, 1996).

Page 7. **Exiles and Westerners who were their scribes**: Many accounts of the lives of exiled Tibetans produced in English have relied on ghostwriters not very familiar with Tibetan. However, there are some notable exceptions, such as Tsewang Pemba's autobiography, *Young Days in Tibet* (London: Jonathan Cape, 1957) and Palden Gyatso's collaborative autobiography with Tsering Shakya, *Fire Under the Snow: The Testimony of a Tibetan Prisoner* (London: Harvill Press, 1998), published in the United States under the title *The Autobiography of a Tibetan Monk* (New York: Grove Press, 1997). An earlier, lesser-known example is Tashi Khedrup (compiled by Hugh Richardson), *Adventures of a Tibetan Fighting Monk* (Bangkok: Tamarind, 1986); Richardson was fluent in Tibetan. Two important collaborative autobiographies of Tibetans who remained within Tibet (Tashi Tsering, *The Struggle for Modern Tibet* and Baba Phuntsog Wanggyal, *A Tibetan Revolutionary*) have been produced by Melvyn Goldstein, also a fluent speaker.

Page 7. **Modern Chinese accounts of their non-Chinese nationalities**: Chinese views of their "minority nationalities" have been discussed by Western anthropologists in some detail since the late 1980s. See Chiao Chien and Nicholas Tapp, eds., *Ethnicity and Ethnic Groups in China* (Hong Kong: Chinese University of

Hong Kong, 1989); Dru Gladney, "Representing Nationality in China: Refiguring Majority/Minority Identities," *Journal of Asian Studies* 53, no. 1 (1994): 92–123; Stevan Harrell, "Civilizing Projects and the Reaction to Them," in Stevan Harrell, ed., *Cultural Encounters on China's Ethnic Frontiers* (Seattle: University of Washington Press, 1995), 3–36; Melissa Brown, ed., *Negotiating Ethnicities in China and Taiwan* (Berkeley: East Asian Institute, University of California, 1995); Louisa Schein, "Performing Modernity," *Cultural Anthropology* 14, no. 3 (1997): 361–95; and Susan Blum, *Portraits of "Primitives"* (New York: Rowman and Littlefield, 2001).

Page 7. **Publishing the seen impressions of foreign visitors**: For some time after the establishment of the PRC, Chinese officials based their work with foreigners on a principle that they termed "seeing is believing." Until the 1980s, however, this was in practice limited to those already considered friendly to official views. Tsan-Kuo Chang notes how supporters of China in the 1960s used this idea to discredit American journalists who were then not allowed to enter China, and shows how the writer and filmmaker Felix Greene, who made three trips to China before 1964, was able to question "the accuracy of some of the reports about Communist China conveyed to the American people by the press. He had been there in China and thus knew better. For most American journalists who had never visited China, Greene's charges were difficult to refute" ("China from Here and There: More Than Two Decades of Closed Borders and Narrowed Vision," *Media Studies Journal* [Winter 1999]). Chinese officials modified this approach in the late 1990s, when it was decided to try to convey information concerning Tibet to the West by developing closer relations with Western universities and with scholars of Tibetan studies, rather than by relying on visits by Western politicians or friendly journalists. The policy change is documented in International Campaign for Tibet, *China's Public Relations Strategy on Tibet: Classified Documents from the Beijing Propaganda Conference* (Washington: International Campaign for Tibet, November 15, 1993), which includes a translation of "Speech by Comrade Tenzin" (TAR Conference on External Propaganda Work Document No. 8, Regional Conference on External Propaganda Work, Beijing, March 11, 1993).

The emphasis on visual impressions persists in some journalistic and literary accounts, as, for example, in this article from *China Daily*, China's main English-language newspaper: "The Tibetan people always take great pride in their dress and the accessories they wear. This is evident in the heavy and well-preserved dresses passed down across generations and still shining on happy Tibetans.... Women on the prairie of northern Tibet look the most beautiful in summer when the flowers are in full bloom" ("Tibetan Finery Brightens an Austere Land," *China Daily*, May 24, 2004).

Page 70. **A Mexican senator**: The quotation from the Mexican visitor to Tibet is taken from "Great Changes Seen in Tibet—Moreno," *China Daily*, August 19, 1997.

Page 8. **Happy smiles on their faces**: Statements by Chinese officials about the happiness of Tibetans after 1980 can be found in governmental policy statements as well as in the official press. The phrase "the people of Tibet highly value their happy life today" was used frequently in official texts in the 1990s; see, for example, "Tibet University Campaign to Fight Separatism, Get Rid of Dalai Lama's Influence" (Tibet People's Broadcasting Station, April 14, 1997; published in translation in *BBC Summary of World Broadcasts*, April 15, 1997). Chen Kuiyuan, the Party Secretary of Tibet from 1992 to 2000, in a famous speech about art and the media in 1997, described a good radio program as one that "accords with the happy mood and mental attitude of the Tibetan people" ("Tibet Party Secretary Criticizes 'Erroneous Views' of Literature, Art," *Xizang Ribao (Tibet Daily)*, July 16, 1997, 1, 4, published in translation and retitled by the *BBC Summary of World Broadcasts*, August 5, 1997). Li Kai and Zhao Xinbing, in their booklet *Spectacles on the Snowy Plateau* (Beijing: China Intercontinental Press, 1995), refer to "the rich and happy life [that] is fully reflected in every aspect of the daily activities of the Tibetan people" (21).

Page 11. **Stories of monkish misbehavior**: Several episodes involving significant conflict or unrest in early twentieth-century Tibetan politics are described by Melvyn Goldstein in *A History of Modern Tibet: The Demise of the Lamaist State* (Berkeley: University of California Press, 1989). The protest by the monks of Loseling arose ostensibly over a dispute concerning land leases but really was a result of government disapproval of the monks' earlier support of the Chinese during the 1910–12 occupation of Lhasa. The episode is described in *History of Modern Tibet*, 104–109, and in Goldstein's earlier article, "Religious Conflict in the Traditional Tibetan State," in Lawrence Epstein and Richard F. Sherburne, eds., *Reflections on Tibetan Culture: Essays in Memory of Turrell V. Wylie* (Lewiston, ME: The Edwin Mellen Press, 1990), 231–47. The Dalai Lama's references to small incidents of theft and irritation among his retinue during his early years can be found in his second autobiography, *Freedom in Exile* (London: Hodder and Stoughton, 1990; San Francisco: HarperSanFrancisco, 1991, pp. 14–15, 48–49). An account of a dispute between the leading Tibetan officials and younger reformers is given in Alex McKay, "Tibet 1924: A Very British Coup Attempt?," *Journal of the Royal Asiatic Society*, Series 3, 7, 3 (November 1997).

Page 11. **Struggles to get control of the Sakya dynasty**: The dispute between the two lines of the Sakya family is described by Jamyang Sakya in her autobiography, *Princess in the Land of Snows*. Melvyn Goldstein adds a note about the dispute in his article "The Balance Between Centralization and Decentralization in the Traditional Tibetan Political System: An Essay on the Nature of Tibetan Political Macro-Structure," *Central Asiatic Journal* XV (1971): 170–82. Goldstein suggests that the losers in this dispute were among the main informants used by C. W. Cassinelli and Robert B. Ekvall in their study of Sakya politics, *A Tibetan Principality: The Political System of Sa sKya* (Ithaca: Cornell University Press, 1969), and that the findings of that study may have been skewed.

Page 11. **Outsiders in the manufacture of Tibetan myths**: I am grateful to Losang Rabgey for her insights on this question.

Page 12. **Six government officials executed**: The fighting with the Chinese began in late 1911 and continued for a year. In January 1912, *Tsipön* (Finance Minister) Trimon and Champa Tendar were appointed by the thirteenth Dalai Lama—then living in exile in India—as his representatives in the war effort. Champa Tendar ordered the execution of Tsarong, a *kalön* or cabinet minister, as well as of his son and of the cabinet secretary, Tsashagpa, for having had close relations with the Chinese, according to the account given by the former finance minister in W. D. Shakabpa, *Tibet: A Political History* (New Haven: Yale University Press, 1967; reprint, New York: Potala, 1984), 241. Three other senior officials were executed for having been on friendly terms with the monks of Tengyeling—Phunrabpa, the chancellor; Mondrong, a member of the national assembly; and Lobsang Dorje, a monk official. Goldstein describes these "executions" as "murders [by] pro-Dalai Lama forces" (*History of Modern Tibet* 64). An account by the former *kalön* Wangchen Gelek Surkhang suggests that these killings involved little or no official procedure, and notes that the executions of Tsarong's son, Phunrabpa, and Tsashagpa were carried out by Sera monks. Surkhang's account is given in his article "Tibet in the Early 20th Century" (*Tibetan Studies Internet Newsletter* 1, no. 2 [January 12, 1999]: part IV, also available at www.cwru.edu/affil/tibet/booksAndPapers/early20thtibet.htm).

Page 12. **The British Public School of Rugby**: The history of the four schoolboys sent with Lungshar to England in 1913 is discussed by Tsering Shakya in his article, "The Making of the Great Game Players: Tibetan Students in England 1912–1916," *Tibetan Review* XXI, no. 1. (1986): 12–17, and in Clare Harris and Tsering Shakya, eds., *Seeing Lhasa: British Depictions of the Tibetan Capital 1936–1947* (London: Serindia, 2003), 99ff. Changnöpa Ringang returned in 1924 with a degree in electrical engineering, the first graduate in Tibet; Kyibuk Wangdu Norbu had greater difficulty in adapting to English conditions and returned seven years earlier. See also Goldstein, *History of Modern Tibet*, 157 (fig. 19) and 159*n*24.

Page 12. **Lungshar returned...with notions of modernity**: An account in Tibetan of the Lungshar episode is given by Lungshar's son, Lhalu Tsewang Dorje, in *"Nga'i pha lung shar rdo rje tshe rgyal dran gso byas pa"* (Recollections of my father, Lungshar Dorje Tsegyal) in Bod rang skyong ljongs srid gros lo rgyus rig gnas dpyad gzhi'i rgyu cha zhib 'jug u yon lhan khang, *Bod kyi lo rgyus rig gnas dpyad gzhi'i rgyu cha bdams bsgrigs* (*Materials on the History and Culture of Tibet* [Beijing: Nationalities Publishing House, 1983], 2:93–109). The most extensive description of the Lungshar affair in English is given in Goldstein, *History of Modern Tibet*, 186–212, 819. In Chinese, a fictionalized account has been written by Yangdron (Tibetan: Dbyangs sgrol, Chinese: Yangzhen) in *Wu xingbie de shen* (*God Without Gender* or, in Tibetan, *'phrul kun 'dzoms kyi lha*). Her novel was turned into a twenty-episode television drama series, *Lasa Wangshi* (Tibetan: *lha* *sa'i sngon byung gtam rgyud*) or *The Tale of Lhasa's Past*, with script by Huang Zhilung, Zhen Lu, and Wang Zhangbo (CCTV/Tibet TV, 2001).

Lungshar seems never to have complained about what was done to him, according to the account given in Goldstein, *History of Modern Tibet*, 211–12. Shakabpa, the former finance minister writing in exile in the 1960s, was less sympathetic, describing Lungshar and his group as "political bandits" who were meddling in "highly confidential matters." He claims that their plans had included assassinating the regent. Kabshöpa, the official who joined Lungshar's group and then denounced them, is seen in some accounts as treacherous, but is described by Shakabpa as a "sagacious man" for revealing the conspiracy (*Tibet: A Political History* 275).

Page 12. **The tacit approval of the British**: There is no explicit evidence that the British encouraged the Tibetan government in the many allegations against Lungshar, but Hugh Richardson, a member of the British mission in Lhasa for most of the 1940s and later of the Indian mission, attributed to Lungshar the policy of "turning away from innovations and the British connection," referring to him as "a flamboyant daemonic figure" who exhibited "dazzling impetuosity" and had "simply a lust for power." In his later writings Richardson publicly endorsed the accusations of Bolshevism against Lungshar, and said he had been prepared to use "bribery, murder and sorcery" (*Tibet and Its History*, 2nd ed. [Boulder: Shambhala, 1984], 138, 141). The rumor concerning the crushing of Retring's testicles is reported in Richardson, *High Peaks*, 719.

Page 13. **The civil war in 1947**: The events that culminated with the death of the regent, Retring Rinpoche, are described in Goldstein, *History of Modern Tibet*, 464–521; in Shakabpa, *Tibet: A Political History*, 292–94; and in Richardson, *Tibet and Its History*.

Page 14. **The Japanese spy-explorer Hisao Kimura**: Kimura's recollections of his life in Tibet in the 1940s were given to Scott Berry some forty years later, after Kimura had become a professor of Tibetan studies in Japan. The account—one of the most insightful foreign descriptions of life in 1940s Lhasa—is published as Hisao Kimura and Scott Berry, *A Japanese Agent in Tibet: My Ten Years of Travel in Tibet* (London: Serindia, 1990).

Page 14. **The fourteenth Dalai Lama describes having heard the sound of gunfire**: The Dalai Lama refers to the conflict with the monks of Sera Je in *Freedom in Exile*, pp. 32–33. The number of Sera monks killed in this incident is given as 200 in Richardson, *Tibet and Its History*, 169ff, and as 300 in Richardson, *High Peaks*, 718.

Page 15. **The paramount place granted to religion in the Tibetan political system**: The Tibetan system of government rested on a specific theory of integrating politics with religion, known in Tibetan as *chos srid zung 'brel* or "religion and politics combined." A history of Tibet examining this principle was written by Dung-dkar blo-bzang 'phrin-las (Dungkar Lobsang Thrinley) under the title *Bod kyi chos srid zung 'brel skor bshad pa* (Beijing: Nationalities Publishing House, 1981; published in English as *The Merging of Religious and Secular Rule in Tibet* [Beijing: Foreign Languages Press, 1991]). This governmental idea was articulated from the time when the fifth Dalai Lama was installed by the Mongol leader Gushri Khan as the political ruler of Tibet in 1642. It lasted until sometime after the Chinese arrived in 1950. In a communiqué addressed to Chiang Kai-shek in 1946 and copied to the British mission in Lhasa, the Tibetan National Assembly described their pride in this political arrangement: "There are many great nations on this earth who have achieved unprecedented wealth and might, but there is only one nation which is dedicated to the well-being of humanity in the world, and that is the religious land of Tibet which cherishes a joint spiritual and temporal system.... We shall continue to preserve and protect our joint spiritual and temporal system and our territories as we have done hitherto" (cited in Goldstein, *History of Modern Tibet*, 542).

Page 15. **Tibet and the League of Nations:** The Tibetan decision to reject Gilbert Murray's suggestion in the 1920s that they apply to join the League of Nations is documented in Tsering Shakya, "Tibet and the League of Nations," *The Tibet Journal* X, no. 3 (1985): 48–56. The Tibetan government sent an official to London to assess the proposal in 1927 but finally decided to turn it down, anticipating that the international community would pressure it to end the politico-religious system.

Page 15. **"Better an enemy who is close":** The version of this proverb that Kabshöpa used in recommending nearby enemies over faraway friends was *thag ring gnyen las mdron pa'i dgra dga'*. A similar concept is found in the variant form given by Lhamo Pemba in his collection of Tibetan sayings: *gsar 'grogs che ba'i gnyen las / phyi thag ring ba'i dgra bo dga'*—"The steady animosity of an old enemy is better than the affection of a new friend." See Lhamo Pemba, *Tibetan Proverbs* (Dharamsala: Library of Tibetan Works and Archives, 1996), 199.

Page 17. **Technology and its incursions:** The extension of telecommunications to Tibet and Chapman's comments on this are discussed by Bishop in *The Myth of Shangri-La*, 185–93. The three-hour gap between the publication of news in London and its arrival with the British expedition is noted in Francis Younghusband, *India and Tibet*, 197–200. The extension of the telegraph line to Lhasa is described in W. King, "The Telegraph to Lhasa," *The Geographical Journal* 63 (1924): 527–31. The Dalai Lama's telephone and his two cars are described in F. Spencer Chapman, *Lhasa: The Holy City* (London: Chatto & Windus, 1938), 11 and 185–86.

Page 18. **The radical nationalist Gendun Chöphel:** The most important study of Gendun Chöphel is Heather Stoddard's book, *Le Mendiant de l'Amdo* (Paris: Société d'Ethnographie, Université de Paris X, 1985). Besides Stoddard's work, a number of studies have been written on this famous literary and religious figure among Tibetan progressives. They include K. Dhondup, "Gedun Chophel: The Man Behind the Legend," *Tibetan Review* 12, no. 10 (1978): 10–18, and Donald Lopez, "Madhyamika Meets Modernity: The Life and Works of Gedun Chopel,"

Tricycle (Spring 1995):42–51. Irmgard Mengele has published a short biography under the title *dGe-'dun-chos-'phel. A Biography of the Twentieth-Century Tibetan Scholar* (Dharamsala: Library of Tibetan Works and Archives, 1999), and Toni Huber has published a translation of one work together with an introduction to Gendun Chöphel's life in *The Guide to India: A Tibetan Account by Amdo Gendun Chöphel* (Dharamsala: Library of Tibetan Works and Archives, 2000).

There are several Tibetan biographies of Gendun Chöphel, including Dorje Gyal (rdo rje rgyal), '*Dzam gling rig pa'i dpa' bo rdo brag dge 'dun chos 'phel gyi byung ba brjod pa bden gtam rna ba'i bcud len* (*A Hero of World Knowledge—The Essence of the Heard Account of Dodrag Gendun Chöphel's True Life and Sayings* [Lanzhou: Gansu Nationalities' Publishing House, 1997]). A Chinese biography of Gendun Chöphel has been written by Du Yongbin, *Xizang de ren wen zhu yi xian qu geng dun qun pei da shi ping zhuan* (*A Critical Biography of Master Gedun Chophel, Pioneer of Humanism* [Beijing: China Tibetology Publishing House, 1999]).

Page 18. **The former dancer Tashi Tsering**: The views and experiences of Tashi Tsering are described by Melvyn Goldstein, Tashi Tsering, and William Siebenschuh in their joint publication, *The Struggle for Modern Tibet: The Autobiography of Tashi Tsering* (Armonk, NY: M. E. Sharpe, 1997).

Page 18. **A small, dissident group of Tibetans with progressive ideas**: Extensive accounts of Tibetan progressives and radicals besides Gendun Chöphel who were active in Tibet or northern India during the early twentieth century can be found in Heather Stoddard's *Le Mendiant*. Shorter descriptions of some of these figures are given in T. N. Takla's article, "Notes on Some Early Tibetan Communists," *Tibetan Review* II, no. 17 (1969): 7–10, and in Heather Stoddard's paper, "Tibet: Transition from Buddhism to Communism," *Government and Opposition* 21, no. 1 (Winter 1986): 75–95.

Prominent among these Tibetans was Rabga Pangdatsang (also spelled Pomdatsang), whose history has been studied by Carole McGranahan in *Arrested Histories: Between Empire and Exile in Twentieth-Century Tibet* (Ph.D. diss., University of Michigan, 2001), and in "*Sa sPang mda' gNam sPang mda'*: Murder, History, and Social Politics in 1920s Lhasa," in Lawrence Epstein, ed., *Khams pa Histories: Visions of People, Place and Authority* (Leiden: E. J. Brill, 2002), 103–26. Her studies have expanded the work done by Heather Stoddard on Rabga Pangdatshang in *Le Mendiant*. The founding of the Tibet Progressive Party is also described in Goldstein, *History of Modern Tibet*, 450–61. For a study of Uighur progressives in this period, and the complexities of their relationships with the Chinese state, see Linda Benson, "Uygur Politicians of the 1940s: Mehmet Emin Bugra, Isa Yusuf Alptekin, and Mesut Sabri," *Central Asian Survey* 10, no. 4 (1991): 87–114.

A Chinese writer's view of three Tibetan progressives is given by Ma Lihua in *Old Lhasa: A Sacred City at Dusk* (Beijing: Foreign Languages Press, 2003), 195–224. Ma deals with the tenth Demo, Kunphel-la, and Gendun Chöphel;

only the last two are included in most Western accounts of Tibetan progressives in this period. Her account of them is based on the Chinese translation of Goldstein's *History of Modern Tibet* (translated by Du Yongbin as *Lama Wangguo de Fumie* [Beijing: Current Affairs Publishing House, 1994]). Ma criticizes British interference in these Tibetans' efforts to reform aspects of Tibetan culture or society.

Ma also presents one of China's *ambans* to Tibet, Zhang Yintang, as an early reformer. He had served in Lhasa as the *Amban* or Imperial Commissoner for seven months in 1904–5, and was the first ethnically Chinese *amban*, all his predecessors having been Mongolian or Manchurian. He had worked as a diplomat for China in the United States, and is said by Ma to have given lectures at the Jokhang on evolution and on British colonialism. He published a pamphlet in Lhasa called *Elementary Ethics* and another called *Change Your Habits and Ways*. According to Ma, he "failed to change the backward social habits of the Tibetans," but "his spirit will be remembered forever by both the Tibetan and Han peoples" (Ma, *Old Lhasa*, 133–43), though she does not offer evidence to support the latter claim.

A similar but more nuanced case for Zhang had been presented twenty years earlier in Wang Furen and Suo Wenqing, *Highlights of Tibetan History* (Beijing: New World Press, 1984). Wang and Suo are more critical than Ma of Zhang's efforts to impose new standards on Tibetans: they describe his pamphlets and proposals as "written from the standpoint of Han chauvinism" and say that he "dismissed Tibet's language, customs and time-honoured moral standards, while imposing those that prevailed in the Han areas" (142).

Page 18. *Baba* **Phuntsog Wanggyal**: Phuntsog Wanggyal came from Bathang in eastern Tibet, now part of Sichuan; the epithet *Baba* refers to his birthplace. He was the only early Tibetan progressive to hold a significant position after 1950: he was appointed to the Tibet Work Committee, the shadow organization set up by the Communist Party to run Tibet in the 1950s, and was the only Tibetan member for most of its life. He was purged after eight years and spent eighteen years in prison, technically for having had a copy of Lenin's treatise on nationality policy among his possessions. The current Dalai Lama describes him with some warmth in *Freedom in Exile*, but the first detailed account of his life came only with the emergence in 1999 of a handwritten manuscript from Beijing that was attributed to one Zla ba'i shes rab (Dawei Sherap, a pseudonym meaning "Knowledge of the Moon"). The manuscript, which gave an important account of Phuntsok Wanggyal's life, was entitled *Sgor ra nang pa phun tshogs dbang rgyal (phun dbang) gyi mdzad rnam mtor bsdus (A Brief Biography of Phuntsog Wanggyal Goranangpa)*. This text later appeared as appendix II of the English-language publication of an obscure philosophical treatise on dialectics by Phuntsog Wanggyal, *Liquid Water Does Exist on the Moon (Zla ba'i nang gsher gzugs yod* [Beijing: Foreign Languages Press, 2002]), 434–80. A similar but less detailed biography had earlier appeared in an article by Wang Fan and Chen Shumei, "The Man Whom Time Forgot," *Renwu (Personalities)* 3 (1996). These articles indicated for the first time that a Tibetan Communist Party had been established by Phuntsog Wanggyal and others in eastern Tibet in 1939 or shortly after, and, more important, that the fledgling organization had had no direct connections with the Chinese Communist Party. This claim has not apparently been accepted by the CCP. A major and authoritative account of Phuntsog Wanggyal's life was published by Melvyn C. Goldstein, Dawei Sherap, and William R. Siebenschuh as *A Tibetan Revolutionary—The Political Life and Times of Bapa Phüntso Wangye* (Berkeley: University of California Press, 2004).

Page 19. **The Tibetan People's Unified Alliance**: This was the name of Phuntsog Wanggyal's front organization in Lhasa, but it included as its secret core group an organization called *Gangs ljong bod rigs gung khran ring lugs gsar brje tshogs chung*—"The Tibetan Snowland Communist Revolutionary Association" (see Dawei Sherap, *A Brief Biography*, and Goldstein, Dawei Sherap, and Siebenschuh, *A Tibetan Revolutionary*, 70). "The Communist Group resolved that to fight for national liberation and make democratic reforms were its immediate and principal tasks," according to Dawei Sherap's *Brief Biography*. The core group had been formed earlier at a house called the Chubagang in Lhasa, and Phuntsog Wanggyal says that it later included the young Lhasa aristocrat Tomjor Tethong, at whose house the front organization's meetings were held.

Page 19. *Kalön* **Surkhang**: Phuntsog Wanggyal's meetings with Surkhang, the brother of Dorje Yuthok, are described in Goldstein, Dawei Sherap, and Siebenschuh, *A Tibetan Revolutionary*, 76–77. Goldstein also gives the full text of Phuntsog Wanggyal's revolutionary song calling for the creation of a Tibetan state that would include all the traditional Tibetan areas.

Page 20. **The Tromsikhang**: The history of the Tromsikhang and its demolition, apart from its façade, is documented in André Alexander and Pimpim de Azevedo, *The Old City of Lhasa—Report from a Conservation Project (98–99)* (Tibet Heritage Fund at www.asianart.com/lhasa_restoration/report98/index.htm), part 8. The Lhasa Municipal Planning Office had called for most of the Tromsikhang to be demolished, except for the frontage on the Barkor, according to Alexander and de Azevedo, despite the fact that officials in the TAR Cultural Relics Bureau had recommended preservation of the building. The writers note that some elements of the building were preserved within the new structure when it was completed in 1998. "The Tromsikhang is only the second non-monastic building in the old city to be restored by the government (the first one was the old courthouse, Nangtseshar, in 1995)," they add. See also "Historic Lhasa Palace Demolition," Tibet Information Network, June 18, 1997, and "Lhasa Palace's Future in Dispute," Associated Press, June 20, 1997. The early history of the Tromsikhang and the murders of the two Ambans in 1751 are described in Luciano Petech, *China and Tibet in the Early XVIIIth Century*.

Page 21. **The Chinese Military Headquarters in Lhasa**: There were only four military bases in or near the city in the 1950s: at Drib on the south side of the river, at Danpa just below Drepung, at Beding, and the *junqu* or headquarters on the south side of the Lingkor opposite the Yamen. From the mid-1960s there was an army camp at Parikhu near Gönpasar, which also included a work camp for aristocrats and other members of the Political Consultative Conference. At least a dozen other bases were added later, most notably the half-mile-long military camp built in 1991 at Dongkar Bridge, near Toelung, on the western approach road to Lhasa (see "New Military Headquarters: Tibet Construction Boom," in *TIN News Compilation, October 1993 Reports from Tibet 1992–3*, London: Tibet Information Network, 97).

Page 21. **The Kyitöpa**: Phuntsog Wanggyal refers to the school at the Kyitöpa where he taught in Goldstein, Dawei Sherap, and Siebenschuh, *A Tibetan Revolutionary*, 114–15. An account by Chen Xizhang, "My Work as Secretary General of the KMT Tibet Office (II)" was published in English in *China's Tibet* 4 (2000), but this version did not include comments on the espionage networks in Lhasa. Kimura gives extensive details of the feuds between the Chinese intelligence services, and refers to several murders, in Kimura and Berry, *A Japanese Agent in Tibet*, 150–51.

Page 22. **The British spy network**: Claims that the British supplied the Tibetan government with details about Communist sympathizers in Lhasa in 1949 are made by Xirab Nyima in his contribution to Wang Jiawei and Nima Jianzhan's compilation, *The Historical Status of Tibet* (Beijing: China Intercontinental Press, 1997; published in Chinese as Wang Gui, Xiraonima, and Tang Jiawei, *Xizang Lishi Diwei Bian—Ping Xiageba "Xizang Zhengzhishi" he Fanpulahe "Xizang de Diwei"* (*The Historical Status of Tibet—A Response to Xiageba's [Shakapba's] "Political History of the Tibetan Region" and Fanpulahe's [Van Walt's] "The Status of Tibet"* [Beijing: Nationalities Publishing House, 1995], chapter VI, part 13).

Richardson denied that the British had any prior knowledge of the 1949 expulsion of Communist sympathizers and Chinese. The Chinese authorities later claimed that Robert Ford had been a spy for the British, especially while he was a radio operator for the Tibetan government in Chamdo in 1950. Similar accusations were made about his colleague Reginald Fox, then working in Lhasa. See Robert Ford, *Wind Between the Worlds: The Extraordinary First-Person Account of a Westerner's Life in Tibet as an Official of the Dalai Lama's Government* (New York: David McKay, 1957), later published as *Captured in Tibet* (Oxford: Oxford University Press, 1990).

Page 23. **Jiang Xinxi**: Hisao Kimura gives a description of Phuntsog Wanggyal's uncle, the spymaster and general Jiang Xinxi. Kimura thought that Jiang's lack of loyalty to the Republican cause (which Kimura inferred from the fact that Jiang lied about his nephew's political affiliations) was a result of discrimination that he had experienced as a Tibetan, and his sense that he had therefore been denied promotion. Kimura became close to Phuntsog Wanggyal and his circle, and even invested in Jiang's failed restaurant (Kimura and Berry, *A Japanese Agent in Tibet*, 205). He described daily meetings with Phuntsog Wanggyal at which they discussed detailed plans for a new constitution for Tibet, borrowing in part from the Japanese model, which Kimura felt had much to offer to the Tibetans (201). But neither Kimura nor any Japanese precedents are mentioned in Phuntsog Wanggyal's biographies.

Page 23. **Radical Indian intellectuals**: An important influence on Gendun Chöphel was Rahul Sankrityayana, the only figure in modern Indian studies known to have gone to Tibet before 1950 to study the Sanskrit texts preserved there. He was born Kedarnath Pandey in Azamgarh, Uttar Pradesh, in 1893 and learned thirteen languages (some followers claim that he knew thirty). He became a major scholar of Sanskrit and Buddhism, as well as a leading organizer and activist in the Communist Party of India. He is said to have brought back some 2,000 texts to India on his return from Tibet in the 1930s. He later held the position of professor of Indology at the University of Leningrad from 1937 to 1938 and from 1947 to 1948. By the time of his death in 1963 he had published some 150 books and pamphlets, mostly in Hindi, including *Meri Jeewan Yatra* (*My Journey Through Life* [Allahabad, 1961]) and Rahul Sankrityayan et al., *Buddhism: The Marxist Approach* (New Delhi: People's Publishing Ho use, 1970).

2. FOREIGN VISITORS, OSCILLATIONS, AND EXTREMES

Page 27. **The writings of Western visitors to Lhasa**: The first eyewitness account of Tibet to appear in a Western language was Antonio de Andrade's *Relatione del Novo Scoprimento del Gran Cataio, overo Regno di Tibet* (Rome: Corbelletti, 1627) and *Prosigue el descubrimento del gran Catay, o Reynos del gran Thibet, por el Pade Antonio Andrade. de la Compagñia de Iesus, Potugues...*(Segovia: Diego Flamenco, 1628). These were based on his work as a missionary in western Tibet. The first description of Lhasa by a foreign visitor came in the letters of the Jesuit missionary Desideri, who spent nearly seven years in the city in the early eighteenth century and became fluent in the local language. The letters were later published in Ippolito Desideri (edited by Filippo de Filippi), *An Account of Tibet. The Travels of Ippolito Desideri of Pistoia, S.J., 1712–1727* (London: George Routledge & Sons, Ltd., 1937) and H. Hosten, S.J. (editor and translator), *Missionary in Tibet: Letters and Other Papers of Father Ippolito Desideri, S.J. (1713–21)* (New Delhi: Cosmo Publications, 1999). The Capuchin father Francesco Orazio della Penna di Billi wrote an account of his time in Tibet following his stay in Lhasa as a missionary in the early eighteenth century, *Brief Account of the Kingdom of Tibet* (1730), reproduced in appendix III of Markham's collection of visitors' accounts to Lhasa. The collection includes Thomas Manning's account of his 1811 visit; see Clements Markham, *Narratives of the Mission of George Bogle to Tibet, and of the Journey of Thomas Manning to Lhasa* (London, 1879).

The writings of early Catholic missionaries are collected in Luciano Petech, *I Missionari Italiani nel Tibet e nel Nepal* (Rome: Istituto Italiano per il Medio ed Estremo Oriente, 1951–56) and are summarized in C. Wessels, *Early Jesuit Travellers in Central Asia, 1603–1721* (The Hague, 1924; reprint, New Delhi: Asian Educational Services, 1992). The history of the Capuchin mission has been presented in Fr. Fulgentius Vannini, O.F.M., *The Bell of Lhasa* (no publisher is given but the reader is referred to the Capuchin Ashram, Agra; printed at Devarsons, New Delhi, 1976).

Later an account of a much shorter visit to Lhasa was given by Abbé Huc, *Souvenirs D'Un Voyage Dans La Tartarie, Le Thibet Et La Chine Pendant Les Années 1844, 1845* (Paris, 1850). It was published in English as *Recollections of a journey through Tartary, Thibet, and China (1844–6)* (New York, 1852). A Japanese monk's description of his life in Lhasa, which he disliked intensely, was given by Ekai Kawaguchi in his memoir *Three Years in Tibet* (Benares and London: Theosophical Publishing Society, 1909).

English-language writing on Lhasa in the early twentieth century is dominated by the work of those who accompanied the Younghusband expedition. Among the principal accounts are those of Edmund Candler (correspondent for *The Daily Mail*; his name is often misspelled as Chandler), *The Unveiling of Lhasa* (London: Edward Arnold, 1905); Perceval Landon (*The Times* special correspondent), *LHASA: An account of the country and people of central Tibet and of the progress of the mission sent there by the English Government in the year 1903–1904* (London: Hurst and Blackett, 1905), published in the United States as *The Opening of Tibet: An account of Lhasa and the people of central Tibet...*(London: Doubleday, Page & Co., 1906); William Ottley, *With Mounted Infantry in Tibet* (London: Smith, Elder & Co., 1905); and L. Austine Waddell (his name is often given incorrectly as Augustine), *Lhasa and Its Mysteries: With a Record of the Expedition of 1903–1904* (London: John Murray and New York: Dutton, 1905). Waddell was officially the medical officer on the expedition, but went on to become the first university professor of Tibetan in Britain. Younghusband published his own *apologia* for the expedition, *India and Tibet*, in 1910.

Several later British officials also published accounts of their time in Tibet, including Charles Bell, *Portrait of a Dalai Lama: The Life and Times of the Great Thirteenth* (London: William Collins, 1946) and *Tibet Past and Present* (Oxford: Clarendon Press, 1924); David Macdonald, *Twenty Years in Tibet* (London: Seeley Service & Co., 1932); F. Spencer Chapman, *Lhasa: The Holy City* (London: Chatto & Windus, 1938). Hugh Richardson was a prolific scholar and researcher, but he wrote few personal accounts of his time in Tibet apart from the vignette, "The Chapel of the Hat," *Tibet Society Newsletter* (Summer 1983):14–16, republished in *High Peaks, Pure Earth* (London: Serindia, 1998), 726–28.

One account was published by an American: William Montgomery McGovern, *To Lhasa in Disguise: An Account of a Secret Expedition Through Mysterious Tibet* (1924; reprint, London: Kegan Paul, 2004). McGovern's criticisms of the regime led the British to stop Western travelers going to Tibet unless they agreed to submit their texts for censorship; see Alex McKay, "'Truth,' Perception and Politics: The British Construction of an Image of Tibet," in Thierry Dodin and Heinz Räther, eds., *Imagining Tibet*, 67–90.

McKay also notes that there were scores of more junior British staff who served in Tibet whose impressions were never published: "Just as the British imperial process marginalised indigenous 'subaltern' voices, so too were the voices of British 'subalterns' marginalised. More than 100 British clerical, communications and medical staff served at the Trade Agencies. They include the Europeans who spent longest in Tibet (two British telegraph sergeants), and the European who spent the longest time in Lhasa (a British Radio Officer). But all three of these men were what the English call 'working class', and their names—Henry Martin, W. H. Luff, and Reginald Fox—have been forgotten by history" (McKay, "'Truth'," 74–75). The history of British officials in Tibet is discussed in detail in Alex McKay, *Tibet and the British Raj: The Frontier Cadre 1904–1947* (Richmond, Surrey: Curzon Press, 1997).

The most substantial accounts of the Tibetan capital in the later decades of the twentieth century are those of Heinrich Harrer (*Seven Years in Tibet* [New York: Penguin, 1954]) and Robert Ford (*Wind Between the Worlds*), both of whom spoke Tibetan. Brief visits to Lhasa were described in Alexandra David-Néel, *My Journey to Lhasa* (New York: Harper, 1927; reprint, Boston: Beacon, 1986); Theos Bernard, *Penthouse of the Gods: A Pilgrimage Into the Heart of Tibet and the Sacred City of Lhasa* (New York: Scribners, 1940); and Lowell Thomas Jr., *Out of This World: Across the Himalayas to Forbidden Tibet* (New York: Greystone Press, 1950). The visit of two OSS officers in 1942 is documented in Rosemary Jones Tung, *Portrait of Lost Tibet: Photographs by Ilya Tolstoy and Brooke Dolan* (Berkeley: University of California Press, 1980).

In the 1950s and early 1960s a number of Western journalists sympathetic to the Chinese were allowed to visit Lhasa and published admiring accounts of contemporary reforms that they witnessed. These include Alan Winnington, *Tibet* (New York: International Publishers, 1957); Anna Louise Strong, *When Serfs Stood up in Tibet* (Beijing: New World Press, 1960); and Stuart and Roma Gelder, *Timely Rain Travels in New Tibet* (London: Hutchinson, 1964). Toward the end of the Cultural Revolution, sympathetic visitors were again allowed to visit Tibet, such as Han Suyin, who wrote *Lhasa, the Open City: A Journey to Tibet* (New York: Putnam, 1977) and Felix Greene, who produced a documentary film of his visit, *Tibet* (1976). See also Israel Epstein, *Tibet Transformed* (Beijing: New World Press, 1983), a polemical work based on three visits to Lhasa.

In the 1980s the most significant first-person account was by Catriona Bass, *Inside the Treasure House* (London: Gollancz, 1990); Bass spent a year teaching in Lhasa and spoke some Chinese and Tibetan. An important study was produced in French by Pierre Julien Quiers, *Histoires Tibétaines* (Paris: Éditions Florent-

Massot, 1997). See also Heinrich Harrer, *Return to Tibet—Tibet After the Chinese Occupation* (London: Phoenix, 1984) and Alec Le Sueur, *Running a Hotel on the Roof of the World* (London: Summersdale, 1998). The history of travel writers in Tibet has been discussed in Peter Hopkirk, *Trespassers on the Roof of the World: The Secret Exploration of Tibet* (Boston: J. P. Tarcher, 1982).

Page 27–28. **Descriptions oscillate between two extremes**: The oscillation of emotions in Western writings on Tibet has been noted by Bishop and by Lopez, who describes it thus: "Tibet's complexities and competing histories have been flattened into a stereotype. Stereotypes operate through adjectives, which establish chosen characteristics as if they were eternal truths....With sufficient repetition these adjectives become innate qualities, immune from history. And once these qualities harden into an essence, that essence may split into two opposing elements" (*Prisoners of Shangri-La* 10).

Page 28. **Dirt**: Manning, Landon, MacDonald, and Younghusband all refer copiously to what they saw as the filthiness of Lhasa and/or of Tibetans in general. Chapman's discussion of Tibetan dirtiness can be found in *Lhasa: The Holy City*, 145–46. Younghusband's description of the Tibetans as "obtuse and ignorant" and of the city streets as "filthy dirty, and the inhabitants hardly more clean than the streets" is in *India and Tibet*, 246–47. Waddell gives his view of Phari as perhaps the dirtiest town in the world in *Lhasa and Its Mysteries*, 100–101. He goes on to describe the women as "more like hideous gnomes than any human beings," and adds that none would be "so indiscreet as to wash."

The classical Chinese view of Tibetans may have been similar, according to a fourteenth-century Tibetan history that cites a Chinese aristocrat who described Tibet as "a place of outcasts, where there is no difference between clean and unclean." The history was written by Lama Dampa Sonam Gyaltsen (*Bla-ma dam pa* bSod-nams rgyal-mtshan) (1312–1375) and has been translated into English by Per K. Sørensen as *The Mirror Illuminating the Royal Genealogies— An Annotated Translation of the XIVth Century Tibetan Chronicle: rGyal-rabs gsal-ba'i me-long* (Asiatische Forshungen, Vol. 128, Wiesbaden: Harrasowitz Verlag, 1994), 230.

Visitors to Lhasa of less patrician origins do not seem to have mentioned dirt in their descriptions of the city. Phuntsog Wanggyal, the earliest Tibetan communist in Lhasa and by no means a sentimentalist, gives an extended description of the city after his first visit in 1943 without any reference to dirt. In fact, he specifically mentions "the smell of the incense in the Barkor" alongside other impressions that delighted him (Goldstein, Dawei Sherap, and Siebenschuh, *A Tibetan Revolutionary*, 69). In 1923 Alexandra David-Néel describes the streets of Lhasa as "relatively clean" (*My Journey* 273). Robert Ford, a long-term resident of Lhasa in the 1940s, and not in origin a member of the British officer class, also makes no mention of dirt or lack of hygiene; neither does Kimura. Both of them were fluent in Tibetan. Heinrich Harrer provides a useful discussion concerning foreigners' complaints about Tibetan dirtiness in *Lost Lhasa* (New York: Abrams, 1992), 92–93.

The attitude of Westerners toward Tibetan hygiene is discussed in Bishop, *The Myth of Shangri-La*, 171, and in Robert Barnett, "A City, Its Visitors, and the Odour of Development," in Françoise Pommaret, ed., *Lhasa in the Seventeenth Century—The Capital of the Dalai Lamas* (Leiden: Brill, 2003), 199–226. The latter includes examples from Western "fellow-travelers" who visited Tibet in the 1960s, such as Anna Louise Strong and Stuart Gelder, who were disgusted by various smells and odors. For these writers, as for the English military writers who preceded them and the Chinese who followed them, an important purpose of their accounts was to convey their fortitude in overcoming the rigors of their journey to such a "remote" place. Tsering Shakya notes the legacy of Victorian travel writing in such accounts: "From Savage Landor onwards the great majority of western travel writers have sought to emphasise the difficulties of their journey and the uniqueness of their encounter with the Tibetan environment. What struck these writers was a combination of their personal fortitude and the exclusivity of their experience.... The travellers were struck primarily by the landscape, referring to the harshness of the environment and the splendour of the mountains. These they saw reflected in the essential nature of the Tibetan character and philosophy" ("Introduction: The Development of Modern Tibetan Studies," in Robert Barnett, ed., *Resistance and Reform in Tibet* [London: Christopher Hurst and Bloomington: Indiana University Press, 1994], 1–14).

Page 28. **Ants at work**: The tendency to describe Tibetan monks as ants is noted by Bishop, *The Myth of Shangri-La*, 170–71, where he cites, for example, Landon, *LHASA*, 2:283–84. Waddell more than once describes Tibetan soldiers, before they commenced battle, as resembling bees.

Page 28. **720 pounds of soap**: The figures for soap imports are given in Waddell's *Lhasa and Its Mysteries*, Appendix X, 476. He describes the discovery of soap in the soldiers' packs with some astonishment, and suggests that the relative cleanliness of the people in Lhasa itself might have been due to the coincidence of a recent rainstorm preceding his inspection (347). Nevertheless, he also notes that soap was available at "most of the stalls and has for years been one of the cheap imports," an observation that contradicts those of the French linguist and explorer Fernand Grenard, who wrote that he had found "a box containing six cakes of scented soap, which were the only specimens of soap that could be discovered within the radius of Lhasa in the month of January 1894 and which their purchaser was delighted to sell to us after having them for forty years in his shop" (*Le Tibet; le pays et les habitants* [Paris: Librairie Armand Colin, 1904]; published in English as *Tibet: The Country and Its Inhabitants* [London: Hutchinson & Co., 1904], 301; cited in Bishop, *The Myth of Shangri-La*, 154). Grenard in fact never reached Lhasa.

Page 28. **The British seem to have pillaged the corpses**: The looting and pillaging of treasures and manuscripts during the Younghusband campaign has been discussed by Charles Allen in *Duel in the Snow*, where he cites Arthur Hadow's explicit descriptions of looting (224ff.). A more detailed discussion is given in Michael Carrington's article, "Officers, Gentlemen and Thieves: The Looting of Monasteries During the 1903/4 Younghusband Mission to Tibet," *Modern Asian Studies* 37, no. 1 (2003): 81–109. In *Twenty Years in Tibet*, the British official David Macdonald records that more than 400 mule-loads of "rare and valuable manuscripts of Lamaist sacred works, images, religious paraphernalia of all descriptions" collected by him and Waddell were brought back to India in 1904 (Allen, *Duel in the Snows*, 305–308).

Page 29. **The princess Pemá Chöki**: Maraini describes his journeys to Tibet and his meeting with the Princess of Sikkim in *Secret Tibet* (New York: Viking, 1952). For the description of the peas and his discussion of what he saw as an inexplicable relationship between the princess and the *gönkhangs*, see *Secret Tibet*, 48 and 51–53. Berenson's comments on Maraini's writings are on page xiii.

Page 31. **Contradictory emotions**: Landon's concessions to the potential worth of Tibetan Buddhism appear in *LHASA*, 2:190. The views on Tibetan Buddhism of Heinrich Hensoldt, a professor of Eastern religions in Germany and the author of "Occult Science in Tibet" (*Arena* 10 [1894]), are cited by Bishop in *The Myth of Shangri-La*, 169, as are those of the explorer Sven Hedin.

Page 31. **Three Russian rifles and a few cartridges**: The discovery of Russian rifles was reported by Landon, seemingly with some relief, in his article for *The Times* on the "regrettable" massacre at Chumik Shenko. "One most significant fact," he wrote, "is that three of the escort of the Tibetan general were armed with rifles bearing the Russian Imperial stamp. I have personally secured one from a dead Tibetan. Russian ammunition was also found" ("Latest Intelligence: The Mission to Tibet. Colonel Younghusband's Passage Opposed. Heavy Losses of the Tibetans," *The Times*, April 1, 1904). Allen discusses the issue in *Duel in the Snows*, 124. The stories of a Russian conspiracy to gain a foothold in Tibet had been based on the presence in Lhasa of the Buryat, Agwan Dorjief, whom *The Times* described as the "evil adviser" to the "dreamy and headstrong" Dalai Lama. The paper "fervently prayed" that the Dalai Lama was in his "final transmigration" (Editorial, August 13, 1904). Richardson later defended the British position, writing that the thirteenth Dalai Lama, while "rejecting Curzon's overtures, was busily exchanging amicable messages with the Czar" through Dorjief (*Tibet and Its History* 82–83). Richardson refers also to the "genuinely accepted...circumstantial rumours" of Russian arms consignments to Tibet.

Dorjief's role is discussed in John Snelling, *Buddhism in Russia: The Story of Agvan Dorzhiev, Lhasa's Emissary to the Tsar* (Boston: Element Books and Dorset: Shaftesbury, 1993); Alexandre Andreyev, "A Debacle of Secret Diplomacy," *The Tibet Journal* XXI, no. 3 (Autumn 1996): 4–34; Alexandre Andreyev, "Agwan Dorjiev's Secret Work in Russia and Tibet," *Tibetan Review* (September 1993): 11–14; Nicolai S. Kuleshov, "Agvan Dorjiev, the Dalai Lama's Ambassador," *Asian*

Affairs 23, no. 1 (1992): 20–33; and Nikolai S. Kuleshov, "Russia and Tibetan Crisis: Beginning at the Twentieth Century," *The Tibet Journal* XXI, no. 3 (Autumn 1996): 47–59.

Page 32. **Gunned down as they walked away**: A detailed account of the killings at Chumik Shenko carried out at the order of Francis Younghusband in 1904 is given in Charles Allen, "The Myth of Chumik Shenko," *History Today* 54, no. 4 (April 2004): 10–17. Younghusband himself used the term "massacre" in his private letters to describe the event. Accounts of the battle of Chumik Shenko (literally, "the crystal tears") differ widely in their explanations as to why so many Tibetans were killed for the loss of so few on the British side. Allen notes that there were intense arguments among the British soldiers during the night after the battle about how this had been allowed to happen. He provides some evidence that Arthur Hadow, one of the machine gunners, eventually pretended that his weapon had jammed rather than continue to obey orders to fire on the retreating Tibetans (*Duel in the Snows* 117–18).

Two fictionalized versions of the massacre at Chumik Shenko have appeared in Chinese, one a short story and the other a film, both with some attention to historical records of the incident. Both deal mainly with the Younghusband invasion and are much looser with historical materials. The short story is Ge Fei's *Encounter*, translated by Herbert Batt in Herbert Batt, ed., *Tales of Tibet: Sky Burials, Prayer Wheels and Wind Horses* (New York and Oxford: Rowman and Littlefield, 2001), 77–104. The film is *Hong he gu* (*Red River Valley*; 1997), directed by Feng Xiaoning. It is largely fanciful except for a reconstruction of the Chumik Shenko massacre. There is also a novel about the British invasion by Yeshe Tenzin, *Sword in Snowy Twilight* (Lhasa: Tibetan People's Publishing House, 1996).

Page 32. **Cajoled to give up their defensive positions**: Candler reported that in the build-up to the battle of Chumik Shenko, the Tibetans were "quietly induced to retire" from their defensive positions (*The Times*, April 1, 1904). Waddell says that the Sepoys physically pushed the Tibetans out of their *sangars* or defensive positions overlooking the British during the negotiations, indicating that the British thus replaced the Tibetans on the hillsides (*Lhasa and Its Mysteries* 156–61). The Tibetan soldiers were under strict orders from Lhasa not to fire unless fired upon, and were led by the British to believe that their generals would hold negotiations. Chinese histories claim that the British soldiers each removed a bullet from their rifles and so tricked the Tibetans into extinguishing the fuses on their muskets, since the Tibetans did not realize the British rifles could instantly be reloaded (Xirab Nyima in Wang and Nima Jianzhan, *The Historical Status of Tibet*, chapter VI, part 8).

Page 32. **Lost only 34 of them in battle**: Waddell notes that the expedition had 16 engagements, which resulted in 202 casualties to his men, of whom 23 were officers. He does not give a figure for deaths except to say that five of the wounded officers died (*Lhasa and Its Mysteries* 442). Charles Allen cites the official death count on the British side as 34, of whom 29 were "natives," meaning Indians or Nepalis. Several soldiers died of frostbite, but their numbers are not given. Thousands of pack animals perished—of 3,500 yaks, for example, only 150 survived (Bishop, *The Myth of Shangri-La*, 152, citing Candler, *Lhasa*, 86–87). Xirab Nyima's chapter in *The Historical Status of Tibet* claims that 280 British troops were killed in one skirmish alone and 121 in another, but this seems unlikely (Wang and Nima Jianzhan, *The Historical Status of Tibet*, chapter VI, section 8).

Page 32. **"I went off alone to the mountainside"**: Francis Younghusband's epiphany as he departed from Tibet is described in *India and Tibet*, 305.

Page 35. **"Is there no light that cuts through the demonic darkness"**: The missionary pamphlet calling on evangelists to go to Tibet was produced by a fundamentalist Protestant missionary organization called The Sowers' Ministry in the early 1990s. Founded in Nepal in 1986 by Americans born in India who were ordained in Texas, it mainly targets people in Nepal, India, Tibet, China, and Bhutan. It describes itself as a "mission organization involved in evangelism, training and church planting [whose] goal is to preach Christ where His name is not known and plant churches," though it also invites followers to "pray against the spreading of Tibetan Buddhism into other countries" (www.sowers.org/test-tibet.html). The text of the pamphlet is reproduced as an appendix to my article on Protestant missionaries in Tibet in that period; see Robert Barnett, "Saving Tibet from 'Satan's Grip': Present-Day Missionary Activity in Tibet," *Lungta 11: Christian Missionaries and Tibet* (Winter 1998):36–41.

The history of early Catholic missionaries has been studied by Luciano Petech in *I missionari italiani*, by Wessels in *Early Jesuit Travellers*, and by Vannini in *The Bell*. There is an extensive literature on Protestant missionaries in the Himalayan areas, including several short studies by John Bray, such as "Christian Missions and the Politics of Tibet, 1850–1950," in Wilfried Wagner, ed., *Kolonien und Missionen—Referate des 3. Internationalen Kolonialgeschichtlichen Symposiums 1993 in Bremen* (Bremer Asien-Pazifik Studien, vol. 12, Bremen: Universität Bremen, n.d.), 180–95. Several autobiographical accounts have been published by missionaries who worked in the Tibetan borderlands in the 1940s and early 1950s, including George Patterson. He worked first as a Protestant missionary in Bathang in eastern Tibet and then, in a remarkable move, offered himself for many years as an unofficial liaison between the Tibetan rebel army and the CIA. His experiences are described in several books, including George Patterson, *God's Fool* (London: Faber and Faber, 1956).

The most famous Tibetan convert to Christianity was Tharchin *babu*, who was converted by Moravians in Kinnaur, northern India, and later ordained a Minister of the Church of Scotland Mission in Kalimpong, West Bengal. For over thirty years, Tharchin produced an influential Tibetan-language newspaper called *Sargyur Melong* or *The Mirror*. The paper helped Kalimpong become a center for exiled Tibetan progressives in the middle decades of the twentieth century. See H. Louis Fader, *The Life and Times of a True Son of Tibet, Gergan Dorje Tharchin* (Kalimpong: Tibet Mirror Press, 2002).

Page 36. **They do not have the words of any God to help them**: In his early writings Wang Lixiong, a noted Chinese intellectual and critic of Beijing's Tibet policies, described pre–1980 leftist policies as relatively effective in Tibet because they had been able, in effect, to replace one god with another: "It was impossible to overthrow centuries of worship without playing the role of a new god....It was simply that Mao had replaced the Dalai Lama as the god in their minds." Since after liberalization this option no longer remained, Wang suggests that the problem can only be resolved by including the Dalai Lama: "Today, the person who controls the two banners [of religion and nationality] is none other than the Dalai Lama.... With the Tibetan populace coalesced behind these banners, there existed no opposition force that could counter the exiled deity. Only Mao had succeeded in dissolving the religious and ethnic unity of the Tibetans, by introducing the element of class struggle. Renouncing this without creating any new ideology has left a vacuum that can only be filled by a combination of lamaist tradition and ethnic nationalism." Wang Lixiong, "Reflections on Tibet," *New Left Review* 14 (March–April 2002).

Page 37. **Translation of works from Chinese**: The question of Tibet's cultural or religious links with China has not been much studied by Western scholars of religion and culture apart from a major work by Gray Tuttle, *Tibetan Buddhists in the Making of Modern China* (New York: Columbia University Press, 2005). Tuttle documents the rapid emergence of Chinese interest in Tibetan Buddhism in the 1920s, at the same time that Chinese nationalist leaders—some of whom also became Tibetan Buddhist devotees—were looking for ways to refashion China as a modern nation-state and to encourage the integration of Tibet within it.

R. A. Stein notes in his *Tibetan Civilization* (translated from the French by J. E. Stapleton Driver, London: Faber, 1972) that there were translations of Chinese works into Tibetan in the eighth and ninth centuries (59), as do many Chinese authors. Buddhism had come to China much earlier than to Tibet, and later Tibetan literature explains the absence of Chinese influence in Tibet after the eighth century mainly by referring to accounts of a debate staged by the Tibetan king Trisong Detsen in about 792. The debate was between Indian and Chinese Buddhist scholars and was held to decide which school should be followed in Tibet. Most Tibetan histories, such as the fourteenth-century *Bu ston chos 'byung*, say that it was won by the Indians and that the Chinese protagonists were expelled from the country, along with their texts. Some other histories, such as the *Nyang chos 'byung*, say that the main Chinese scholar was not penalized and that the Tibetans continued to revere him (see Pasang Wangdu with Hildegard Diemberger [translators], *dBa' bzhed: The Royal Edict Concerning the Bringing of Buddha's Doctrine to Tibet* [Vienna: Verlag der Österreichischen Akademie der Wissenschaften, 2000], 88*n*331). The *Dba' bzhed*, a history dating probably from the tenth century, ends, in one version, with the same king who had earlier decided to only have texts from India translated saying a few years later, "I regret the fact that the doctrinal scriptures of China were not translated." Matthew Kapstein has given a detailed account of the Tibetan borrowings from Indian literary culture in "The Indian Literary Identity in Tibet" in Sheldon Pollock, ed., *Literary Cultures in History: Reconstructions from South Asia* (Berkeley: University of California Press, 2003).

Page 37. **An innovative and irrefutable division of time**: The politics of periodization have been studied by a number of writers, in particular, in the Chinese context, by Prasenjit Duara in *Rescuing History from the Nation: Questioning Narratives of Modern China* (Chicago and London: University of Chicago Press, 1995), where he describes periodization "as rhetorical strategies to conceal the aporias and repressions necessitated by the imposition of a master narrative" (27–28; also cited in Tuttle, "Modern Tibetan Historiography," *Papers on Chinese History* [Spring 1998]:104). See also Prasenjit Duara, "The Régime of Authenticity: Timelessness, Gender, and National History in Modern China," *History and Theory* 37, no. 3 (1998): 287–308, and Jonathan Unger, ed., *Using the Past to Serve the Present: Historiography and Politics in Contemporary China* (Armonk, NY: M.E. Sharpe, 1993), which includes Geremie R. Barmé's essay, "History for the Masses." Soviet approaches to time divisions in historiography are discussed in Cyril E. Black, *Rewriting Russian History: Soviet Interpretations of Russia's Past* (New York: Vintage, 1962). Q. Edward Wang discusses Chinese Marxist historians in "Between Marxism and Nationalism: Chinese Historiography and the Soviet Influence, 1949–1963," *Journal of Contemporary China* 9, no. 23 (March 1, 2000): 95–111. A discussion of this issue in another field can be found in Linda Georgianna, "Periodization and Politics: The Case of the Missing Twelfth Century in English Literary History," *Modern Language Quarterly* 64, no. 2 (June 1, 2003): 153–68 (16).

Page 38. **The ruling that practice rather than Mao's dictums should be the "sole criterion of truth"**: The 1978 decision by the Chinese Communist Party on "practice as truth" led to the passage of a "Resolution on Certain Historical Issues Concerning the Party Since the Founding of New China" in June 1981. The resolution ruled that Mao had been correct 70 percent of the time. It in effect formalized the end of the previous era and marked the third Plenum of the eleventh Congress as the moment of transition from that era to the next.

Page 38. **Tibetan leaders appointed during the Cultural Revolution**: The two Tibetan leaders who survived the purge of leftist officials and the fall of the Gang of Four in October 1976 were Ragti and Pasang (the names are romanized in Chinese publications as Raidi and Basang). Ragti had been made the equivalent of a party secretary of the TAR in 1975, and in 1977 had been placed on the Central Committee of the national CCP. He remained in these positions until after the turn of the millennium. Pasang had become a vice chairwoman of the newly established TAR Revolutionary Committee in September 1968. In 1971 she was made a deputy party secretary in the TAR Party Committee, a position she held until her retirement in 2002. She had been given a national position on the CCP Central Committee in 1973 and had served continuously until her retirement. Tsering Shakya, in *The Dragon in the Land of Snows*, discusses the explanation given by Hu Yaobang at the Second National Work Forum in 1984 for keeping these two Tibetans in their positions despite their Cultural Revolution associations: "It was clear that even the most liberal leader was not prepared to carry out a purge of Tibetan leftists, perhaps because...only those Tibetans who had gained most under the Communists could be relied upon to support Beijing" (349, 365–66).

Page 39. **Participants whose memories are more likely to be ordered by experience**: The tenth Panchen Lama, the most important Tibetan dignitary to have remained within China after 1959, gave a famous speech to officials in Shigatse in January 1989, a few days before he died, which summarized Tibetan experience without allowing for any temporal divisions since 1951. According to Isabel Hilton in her book *The Search for the Panchen Lama* (London: Viking, 1999), his actual words were: "Since liberation, there has certainly been development, but the price paid for this development has been greater than the gains" (194). The remark was one of the rare occasions when a Tibetan within Tibet referred publicly to modern history without using the years 1978 or 1980 to mark a radical break in time.

3. THE SQUARE VIEW AND THE OUTSTRETCHED DEMONESS

Page 41. **"To the east, in China, is the king of divination"**: Stein's summary of what he called "the square-based view," based on his study of Tibetan histories dating from the twelfth to the seventeenth centuries, is given in *Tibetan Civilization*, 39. The description of the four kings given here is an abbreviated version of F. W. Thomas's translation of a section of the *Rgyal po bka' thang*, dating from before the fifteenth century, cited in Stein, *Recherches sur l'Épopée et le Barde au Tibet* (Paris: Presses Universitaires de France, 1959), 244. Stein noted that the scheme appeared in eleventh-century poems by Milarepa. Geza Uray later noted that it also exists in the Dunhuang manuscripts from the dynastic era (the seventh to the ninth centuries), as he demonstrated in his article, "*Vom Römischen Kaiser bis zum König Gesar von gLing*," in Walther Heissig, *Fragen der Mongolischen Heldendichtung* (Wiesbaden: Harrasowitz Verlag, 1982), 3:530–48.

The fourfold pattern is found repeatedly in Tibetan historical texts, such as those describing the leaders of the twelve tribes when they welcomed the first Tibetan king descending from the sky, the four tribes that formed the early army, the four tributary kings conquered by Trisong Detsen in the early ninth century, and the four horns or banners that were used for military administration in the dynastic era. In Buddhist thought the scheme related to the Protector Kings of the Four Directions, and in Buddhist geomancy it related often to the eight-spoked wheel and the eight-petaled lotus. Stein also notes that this horizontal view was often combined (as in an offering mandala) with a vertical model that had three levels (often sky, earth, and "the world under the earth") or, at other times, seven levels (*Tibetan Civilization* 41).

Page 43. **"The heart of the continent, the source of all rivers"**: An alternative translation of the dynastic-era poem describing Tibet as the central realm is given in David Snellgrove and Hugh Richardson, *A Cultural History of Tibet* (Boston: Shambhala, 1995): "This centre of heaven, / This core of earth, / This heart of the world, / Fenced round by snow, / The headland of all rivers, / Where the mountains are high and the land is pure...." Another poem from the same period goes: "From mid-sky, seven stage high, / Heavenly sphere, azure blue, / Came our King, Lord of men, Sun divine, to Tibet. / Land so high, made so pure, / Without equal, without peer, / Land indeed! Best of all! Religion too surpassing all!" (*Cultural History* 23, 24).

Page 43. **Their perception of themselves was reordered**: The view of Tibetans as northern savages and the relocation of their spiritual focus to the south are associated with specific moments in Tibetan history. One of these is the decision after the death of the Tibetan monarch Trisong Detsen in about 802 that Buddhist rather than Bonpo rites should be performed at the royal funeral. According to the *Dba' bzhed*, the debate was held between the Buddhist scholar Vairocana and the Bon minister Chimtsen zherlegzig (mChims bTsan zher legs gzigs) in front of the new king, Mu-ne tsenpo. The arguments of the two protagonists were in part geomantic, since they concerned which geographic site offered the greatest source of power to the kingdom. The Bon minister said that Yarlha shampo, a mountain deity in Tibet, "was very mighty and had great magic powers," while Vairocana responded that the temple of Nalendra in India was "more auspicious" and that Buddhist protectors were "possessed with greater magic." The new king accepted Vairocana's view (Pasang Wangdu and Diemberger, *dBa' bzhed*, 98–100). This account of the debate suggests that at least by the tenth century, there was a view in Tibet that retrospectively projected the notional source of moral authority to the south.

Page 44. **"The Emperor looked at mGar with piercing eyes"**: The story of the visit of Minister mGar to the court of the Tang Emperor Taizong in 640–41 to seek a princess as a bride for the Tibetan King Srongtsen Gampo is told in many medieval Tibetan chronicles and histories, notably the *Ma Ni bka' 'bum* (eleventh century), the *Bka' chems ka khol ma*, the *Rgyal-rabs gsal-ba'i me-long* (1368), and the opera text *Rgya-bza' bal-bza'i rnam-thar* (probably sixteenth century). These histories also describe a series of tests that the emperor (629–649) sets for the minister and for competing suitors from other realms. The extracts here, which I have heavily abbreviated, are from Per Sørensen's annotated translation of the *Rgyal-rabs gsal-ba'i me-long*, known in English as *The Mirror Illuminating the Royal Genealogies*, and written by *Bla-ma dam pa* bSod-nams rgyal-mtshan, who lived from 1312 to 1375. The courtesan's explanation of Chinese views of Tibet and the emperor's mocking response to mGar are given in Sørensen, *Mirror Illuminating*, 224 and 217.

The self-deprecating account of Tibet given in the Tibetan sources is a rhetorical strategy by the writers: all the Tibetan texts show mGar as finally outwitting the emperor and winning the grudging admiration of the court. They also show him outwitting the Four Kings of the Four Directions, despite the fact that they are more powerful than the Tibetans by any material or physical measure. mGar arrives at the court at the same time as four ministers representing the King of Religion from India, Gesar the King of War, the King of Wealth from Persia, and the Turkic-Uighur King of Hor, and all of them have come with the same request: a Chinese princess to marry to their monarch. Historically it was in fact the case that the Tibetans had been outmaneuvered in obtaining princesses from the Chinese court by the Turks and the Tu-yu-hun, a people in the Kokonor or Qinghai area. This is discussed in Sørensen, *Mirror Illuminating, n*614, and Christopher I. Beckwith, *The Tibetan Empire in Central Asia: A History of the Struggle for Great Power Among the Tibetans, Turks, Arabs, and Chinese During the Early Middle Ages* (Princeton: Princeton University Press, 1987).

In the version given in the *The Mirror Illuminating the Royal Genealogies*, the four powerful ministers take up their respective positions outside each of the gates of city at its cardinal points. The Tibetans have to pitch their tents between the northern and the eastern gates—not a cardinal point. Thus China becomes, in this account, the center of the Tibetan square (Sørensen, *Mirror Illuminating,* 216), as it was to remain for much of subsequent history. The Tibetan accounts do not ignore Tibetan proficiency in some areas, and mention the excellence of technological skill at the time in metalwork, particularly in the production of armor, weapons, and golden utensils; mGar is supposed to have presented a lapis lazuli coat of mail to the emperor. When mGar finally outwits the other ministers in the tests set by the emperor, he is described as riding his horse around the defeated delegations, saying, "We Tibetans surpass you Indians and Hor people! We shall [take] the princess, so all of you sit down and place your fingers to your mouths!" (Sørensen, *Mirror Illuminating,* 229).

In the earliest extant Tibetan account of mGar's visit to the Chinese court to ask for a princess—the Tibetan history known as the *Dba' bzhed*—there is no mention of any tests of the ministers' wits. Instead, the three pre-written letters, and the Tibetans' ability to predict the Chinese emperor's demands, are sufficient evidence for the emperor to tell his daughter, "Consider the bTsan po [Emperor] of Tibet and the Emperor of China as equals" (Pasang Wangdu and Diemberger, *dBa' bzhed,* 30–31).

Page 45. **Tibetans have not drawn much upon the earlier history of Tibet:** Tibet's imperial might between the seventh and ninth centuries did not disappear from political memory during subsequent periods, but it seems to have been used somewhat sparingly as a nation-building device, and only by the most powerful of Tibetan rulers. Its use is associated, for example, with the fourteenth-century Phagmodrupa power holder in Tibet, Changchub Gyaltsen. Giuseppe Tucci, in *Tibetan Painted Scrolls* (Rome: Librera dello Stato, 1949), saw the practice of discovering *terma* (*gter-ma*) or "hidden treasures" (sacred documents or objects said to have been written centuries earlier) from the twelfth century onward as a way of referring to the dynastic period. "It was his aim to give Tibet a political consciousness, to pacify internal struggles which had turned it asunder so long, to free it from subjection to China. He aspired to restore the ancient kings' monarchic ideal, to revive national law and customs, and he enacted a code by which up to our days justice is administered in Tibet.... This conscious rebirth of ancient traditions...was attended not only by a renewal of historical studies and a vast production of chronicles, but also by research for documents, real or presumed, which might revive, as a reminder, the age of the kings," wrote Tucci (*Tibetan Painted Scrolls* I:23–24).

In the late seventeenth century the fifth Dalai Lama and his regent, Sangye Gyatso, explicitly intended their rebuilding of the Potala Palace to be an evocation of Srongtsen Gampo's era, when the first version of the palace was said to have been erected. As Samten Karmay wrote, "the completion of the building of the Potala as the seat of government [represented] this motivation to restore in a certain sense the former imperial power" ("The Rituals and Their Origins in the Visionary Accounts of the Fifth Dalai Lama," in H. Blezer, ed., *Religion and Secular Culture in Tibet* [Leiden/Boston/Köln: Brill, 2002], 28). The same view is expressed by Hugh Richardson in "The Fifth Dalai Lama's Decree Appointing Sang-rgyas rgya-mtsho as Regent" in *High Peaks*, 448. But sustained references by later rulers to the earlier, more powerful epoch of Tibetan history seem generally to have taken second place to claims of religious legitimacy, usually deriving from connections with India.

Page 48. **"On one auspicious day, at the height of summer"**: Tiley Chodag's description of the founding of Lhasa is taken from his popular summary of Tibetan folklore, translated by W. Tailing and published as *Tibet: The Land and the People* (Beijing: New World Press, 1988). Chodag, born in 1937, studied at Sera monastery until 1953, when he went to study in Beijing at the Central Minorities Institute. He returned to Lhasa in 1958 and worked as an editor at the Tibet People's Press, where he translated the eight main Tibetan opera texts into Chinese and wrote about Tibetan culture and folklore.

Page 50. **The predetermined process of social evolution**: The view of nationalities and peoples as evolving through a series of preordained stages is associated with the American lawyer and anthropologist Lewis Henry Morgan (1818–81), whose theory of cultural evolution or "social Darwinism" viewed human societies as "progressing" in turn through seven stages, of which the main categories were the savage, the barbaric, and the civilized. Marx's comments on the theory were used by Engels in his work *The Origins of the Family, Private Property, and the State* (1884), and these later influenced Chinese Marxist thinking, generating a stage theory of evolution that was particularly significant in China's assessments of non-Chinese nationalities within its borders. These views were later taken up by Fei Xiaotong, China's leading anthropologist, and by the state.

According to Ma Yin, ed., *China's Minority Nationalities* (Beijing: Foreign Languages Press, 1989), an official handbook, "the social and economic development of the Han people in 1949 was more highly developed than that of most of the minorities.... In China before liberation the minorities presented...an illustration of social development in four different socio-economic forms. A feudal landlord economy was practised, as a rule, by those groups that had social and economic structures largely identical with those of the Han. Contrasting with these were a few others that still lived under a feudal serf system or with slavery (Tibetans and Yis); vestiges of primitive communal society were even found among many of the small, primitive tribes" (4–5).

For further details see Gregory E. Guldin, *The Saga of Anthropology in China: From Malinowski to Moscow to Mao* (Armonk, NY: M. E. Sharpe, 1994); Dru C. Gladney, "Representing Nationality in China: Refiguring Majority/Minority Identities," *Journal of Asian Studies* 53, no. 1 (1994): 92–123; Barry Sautman, "Myths of Descent, Racial Nationalism and Ethnic Minorities in the People's Republic of China," in Frank Dikötter, ed., *The Construction of Racial Identities in China and Japan* (Honolulu: University of Hawai'i Press, 1997), 75–95; and Stevan Harrell, "The Anthropology of Reform and the Reform of Anthropology: Anthropological Narratives of Recovery and Progress in China," *Annual Review of Anthropology* 30 (October 2001): 139–61.

Page 50. **"The cultivation of radishes and turnips"**: In the version of the Princess Wencheng story given in *The Mirror Illuminating the Royal Genealogies*, the princess, before leaving for Tibet, asks if the Tibetans already have porcelain clay, silkworm fodder, rose trees, and turnips. The minister mGar replies, "Turnip is not found, but the other things we have," and the narrator adds, "wherefore [it was decided to] take along seeds of radish and turnip" (Sørensen, *Mirror Illuminating*, 223).

Page 50. **The official view of the princess...an industry of its own**: The story of Princess Wencheng's marriage to Srongtsen Gampo has been used as a basis for numerous operas, films, paintings, songs, and literature in China since 1950, and giant statues were erected in the 1990s along the route of her journey from China to Lhasa. Hers is the main story used officially in modern China to describe the Sino-Tibetan relationship. Most if not all of this cultural production is state-sponsored, and in 1986 a play by Huang Zhilong, *Srongtsen Gampo*, was banned by the government, apparently because it failed to emphasize sufficiently the role of Wencheng (see Robert Barnett, "The Secret Secret: Cinema, Ethnicity and Seventeenth-Century Tibetan-Mongolian Relations," *Inner Asia* [Winter 2002]: 277–346).

An account of the cultural politics in post–1950 China that led to the official promotion of stories about the ancient practice of *heqin* or political marriage, and of some of the uses of the Wencheng story, is given in Uradyn Bulag, "Naturalizing National Unity: Political Romance and the Chinese Nation," in *The Mongols at China's Edge: History and the Politics of National Unity* (Lanham, MD: Rowman

& Littlefield, 2002), 63–102. Bulag describes the Chinese Premier Zhou Enlai's efforts to get a drama written about the Wencheng story immediately after the uprising in Tibet in March 1959. A twenty-part television drama describing her life in Tibet was produced as *Wencheng Gonjo* (*Rgya bza' gong jo* in Tibetan, or *Princess Wencheng* in English) by Central China Television in 2000; the series, which seems not to have been well received among educated Tibetans, depicts her as a didactic bringer of civilization to backward Tibetans.

This claim does have some historical foundation—*The Mirror Illuminating the Royal Genealogies* records that Wencheng offered the Tibetans "worldly affairs and architectural refinements, various ways of preparing dishes of food, ornamental design, [and] merits [derived from] tilling and grinding alien harvests" (Sørensen, *Mirror Illuminating*, 247). *The Mirror* also describes specific techniques she is said to have introduced—recipes for curd, butter, and cheese; techniques for pounding rosewood, for making rope from hemp, for making earthenware, for planting turnips, and for setting up watermills (248). But in that text it seems that these are all intended to be understood as embellishments of existing cultural practices, not as innovations.

Page 55. "**The eastern mountain peaks rise in waves**": Wencheng's poem about the mountains around Lhasa can be found in Tiley Chodag, *Tibet: The Land,* 79, and in Sørensen, *Mirror Illuminating,* 260–61. In the latter text Wencheng is described as recognizing a complex series of geomantic forces in the landscape, only some of which relate to the demoness. She identifies not only the three hillocks within the Lhasa valley area that are the "heart bones" (*snying khrag*) of the demoness but also the doors to the caverns or sleeping places of the *nāga*s, the tree that is a meeting place of spirits, the path of the *btsan*-spirits, the five mountains that are *sa dra* (terrestrial antagonists), the four mountains that resemble auspicious signs, the eight mountains bearing each of the eight auspicious symbols, and the four places that each hold or represent supplies of different precious metals. The *Bka' chems ka khol ma* gives a fuller description of Wencheng's recognition of the eight-spoked wheel and the eight-petaled lotus formed by the mountains around Lhasa, and of the five "antagonists" that have to be subdued (see Sørensen, *Mirror Illuminating,* 553–60). At least according to these post-tenth century texts, it seems that the technology the Tibetans mainly wanted from China was skill in geomantic divination.

Page 55. **The outstretched *srinmo* or demoness**: The recognition of the inner hillocks or spurs of the Lhasa Valley—Marpori, Chagpori, and Bemari—as the breasts and genitals of the prostrate *srinmo* or demoness is not found specifically in *The Mirror Illuminating the Royal Genealogies*. But another chronicle, the *Bka' chems ka khol ma*, says, "the three parts of hillocks towering [around Lhasa] are known to be the nipples of her breast and the vein of the life [force] of the demoness.... dMar-po-ri and lCags-kha-ri, the two, resemble the tail of a lion [and a tiger] tied together. These two...are the heart-bones of the demoness, recognized to devour the life of sentient beings" (Sørensen, *Mirror Illuminat-*

ing, 556). This text does not name Bemari as the third hill, but this is clarified by Keith Dowman, *The Power-Places of Central Tibet* (London: Routledge, 1988). Dowman notes that Bemari is variously spelled *dbong po ri*, *bong pa ri*, or *spar ma ri*, and that it can also be pronounced "Bompori" or "Bhamari" (284); it is consequently sometimes confused with the more prominent Bumpari, one of the eight mountains surrounding Lhasa. An influential interpretation of the *srinmo* myth is given by Janet Gyatso in her article, "Down with the Demoness: Reflections on a Feminine Ground in Tibet," *The Tibet Journal* XII, no. 4 (Winter 1987): 38–53, also published in Janice Willis, ed., *Feminine Ground: Essays on Women and Tibet* (Ithaca, NY: Snow Lion, 1989).

Page 55. **A series of nesting squares**: The system of the Thandul (*mtha' 'dul*) and the Yangdul (*yang 'dul*) temples that pin down the demoness is discussed in detail in Michael Aris, *Bhutan: The Early History of a Himalayan Kingdom* (Warminster: Aris and Philips, 1979), 3–33, and in Sørensen, *Mirror Illuminating*, notes 770–78 and 832–58 to the main text, and note 770 in the appendix (pp. 561–77). There are multiple versions of the demoness story, of which the earliest so far discovered is probably the *Ma Ni bka' 'bum* (eleventh century). Several name the first set of four temples, with some variations, as Katsel (Ka rtsal) in Medrogongkar county (this is in the central *ru* or horn) pinning down the right shoulder; Trandrug (Khra 'brug) in Nedong county (in the left *ru*) pinning down the left shoulder; Tsangdrang (Gtsang 'phrang) in Namling county (in the right *ru*) pinning down the right hip; and Drumpa Gyang (Grum pa rgyang) in Lhatse county (in the *ru lag* or western *ru* of Tsang) holding down the left hip. Diagrams or pictures illustrating the demoness or the squares pinning her down are given in Dowman, *Power-Places*, 284; Victor Chan, *The Tibet Handbook: A Pilgrim's Guide* (Chicago: Moon Publications, 1994), 44; and Pommaret, ed., *Lhasa in the Seventeenth Century*, 17.

The *Dba' bzhed*, which could be a century earlier than the *Ma Ni bka' 'bum*, refers to a similar scheme, but it says that this consisted of 42 temples built by Srongtsen Gampo. It implies that they were built before the king sent mGar to sue for the hand of Princess Wencheng (Pasang Wangdu and Diemberger, *dBa' bzhed*, 26 and 30–32). Some other texts refer to attempts to establish 108 temples in this period, while others say that some of the temples were built a century later. Most writers agree that these temples were related to the system of the four *ru* or horns—these were the main units in the administration of central Tibet during the period of the Tibetan Kingdom. This connection is noted in Stein, *Tibetan Civilization*, 40ff. See also Geza Uray, "The Four Horns According to the Royal Annals," *Acta Orientalia Academiae Scientiarum Hungaricae* X:31–57; and Robert J. Miller, "'The Supine Demoness' (Srin mo) and the Consolidation of Empire," in Alex McKay, ed., *The History of Tibet* (London: Curzon, 2003), 336–53.

Page 56. **The name Lhasa, the place of the Gods**: The term "Lhasa" is first encountered on the pillar bearing the text of the Sino-Tibetan treaty of 822. This was placed at the foot of the Marpori, the Red Hill, on which the Potala Palace was built. In that text and in some later documents the name Lhasa referred only to the Jokhang. Before 822 the name Rasa had been used. *Ra* is the Tibetan word for goat, and this name is understood by later writers to have meant "the place of the goats," because white goats were used to carry the earth for the foundations of the Jokhang. Anne Marie Blondeau and Yonten Gyatso suggest that "Rasa" may have been a contraction of *rawe sa,* "a place surrounded by a wall" ("Lhasa, Legend and History," in Pommaret, ed., *Lhasa in the Seventeenth Century,* 15–38; the discussion of Lhasa's names is at 21–22).

Page 56. **The persistent problem of water:** The constant danger of flooding throughout Lhasa's history, and the prophecies connected to that threat, are discussed in Blondeau and Yonten Gyatso ("Lhasa, Legend" 29–31). They note that the biographies of many lamas describe their efforts, practical or mystical, to maintain the dikes. In particular, according to his biography, a "treasure-finder" lama called Zhikpo Lingpa built a temple in Lhasa in 1554 that was designed to protect the city from floods. The temple seems not to have been powerful enough, because in 1562 the Kyichu burst its dikes and flooded the town, motivating Sonam Gyatso (1543–88), later to be recognized as the third Dalai Lama, to establish the practice of the Drepung monks reinforcing the dikes on the last day of the Great Prayer Ceremony each spring. This was done every year until recent times ("Lhasa, Legend" 36). Although ten feet thick, the dikes could not withstand the monsoon rains and would collapse each year. In the 1940s, at the request of the Tibetan government, Heinrich Harrer and Peter Aufschnaiter built a new, longer-lasting dike system with a sloping earthen wall, using up to 700 laborers at a time (Harrer, *Lost Lhasa,* 74–77).

The history of the Lhalu (or Lhaklu) pasture land and a discussion of its environmental qualities is given in Emily Yeh, "The Lhalu Wetland Nature Reserve: Land Use Change and State Environmentalism in Lhasa, Tibet," paper presented during the panel "The Construction of Nature Reserves in Western China," Association of Asian Studies Annual Meeting, New York, March 2003.

Page 57. **Not the political capital or administrative center of the country:** From the fall of the Tibetan line of kings in 842 until the accession of the fifth Dalai Lama in 1642, Lhasa's significance was religious rather than political, since in that period power moved to different areas within the central region as different local princes or lamas vied to become the dominant leader in Tibet. After the end of the royal dynasty, Lhasa thus declined as a city or physical center for more than a century, and it is not clear when lay buildings were erected besides the Jokhang, the Ramoche, and the other temples built near them. There was certainly a palace on the Marpori in Lhasa (the hill now dominated by the Potala) in the seventh or eighth century, known as the Lha sa'i sku mkhar and mentioned in the *Dba' bzhed* (Pasang Wangdu and Diemberger, *Dba' bzhed,* 46). But many visitors and inhabitants may have lived in tents, and some of the kings may not have had fixed residences during the dynastic era, since they moved frequently and had palaces elsewhere. The physical shape of the town before the seventeenth century is not clearly documented. But it is probable that by then "a town was built up gradually around these prestigious monuments, accommodating the craftsmen who worked on their improvements" and those who catered to the pilgrim trade as well as to the monasteries founded by Tsongkhapa and his followers (Blondeau and Yonten Gyatso, "Lhasa, Legend," 25ff.).

Except in the anti-Buddhist period of the late ninth and early tenth centuries, when it is said that the Jokhang and the Ramoche were turned into stables, Lhasa must have remained a place of exceptional importance to Tibetans. One of the stone pillars engraved with the text of the Sino-Tibetan peace treaty of 822 was placed there, the great Bengali Buddhist teacher Atisha taught there for some time before his death in 1054, Gompa Tsultrim Rinchen (1116–62) restored the Jokhang in the twelfth century, and his student Lama Zhang founded the monasteries of Tsel (1175) and Gungthang (1187), some 7 miles east of Lhasa, to ensure the protection of the city's temples (Blondeau and Yonten Gyatso, "Lhasa, Legend," 25–31).

The increasing importance of the town in medieval times is further shown by Tsongkhapa's choice of Lhasa as the site for his main monasteries. The most powerful town at that time in political terms was Ne'udong, but he chose the slope of the mountain to the north of Lhasa, where Sera is now, for a retreat, and while there had a vision that led him to establish the *Mönlam chenmo* or Great Prayer Ceremony at the Jokhang.

The festival was held for the first time in 1409, after the temple's interior and statues had been refurbished; it lasted 16 days and is said to have attracted 10,000 people. The event became an important factor in Lhasa's revival in the fifteenth century and remained the city's principal calendrical event until it was banned by the Chinese state in 1959. The other major factor in the revival of Lhasa was the founding of the three great monasteries of Ganden, Drepung, and Sera in 1409, 1416, and 1419 respectively. The first was established by Tsongkhapa himself; Drepung and Sera were established by his disciples (Blondeau and Yonten Gyatso, "Lhasa, Legend," 33–35). The Dalai Lama lineage was based in Drepung monastery, from where it built up major relations with the most powerful khans in Mongolia. Lhasa became a political center again and a built city after Gushri Khan enthroned the fifth Dalai Lama as the head of the Tibetan government, then based in Drepung, in 1642. The Dalai Lama began the construction of the Potala Palace, later the seat of the government, three years later.

Page 57. **They considered the city to be almost totally devoid of men**: The population of Lhasa in 1904 was estimated by the British at 30,000 people, of whom 20,000 were said to be monks. This claim is discussed in Blondeau and Yonten Gyatso, "Lhasa, Legend," 26. In 1936 Spencer Chapman estimated the population at 50,000 to 60,000, consisting of 20,000 residents and 30,000 to 40,000 monks, according to Ma Rong, "Han and Tibetan Residential Patterns in Lhasa" (*China Quarterly* 128 [December 1991]: 814–36). Ma suggests that the population in 1952 was approximately the same as in Chapman's day. In 1986 the official population of Lhasa was 107,725, and 52.5 percent of the 72,349 Chinese in the TAR—about 38,000—were living in the city (832, 815). These sources do not specify the number of nuns.

4. THE CITY, THE CIRCLE

Page 65. **The constant risk of being kidnapped by senior monks**: Tashi Tsering's accounts of his attempts to avoid kidnapping by monks in the 1950s are given in his autobiography (*The Struggle for Modern Tibet* 26–30). The issue is also discussed in the biography of the former *dobdob* Tashi Khedup, published in English as Tashi Khedrup, *Adventures of a Fighting Monk*. See also Melvyn Goldstein, "A Study of the *Ldab Ldob*," *Central Asiatic Journal* 9, no. 2 (1964): 125–41.

Page 65. **"There is nothing one cannot buy"**: Heinrich Harrer's description of Lhasa shopping is from Harrer, *Seven Years in Tibet*, 126. The hand grenades are described in Kimura and Berry, *A Japanese Agent in Tibet*, 119. Tashi Tsering's descriptions of the city streets as he saw them on his return to Lhasa after years in the United States are in *The Struggle for Modern Tibet*, 108.

Alexandra David-Néel, when she finally reached Lhasa in 1923, complained volubly about the lack of shops where she could buy antiques. But she confirmed that international trade was quite active: "Nowadays the most conspicuous articles in the Lhasa market are aluminum wares. For the rest, the display is exclusively composed of inferior goods exported from India, England, Japan, or a few other European countries. I have never seen elsewhere uglier cotton cloth, more hideous crockery than that which one finds on the stalls of the Lhasa merchants" (*My Journey* 267).

Page 66. **"This city of gigantic palace and golden roof"**: Perceval Landon's description of the marshes around Lhasa is given in *LHASA*, 11:182.

Page 66. **A circle of some twenty-two *lingkas* or parks**: Zasak J. Taring's *Map of Lhasa* was drawn from memory after he went into exile and published by the University of Tokyo Press in 1984.

5. MONUMENTAL STATEMENTS AND STREET PLANS

Page 71. **Forty-three capital construction projects in Tibet**: The 1984 decision to invest in grand construction in Tibet was announced at a party meeting in Beijing, the "Second National Work Forum on Tibet." Details of the forum are given in Tsering Shakya, *The Dragon in the Land of Snows*, 394–98; Tseten Wangchuk Sharlho, "China's Reforms"; and Warren Smith, *Tibetan Nation*, 586–95.

Page 72. **A wave of destruction would recommence**: The most informed discussions of the state of architectural preservation in Lhasa in the 1990s can be found in the publications or Web sites of the Tibet Heritage Fund. These include descriptions of a few renovation projects that were allowed. The main publication is André Alexander, John Harrison, and Pimpim de Azevedo, eds., *A Clear Lamp Illuminating the Significance and Origin of Historic Buildings and Monuments in Lhasa Barkor Street (Lhasa Old City, Vol. II)* (Berlin: Tibet Heritage Fund, 1999). Another important text is their 1998 report, published as André Alexander and Pimpim de Azevedo, *The Old City of Lhasa—Report from a Conservation Project (98–99)* (Berlin and Kathmandu: Tibet Heritage Fund, 1998), also available at www.asianart.com/lhasa_restoration/report98/index.htm. Other materials, including year-by-year maps of demolitions in the Old City, can be seen at www.tibetheritagefund.org; these show an annual loss of 35 historic buildings in the Old City area, except for the years 1999 and 2000, when losses were lighter. A book by André Alexander, *The Temples of Lhasa: Tibetan Buddhist Architecture from the Seventh to the Twenty-first Centuries* (London: Serindia), is forthcoming.

Page 72. **The final enclosure of what had been the original city**: Details of the history of urban development in Lhasa during the 1980s can be found in Barnett, "Odour of Development," in Pommaret, ed., *Lhasa in the Seventeenth Century*. The stages of urban development in Lhasa are demonstrated most clearly in the three-part map of Lhasa entitled *Tibetan Old Buildings and Urban Development in Lhasa: 1948–1985–1998* (Berlin: VFKA, 1998), produced by the Lhasa Archive Project, part of the Tibet Heritage Fund. These maps are also shown at www.asianart.com/lhasa_restoration/map.html#2. Satellite photographs of these periods and other material concerning Lhasa architecture and the changes it underwent in the 1980s and 1990s can be found in Knud Larsen and Amund Sining-Larsen, *The Lhasa Atlas: Traditional Tibetan Architecture and Townscape* (London: Serindia, 2001).

A detailed survey of old buildings and demolition projects in the city in 1993 can be found in *TIN Background Briefing Paper 23: Demolition and Reconstruction in the Old Quarter of Lhasa 1993* (London: Tibet Information Network, November 1994).

Page 72. **The Tromsikhang**: The name Tromsikhang means "the building from which the market can be seen," and there had for centuries been a marketplace north of the mansion in which the two *ambans* were murdered in the eighteenth century. The Mongol overlord Lhazang Khan and the *ambans* had chosen this mansion for the Chinese Resident, perhaps because they felt the market was the place that, as would-be rulers, they should watch.

Page 74. **The new state appropriated the houses of those who had fled**: The appropriation of rebel properties after the 1959 uprising is described by Ma Rong: "In the late 1950s, the masters and monks of these monasteries fled to India, and the houses and the land were then used for public affairs and government institutions. Some houses belonging to nobles who had fled were distributed among the homeless urban Tibetans. Many new units have been established in the zone around the urban district and gradually expanded into suburbs along the newly constructed roads" ("Patterns" 833). In the 1990s, some of the mansions confiscated in 1959 were given back to the original owners if they returned to Tibet.

Page 74. **Not so many outward signs of the new regime**: During the new construction initiated by the Chinese authorities, a very considerable portion of the old city was destroyed. This was at the edges, and the new rulers thus left the city's historic center more or less intact. Han Suyin, on her visit in 1975, found that the Lhasa buildings "had not changed their architecture" (she describes their interiors as "sombre" and the courtyards formerly as "toilets") but she acknowledges seeing some demolitions of old buildings: "Today, new Lhasa is growing and the old city is diminishing in size. I saw a bulldozer destroying some houses which will be rebuilt with modern conveniences." She adds in a footnote: "These will have latrines and a modern system of purified running water. One can, if clinging to the exotic, regret that the new houses will probably be in the functional Chinese architecture. However, beautiful old houses belonging to the Tibetan nobility are being kept clean and repaired" (*Lhasa, the Open City*, 38, 176n10).

Page 74. **Satellite conurbations**: The satellite mode of urban expansion before the 1980s—the building of small, noncontiguous developments some distance from the city—had begun twenty years before: "Two industrial districts have taken shape on the northern and western outskirts of the city. Factory buildings and workers' houses now stand on what used to be marshy lands. The famous Potala Hill, covered by the Potala Palace, is now surrounded by new buildings for broadcasting, school, bank office, bookshops and the office of the PCART," reported Xinhua (New China News, the official Chinese news agency) in "Lhasa's New Skyline," January 29, 1964 (in *Tibet 1950–1967* [Hong Kong: Union Research Institute, 1968], 596).

Page 75. **"Three groups live in separate zones"**: The three groups identified by Ma Rong in "Patterns" are "native" Lhasa Tibetans, Chinese or Han migrants, and new Tibetan migrants from other areas of the Tibetan plateau (823). Of the first category, "native" Tibetans, he found that 60 percent (27,500) still lived in the old town and 20 percent (c. 9,900) had moved to work units outside the old town. One quarter (8,000) had moved to the outlying area that Ma calls the "suburbs." The Han group was already larger than the Tibetan group remaining in the old town—37,800, mostly living in the work units. Ma found about 23,300 "migrant" Tibetans, whom he says lived in the work units, which had been constructed in the "middle zone." He says that, largely because of the convenience of stationing Chinese migrants in new buildings outside the traditional area and because the government had failed to spend money on construction in the old town, the government had produced "ethnic residential segregation," and that this consequence "should not be forgotten" by planners (835).

Page 76. **"The urban form of straight lines and rectangular squares"**: This quotation is taken from P. Reed, "Form and Context: A Study of Georgian Edinburgh," in T. A. Markus, ed., *Order in Space and Society: Architectural Form and its Context in the Scottish Enlightenment* (Edinburgh: Mainstream Publishing,

1982), cited in John Rennie Short, *The Urban Order—An Introduction to Cities, Culture and Power* (Cambridge, MA: Blackwell, 1996), 399.

Page 77. **"Lhasa must therefore be built up"**: The description of the "modern socialist city" is given in "Preface to the Maps" in the *Lhasa Municipal Planning Maps*. This volume was published in book form, in Chinese, by the Tibet Autonomous Region Planning Department. It contains outline maps showing the official city plan for Lhasa from 1980 until 2000. No date of publication is given, but it was probably produced in 1981 or shortly afterward. The actual 1980 plans, in text form, have not been published, but fragments of the internal documents that together make up the full text have emerged. One is "Summary of Present Construction Situation" in *Lhasa City Planning Documents* (provisional title), part 9, Lhasa (1980). This is held in the Tibet Information Network archive (London) as TIN Doc. 13 (WZ).

Page 77. **One of the last *ambans* had given 1,000 *taels*:** Zhang Yintang, during the seven months from 1904–5 that he served as *amban*, organized a scheme to plant trees around Lhasa and to have public parks set up, according to Ma Lihua, *Old Lhasa*, 143. Ma claims that the effort failed mainly because of corruption (on the Tibetan side) and lack of planning.

Page 78. **"A decade had passed since I left Lhasa"**: The description by Tashi Tsering of the tree-lined streets is from his autobiography, *The Struggle for Modern Tibet*, 108.

Page 78. **The British residency at Dekyi Lingka**: A description of Dekyi Lingka, and of many aspects of pre–1950 Lhasa life, is provided by Tsering Shakya in "Cities and Thrones and Powers: The British and the Tibetans in Lhasa, 1936–1947," in Harris and Shakya, eds., *Seeing Lhasa*, 79–125. Shakya, a leading modern Tibetan historian, lived in Dekyi Lingka as a child and describes his recollections of its gardens on 124.

Page 78. **Geraniums to Tibet**: Richardson was not the only diplomat in Lhasa to have made an impact on the city's horticulture, if Ma Lihua is correct. According to her, Zhang Yintang "is commemorated in the name of a popular flower in Tibet, the 'Lord Zhang Flower' which can often be seen in residential courtyards and public places in Lhasa. That plant grows chest-high, and has eight petals either red or white. If you look closely, these can be further divided into pink and purple...in Lhasa, there is a Lord Zhang vegetable garden and a Lord Zhang tree" (*Old Lhasa* 135–36). The flower is usually known as coreopsis.

Page 81. **A vast military parade ground**: *China Daily*, the official English-language paper in Beijing, announced the existence of a plan to construct the "new Potala Palace Square" on the site of the village of Shöl (*China Daily*, March 24, 1994). Most of the Tibetan residents had already been evicted from the village by the time the article was published. Construction of the Potala Palace Square began in Lhasa on October 18, 1994, according to Xinhua (*BBC Summary of World Broadcasts*, October 23, 1994): "It will be 600 by 400 m. in area and is expected to cost 110 mln. yuan [c. $13 mln]."

Page 81. **He climbed the flagpole at its center**: For details of the flagpole incident in August 1999, see "Tashi Tsering Hospitalised with Severe Head Injury and a Broken Arm," Tibetan Centre for Human Rights and Democracy, Dharamsala, India, October 8, 1999; Kate Saunders, "Concern for Imprisoned Female Head-Teacher of Children," December 22, 2003, published online in *World Tibet News*, December 23, 2003, part 2; "Death Sentence for Bangri Rinpoche Commuted to Life Imprisonment," Tibetan Centre for Human Rights and Democracy, Dharamsala, December 16, 2004; and *The Tragic Fate of Bangri Rinpoche* (Dharamsala: The Gu Chu Sum Movement of Tibet, 2005).

6. FROM CONCRETE TO BLUE GLASS

Page 85. **Washington's threat to impose trade restrictions on China**: The renewal of China's trading privileges with the United States, known as "most-favored-nation status," in April–May 1994 signaled the end of U.S. efforts to use forceful diplomacy to get China to improve its human rights practices. The previous year, the White House had declared publicly that the privileges would not be continued unless ten changes concerning human rights were implemented, but in due course found itself obliged to renew them with nothing conceded by Beijing. I have written about this period and its consequences for Tibet policy in Robert Barnett and Mickey Spiegel, *Cutting Off the Serpent's Head: Tightening Control in Tibet 1994–95* (London: Tibet Information Network and New York: Human Rights Watch, 1996).

Page 85. **Cement...and the factories that produced it**: "Construction of the Lhasa Cement Plant started in 1960. Completed in 1963, it has already supplied over 10,000 tons of cement for Tibetan construction projects [and] has an annual capacity of 32,000 tons. Nearly all the 200 Tibetan workers trained at the plant were slaves or serfs in the past" ("Tibet Produces Its Own Cement," Xinhua, November 11, 1964, reproduced in the compendium *Tibet 1950–1967* [Hong Kong: Union Research Institute, 1968], 577). In 1980 the Lhasa Cement Factory had 700 workers, and the Prefabrication Factory, built in 1977 to produce cement blocks, had 220 workers, making these probably the most significant factories in Lhasa. At that time one fifth of the workforce was in construction (8,000 people), not including road workers. See "Summary of Present Construction Situation" in *Lhasa City Planning Documents* (1980), 2. As of 2004, the cement factory below Sera monastery and the garbage dump between them were due to be moved to the outskirts of the city. The other major cement factories that had been located beyond the northeastern border of the city had been surrounded by the leading edge of suburban expansion.

Page 86. **The dust from the smokestacks**: The issue of environmental pollution had already been noticed with some concern by local residents. In October 1998, students at the Lhasa Teacher Training School reportedly circulated a petition saying, "Air pollution, deforestation, degradation of grasslands, desertification, acid rain and other environmental perils devastate the environment of Tibet, which directly influences our livelihood.... If we look at the future of industry in Lhasa, there are problems all around: polluted rivers and streams flow in the north of the city, thick clouds of smoke emit in the west, and there is the constant music blaring in the centre of the city. Everybody has seen these problems, but nobody even attempts to solve them. Is this modern civilisation? As human civilisation develops, is it not the human greed for wealth that may ultimately lead to the demise of this civilisation?" The petition was published in translation in "Police Banned Lhasa Students' Procession and Petition for Cleaner Tibetan Environment" (Dharamsala: Department of Information and International Affairs, Tibetan government in exile, January 8, 1999).

Page 86. **Tibetan forests then being cleared**: The timber trade in Tibet and other areas of western China was effectively unregulated until 1998, when the authorities banned logging in areas surrounding the upper reaches of China's major rivers. This followed flooding that led to more than 3,000 deaths in lower China earlier that year. See "The Decision of the CCP Central Committee on Several Major Issues Concerning Agriculture and Rural Work—Adopted by the Third Plenary Session of the 15th CCP Central Committee on 14th October 1998," Xinhua, October 20, 1998, and John Pomfret, "Yangtze Flood Jolts China's Land Policies; Development Curbs Set to Protect Environment," *Washington Post*, November 22, 1998.

Page 86. **The only significant industrial product in Tibet**: The effort to industrialize Tibet was a centerpiece of China's policy in the 1960s and 1970s, and was widely presented in its public relations materials. But besides cement production, it chiefly consisted of a matchstick factory in Kongpo and a wool and textile operation in Nyingtri, 300 miles east of Lhasa. All the components of the textile factory had had to be trucked into Tibet from Shanghai piece by piece, including the workers. A description of the factory is given by Han Suyin in *Lhasa, the Open City*, 124–25.

Page 86. **Tibet's major form of heavy industry**: Economic policy in the TAR by the end of the century was to prioritize the development of "five pillar industries." These were mining, forestry, agricultural and livestock by-products and handicrafts, tourism, and construction. By 2003, after Beijing had imposed a ban on logging in the region, the list had been changed to "six pillar industries," in which forestry was replaced by Tibetan medicine and organic products. The focus of industrialization in Tibet remained on mining, and in 1994 there were 145 mining enterprises in the region, though they were reported to employ only 5,000 people. That year the TAR produced 115,000 tons of chromite, 23,200 tons of borax, 10,300 tons of mineral water, 27,000 tons of lead and zinc, 20.88 kilograms of gold sand, 5,800 tons of coal, and 310,000 tons of limestone. An official of the Tibet Mining Bureau claimed that 94 kinds of minerals had been discovered in 1,719 locations in the TAR, with 39 boasting "impressive reserves." See, for example, *China's Tibet* 6, no. 5 (Winter 1995) and Jane Caple, *Mining Tibet* (London: Tibet Information Network, 2002).

Page 87. **The Spring Tide**: The "Spring Tide" form of economic development was promoted and implemented in the Tibet Autonomous Region by a new party secretary, Chen Kuiyuan, who had been brought from his previous position in Inner Mongolia in March 1992, initially as a deputy secretary. The campaign to spread the rapid marketization approach across China began that month, and Chen's transfer may have been connected to it. He emerged as a forceful exponent of that philosophy, and seems to have seen it as an economic method to contain and suppress forms of Tibetan culture and belief that he considered threatening, as well as to legitimize an increase in non-Tibetan migration to the region's urban areas. An account of this policy shift is given in Barnett and Spiegel, *Cutting Off the Serpent's Head,* and in Robert Barnett, "The Chinese Frontiersman and the Winter Worms—The Traditions of Chen Kuiyuan in the TAR, 1992–2000," in Alex McKay, ed., *Tibet and Her Neighbours* (London: Curzon, 2003), 207–39.

Page 87. **"Individually run enterprises"**: The surge in individual enterprises was announced in "Roundup on Tibet's Private Sector Economy" in *Xizang Ribao (Tibet Daily)*, February 4, 1994, and published in translation by *BBC Summary of World Broadcasts*, March 2, 1994. The business sector in Lhasa has been studied by Hu Xiaojiang in *Little Shops of Lhasa: Migrant Businesses and the Making of a Market in a Transitional Economy* (Stanford: Stanford University Press, forthcoming).

Page 90. **Bars, nightclubs, and 24-hour hair salons**: The dramatic increase in prostitution and gambling establishments was discussed by party leaders in the press, and some attempts were made to regulate the leisure industry. In January 1997, Deputy Party Secretary Tenzin was reported as saying that the focus of the party's work in this respect was "to wipe out pornography, gambling, drug addiction, and other vicious social phenomena [and it] is to inspect ballrooms, karaoke shops, bars, and restaurants; put an end to the providing of women for drinking, dancing, and other activities to customers and prostitution; ban gambling." See "Danzim Listens to Report on Work to Crack Down on Pornographic and Illegal Publications, Calls for Grasping Key Points and Concentrating Efforts on Purifying Society," *Xizang Ribao (Tibet Daily)*, January 23, 1997, 1 (published in translation as "Tibet Cracks Down on Illegal, Pornographic Publications" by the *BBC Summary of World Broadcasts*). Many Tibetans in Lhasa believe that any attempts to regulate or decrease these industries have been purely token.

Page 90. **"On a recent stroll through the streets of Lhasa"**: The letter to "Comrade Editor" is from "Unhealthy Shop Signs in Lhasa Should Be Cleaned Up," *Xizang Ribao (Tibet Daily)*, August 23, 1996, 4. This translation is by Tibet Information Network.

Page 91. **20 square miles**: The figures for the size of the city in 1997—52 square kilometers—are from "Lhasa Makes Great Achievements," *China Daily*, August 19, 1997.

Page 92. **Access to tap water**: A survey of water provision in the Barkor in 1993 can be found in *TIN Background Briefing Paper 23* (London: Tibet Information Network, 1994). The figures for tap water supply in 1997 are from "Lhasa Makes Great Achievements," *China Daily*, August 19, 1997.

Page 92. **City toilets:** Han Suyin discusses toilet practices and the lack of toilet paper in the mid-1970s in her book *Lhasa, the Open City*, where she claims that Tibetans still were defecating in the street as late as 1962, thirteen years before her visit. There was "no domestic drainage system and no arrangement for the disposal of sewage...in 1975 this was changed, with the institution of inconspicuous public latrines and the system of removal" (38). The history of foreign contempt toward Tibetan hygiene and the failure of city planners and developers in the 1980s and 1990s to provide toilets is discussed in Barnett, "Odour of Development," in Pommaret, ed., *Lhasa in the Seventeenth Century*, 218–19. By 2005 the white and orange toilets had been replaced by more attractive buildings in Tibetan style.

7. THE NEW FLAMBOYANCE AND THE TIBETAN PALM TREE

Page 97. **The importation of steel girders**: The development of new Tibetan construction methods in the early twentieth century is discussed in Harris and Shakya, eds., *Seeing Lhasa*. The home that the Ngapö family built in the 1950s still stands between the southeast corner of the campus of Tibet University and the north bank of the Kyichu river.

Page 98. **Wages of all government employees**: The level of salaries in the TAR is discussed in "High TAR Wages Benefit the Privileged," Tibet Information Network, February 10, 2005. The average annual salary in the TAR was 26,931 *yuan* in 2003, close to twice the national average in China that year. This partly reflects higher costs in Lhasa because of the expense of transporting consumer goods and fuel by truck, and also could include "hardship bonuses" and "remoteness allowances" given to all government employees in Tibet. Even so, it represents a major increase in wealth for the Tibetan cadre class.

Page 98. **Cadre class**: The term "cadre"—*ganbu* in Chinese or *las byed pa* in Tibetan—means in the Chinese context any person employed by the government, including schoolteachers, policemen, kitchen staff in work units, and other state employees. They need not necessarily be an administrative official or a member of the Communist Party, though often a cadre might be both.

Page 98. **A private property market**: The reforms that led to the setting up of a housing market in Tibet are discussed in "Housing Reform: Key Policy is to Sell Off State Housing Units," Tibet TV, March 16, 1994, published in translation by the *BBC Summary of World Broadcasts*.

Page 99. **Domestic servants**: The return of domestic labor to Lhasa house-holds and some of its consequences have been examined in a short story, "The Yellow Leaves of Summer," by the leading modern Tibetan writer, Tashi Palden; the plot concerns a disastrous love affair between the husband of a family and the country girl who works for them. For an English version, see Riika J. Virtanen (compiler and translator), *A Blighted Flower and Other Stories: Portraits of Women in Modern Tibetan Literature* (New Delhi: Paljor Publications, 2000), 105–28.

Page 102. **"A song and dance performance"**: The celebrations that were held to celebrate the visit of Hu Jintao, then the vice president of China, to Lhasa in 2001 are described in "Fireworks Show Marks Tibet's Peaceful Liberation Anniversary," Xinhua, July 19, 2001. Entrance to the Potala Square was strictly controlled before and during the main parade, with the deployment of extensive military resources for security. Only designated delegates from work units or schools could enter the square at that time, so most people would only have seen the parade on television.

Page 102. **The first multistory block**: Other skyscrapers were constructed in Lhasa during the 1990s, including a sixteen-story trade center south of the Drepung cement factory, but these were several miles west of the traditional city. The new Lhasa City Public Security Bureau headquarters was the first such block erected close to the historic section of Lhasa.

Page 102. **Dorje Yuthok's family name**: The name Yuthok may have been given to the family because their house was near the covered bridge with the turquoise-colored roof tiles. This family was ennobled in the early nineteenth century because one of their children had been recognized as the tenth Dalai Lama. They then moved to a house near the bridge. Alexandra David-Néel, however, gave a different account of the family's name, writing in 1923 that the family received the title because of the award of a "turquoise knob" from a Chinese emperor (*My Journey* 272).

Page 103. **Lhasa's first official "market street"**: The 1960s development of Yuthok street into a market area was described by Luoga (Loga), then the Mayor of Lhasa, in a magazine article by Liu Tungfen and Wangdu, "How Are You Improving the Living Standard of the People of Lhasa?—Interview with Loga, Mayor of Lhasa Municipality," published in *Grung-go bod ljongs* (the Tibetan-language edition of *China's Tibet*) (Spring 1991):7–16.

Page 104. **An apology**: A disclaimer for earlier pro-Tibetan activism was written by Patrick French in *Tibet, Tibet: A Personal History of a Lost Land* (London: HarperCollins, 2003); French, a former director of a prominent pro-Tibet lobby organization in the United Kingdom, came to believe that outside activism had worsened the situation and that change could only come from inside. Some fundamental claims made by outside commentators, such as the use of the term "colonial" to describe conditions in Tibet and Xinjiang, are attacked in Barry Sautman, "Is Tibet China's Colony?: The Claim of Demographic Catastrophe,"

Journal of Asian Law 15, no. 1 (Fall 2001): 81ff.; and Barry Sautman, "Is Xinjiang an Internal Colony?", *Inner Asia* 2 (2000): 239–71. Sautman also wrote a lengthy critique of the Dalai Lama's credibility, "Association, Federation and 'Genuine' Autonomy: The Dalai Lama's Proposals and Tibet Independence," paper presented at the Association of Asian Studies Annual Meeting, San Diego, California, March 9–12, 2000.

Page 105. **Chinese writers and artists**: The most prominent writings in Chinese about Tibet to have appeared in the 1990s were short stories or novels by Ma Yuan, Ma Jian, Alai, and Tashi Dawa. These authors all wrote in Chinese and in a style they developed from the magical realism of Jorge Luis Borges and Gabriel García Márquez. Ma Yuan worked as a journalist in Tibet from 1982 to 1987 and published a number of short stories with Tibetan themes that became major examples of avant-garde writing in China; three are published in translation in Batt, ed., *Tales of Tibet*, 5–76. Ma Jian was notorious for "Stick Out the Fur on Your Tongue or It's All a Void," a fantasy about Tibet that had to be withdrawn in 1987 because of its salacious accounts of imaginary Tibetan sexuality, which Tibetans complained were insulting. Extracts from the story, together with an important critique by the editors, were published in English in Geremie Barmé and John Minford, eds., *Seeds of Fire: Chinese Voices of Conscience* (New York: Hill and Wang, 1988), 432–52; the title of Ma Jian's piece is given in that volume as "Show Me the Colour of Your Tongue or Fuck All." A longer extract is published in Batt, ed., *Tales of Tibet*, 235–54. Ma Jian's account of traveling in western China is published in English as *Red Dust: A Path Through China* (New York: Anchor Books, 2001).

Tashi Dawa, who is half Tibetan, became famous for his magical realist style in novels such as *A Soul in Bondage* (English translation, Beijing: Chinese Literature Press, 1992) and *The Tumultuous Shambhala* (Beijing: Writers Publishing House, 1993) and short stories such as "The Glory of the Wind Horse," published in translation in *Manoa* 12, no. 2 (2000): 96–113. Alai is a Tibetan writer from Gyalrong in the southeastern Amdo borderlands, now part of Ngaba prefecture in Sichuan, whose novel *Chen ai lou ding* (*When the Dust Settles*), translated by Howard Goldblatt and Sylvia Li-chun Lin as *Red Poppies* (New York: Houghton Mifflin, 2002), won China's main literary prize in 2000 and was turned into a popular television drama series.

Nonfiction in Chinese about Tibet has been dominated by Ma Lihua, who wrote several works of popular ethnography or travel writing, one of which was translated into English by an official publisher as *Glimpses of Northern Tibet* (Beijing: Panda Books, 1991). She also produced a series of television documentaries about Tibet. Not all of the works in Chinese at this time were romantic reveries; the most influential study of Tibet in Chinese has been Wang Lixiong's *Tian Zang* (*Sky Burial*, 1997), the first of many important essays he was to produce on the Tibetan question, among which was the pamphlet "Dalai Lama Is the Key for the Solution for the Issue of Tibet" (May to July 2000).

The most incisive of all PRC-published works in Chinese or Tibetan on contemporary Tibetan culture and politics is Derong Tsering Dondrup's *Wode Xinyuan* (Tibetan: *Bdag gi re smon*; Ganzi [also written as Kandze or Kartse]: Ganzi baoshe yinshuachang [Ganzi Newspaper Office Printing Press], undated, probably November 1995). However, this was issued only as an internal document and never widely circulated in China.

One of the most significant books in Chinese on Tibet is *Xizang Biji* (*Tibet Notes* [Guangzhou: Huacheng Publishing House, 2003]) by the Tibetan writer Oeser (her name can also be transcribed as Woeser; it is written as Weise in Chinese). The book was banned in late 2003. Her earlier poems in Chinese (Weise, *Xizang zai shang* [*For Tibet*] [Xining: Qinghai People's Publishing House, 1999]) have been described by some Chinese as influential in shaping opinions about Tibet. Oeser was born in 1966 in Lhasa but was brought up in the Kham region of Tibet, part of Sichuan province. She graduated in 1988 from the South-West Nationalities Institute in Chengdu and worked in Lhasa from 1989 (see "TAR Authorities Ban Book by Tibetan Author," *TIN News Update*, Tibet Information Network, March 16, 2004 and "Tibetan Stories: Extracts from 'Notes on Tibet'," *TIN Special Report*, Tibet Information Network, May 4, 2004).

Both Oeser and Wang Lixiong published major pieces of highly critical writing on the Internet in 2004 and 2005, including Wang's essay "Tibet Facing Imperialism of Two Kinds: An Analysis of the Woeser Incident—Cultural Suppression from Political Imperialism" (posted on www.asiademo.org, with translation issued online through World Tibet News on December 21, 2004); Oeser's essay "Remembering March 10th: Let's Insist on Our Culture" (posted on www.tibet-cult.org, March 10, 2005); and Oeser's poem "Secret Tibet: Dedicated to the Imprisoned Tenzin Delek Rinpoche, Bangri Rinpoche and Lobsang Tenzin" (posted on New Century Net at www.ncn.org, second draft, November 10, 2004).

Page 105. **A movement widespread in republican China**: The emergence of widespread interest in Tibetan Buddhism among Chinese in the 1930s has been documented in Gray Tuttle, *Tibetan Buddhists in the Making of Modern China*. Public ceremonies were celebrated in the 1930s by the Panchen Lama and other Buddhist teachers in Beijing and Shanghai, sometimes with audiences of up to 75,000 people.

Page 114. *Geshe* **Lamrim**: On the death of *Geshe* Lamrim, see "Leading Religious Teacher Dies," Tibet Information Network, June 14, 1997.

amban (Tibetan: *am ban*): The Manchu term for the commissioners, most of whom were Manchus, who were sent by Beijing as representatives of the Qing emperors to reside in Lhasa from 1727 until 1912, when all Chinese officials and their followers were expelled. The ambans, usually assigned in pairs, regarded their authority in Tibet as extensive, but their influence is said to have become marginal after the mid-nineteenth century. See also **Youtai; Zhang Yintang**.

amchi (Tibetan: *em chi*): A Tibetan term, derived from Mongolian, for a doctor or physician.

Amdo (Tibetan: *a mdo* or *mdo stod*; Chinese: *an duo*): The northeastern area of the Tibetan plateau, one of the three provinces or regions (*mchol kha gsum*) traditionally considered to constitute Tibet. It was divided into semi-independent principalities, most of which were not ruled directly by Lhasa in recent times. Most of Amdo is within Qinghai, which was first administered as a Chinese province around 1723–25, but important parts are in other Chinese provinces, such as Ngaba (Chinese: *Aba*), which is within Sichuan. Areas such as Pari (Chinese: *Tianzhu*), Labrang (Chinese: *Labulengsi*), and Machu (Chinese: *Maqu*) are now within Gansu province. The population is largely nomadic. Many of Tibet's outstanding literary scholars, religious masters, and intellectuals have come from this area, and a number of them studied or worked in Lhasa. See also **Kham; Tibet**.

aristocrat (Tibetan: *sku drag*): A member of one of the 180 to 200 families in central Tibet that owned estates and ran the bureaucracy until 1959. Each family had to submit one son to be an official in the Tibetan government of the Dalai Lamas (known after 1642 as the *Ganden Podrang*, Tibetan: *dga' ldan pho brang*). Ordinary individuals could sometimes be ennobled by the Dalai Lama because of outstanding service (as were Kabshöpa and "new" Tsarong). Twenty-eight of the noble families were of higher status and owned multiple estates; these included six families—known as *yabshi* (Tibetan: *yab gzhis*)—that had been ennobled because one or more of the Dalai Lamas had been born into their families (among these were the Lhalu, Yuthok, Langdun, and Taktser families). The elite group also included the Shatra, Surkhang, Tethong, Taring, Ngapö, and Tsarong families.

Atisha (Tibetan: *jo bo rje* or *dpal mar med mdzad dpal ye shes*) (982?–1054): A prominent Buddhist teacher and scholar from Bengal who traveled to Tibet around the year 1042. Atisha taught widely in central Tibet, including Lhasa, and was a key figure in initiating "the second dissemination" of Buddhism (it had been suppressed by the last king of the Tibetan dynasty, Langdarma, after he came to power in 838). Atisha established the Kadampa school of Tibetan Buddhism, which in the fifteenth century reemerged as the Gelugpa school.

Aufschnaiter, Peter (1899–1973): An Austrian mountaineer who spent eight years in Tibet after escaping with Heinrich Harrer in 1944 from a British internment camp in northern India where they had been placed at the beginning of World War II. Aufschnaiter became a junior Tibetan official, working on irrigation and electricity projects in Lhasa until the Chinese invasion. He also produced an important map of the city, learned Tibetan, and married a Tibetan. He lived the rest of his life in Nepal and India, where he worked as an engineer (see Peter Aufschnaiter and Martin Brauen, *Peter Aufschnaiter, sein Leben in Tibet* [Innsbruck: Steiger, 1983]).

Baba **Phuntsog Wanggyal** (Tibetan: *'ba' ba phun tshogs dbang rgyal*) (born 1922): A radical intellectual from Bathang in Kham (eastern Tibet) who formed a secret Tibetan Communist Party without Chinese support in 1939, later receiving some aid from the USSR. In 1944, he tried unsuccessfully to persuade the Tibetan government in Lhasa to implement social reforms, to stage an uprising in Kham, and to create a greater Tibetan state unifying central Tibet, Kham, and other areas. He also started a clandestine communist cell in Lhasa. In 1949 he joined the Chinese Communist Party (CCP) and became the chief intermediary in its relations with the Dalai Lama. He was given the highest position of any Tibetan within the party in the 1950s but was ostracized in 1957 after a copy of Lenin's work on nationality policy was found in his room. He was imprisoned for 18 years, and spent much of the time writing about dialectical philosophy. In 1980 he returned to a token position in the People's Congress, which he used to push for more moderate policies toward nationalities, working in concert with the Panchen Lama. A first-person account of his life appeared in English under the title *A Tibetan Revolutionary* ([with M. Goldstein et al.] Berkeley: University of California Press, 2004).

Banakshöl (Tibetan: *sbra nag zhol*): A guesthouse situated in an area of that name (literally "Black Tent Below") on the northeastern edge of the Old City of Lhasa after about 1982. The hotel, run by a cooperative, was among the first to open in that era and to be allowed to accept individual foreign travelers. The Snowland, Kirey, and Yak hotels all opened at about the same time in Lhasa and were allowed to accept foreigners.

Barkor (Tibetan: *bar skor*; Chinese: *bajiao*): The alleyway that runs around the four sides of the Jokhang, the main temple in Tibet. The Barkor is the major pilgrimage route in Lhasa as well as the main market area in the old part of the city. Literally "the middle circuit," it is one of at least three pilgrimage routes around the *Jowo* ("Lord"), the statue of the Buddha housed in the Jokhang temple. It was the site of at least 100 pro-independence protests by Tibetans in the period 1987–1996, five of which involved several hundred participants. Chinese references to it as octagonal are due to a coincidental homonymy between the Tibetan word *bar* (middle) and the Chinese word *ba* (eight). See also **Lingkor**.

Barkor Square (Tibetan: *bar skor thang chen*): A modern pedestrianized plaza in front of the main (western) gate of the Jokhang temple complex in Lhasa. The plaza was created in 1985 by demolishing some traditional buildings, apparently in order to provide tourists and traders with a view of the temple.

Bass, Catriona (born 1961): A British woman who was one of the first Westerners to live and work in Lhasa after 1951. Bass had worked as a teacher in China before moving to Lhasa in 1986, where for sixteen months she taught English. She knew some Chinese and Tibetan, and wrote a memoir of her stay in Tibet called *Inside the Treasure House* (London: Gollancz, 1990).

Bathang (Tibetan: *'ba' thang*): An important trading town in the Kham area of eastern Tibet, on the main route from Chengdu to Lhasa (the road runs through Dartsendo, also known as Tachienlu, or nowadays as Kanding, and through Bathang and Chamdo). Tibetans from the area are known as *babas*. The town was the center of several uprisings by Tibetans during the first half of the twentieth century, usually against Chinese or Sichuanese warlords. The People's Liberation Army (PLA) recruited many Tibetans from Bathang to work for its United Front Work Department as translators and intermediaries during and after the army's advance into central Tibet in 1950.

Bell, Charles (1870–1945): The government of India's political officer in Sikkim from 1908 to 1918 and 1919 to 1921. The post included handling British India's relations with Tibet and Bhutan. Bell became fluent in Tibetan and became a close friend of the thirteenth Dalai Lama during the latter's exile in northern India as a result of the Chinese occupation of Lhasa from 1910 to

1912. Bell was a principal adviser during the Simla treaty negotiations with Tibet and China in 1913–14, for which work he was knighted. He spent a year in Lhasa in 1920–21 and wrote at least five books on Tibetan language, culture, and history.

Bemari (Tibetan: *spar ma ri*): The westernmost of the three hills that lie at the center of the Lhasa floodplain. The name is also pronounced "Barmari" or "Bompori"; it means "the Hill of Rocks." On the peak of the hill is a temple to the Chinese god of war, built by a Chinese general in 1792 to celebrate the defeat of the Nepalese invasion but since indigenized and rededicated to the Tibetan epic hero Gesar. Bemari is sometimes confused with Bumpari or "the Hill of the Vase," a much higher mountain south of Lhasa that is one of the eight "auspicious mountains" that surround the city. See also **Chagpori; Red Hill**.

Besant, Annie (1847–1933): A former British socialist leader and labor activist in the 1880s who later moved to India and helped found the Indian Congress Party. She became an ardent follower of Helena Blavatsky, the founder of Theosophy, an eclectic form of Eastern mysticism invented in the late nineteenth century, supposedly with psychic assistance from unseen Tibetan masters.

bodhisattva (Tibetan: *byang chub sems dpa'* [pronounced *chang chub sempa*]): The Sanskrit term for a person who has the "mind of enlightenment"—one who is set on becoming a buddha. In the Tibetan context it often refers to a nonhistorical form of the Buddha that represents an ultimate quality, such as Manjushri or Chenrezig, who are the Bodhisattvas of Wisdom and Compassion respectively and are depicted in "celestial" form, which is more or less indistinguishable from that of a buddha.

Bonpo (Tibetan: *bon po*; Chinese: *ben jiao*): The traditional animist religion of Tibet, which originated before the arrival of Buddhism and is still practiced in many areas. In recent centuries its practitioners incorporated extensive aspects of Buddhist concepts and practice. Bonpo is now regarded by some as a school of Tibetan Buddhism.

cadre (Tibetan: *las byed pa*; Chinese: *ganbu*): The term is used mostly for administrative and political officials, but technically refers to an official or employee of any rank or function in the Chinese government or the Chinese Communist Party.

CCP (Tibetan: *krung go gung khran tang*; Chinese: *Zhongguo gong chang dang*): The Chinese Communist Party, founded in Shanghai in July 1921. It has been the ruling party of China since the founding of the People's Republic of China (PRC) on October 1, 1949.

central Tibet: A term that in English is used loosely to refer to the central and western parts of the area consistently ruled by the Dalai Lamas until 1950, now designated by the current Chinese term for Tibet, the TAR (Tibet Autonomous Region). Central Tibet usually does not include the eastern or northeastern areas of the Tibetan plateau. Some people do not include the western area of Ngari. The Tibetan term Ü (*dbus*) or "center" refers only to the areas around Lhasa, and does not include those around Shigatse (*gtsang*), Ngari, Kham, Amdo, or other regions. See also **Amdo**; **Kham**; **Ngari**; **Tibet**; **Ü**.

Chagpori (Tibetan: *lcags po ri*): Chakpori—literally "the Iron Hill"—is one of the three hills in the center of the Lhasa floodplain. It lies between the other two, Marpori and Bemari. The Tibetan college of medicine and astrology stood on its peak until 1959, when it was destroyed during the fighting at the time of the Tibetan Uprising. It was replaced by a radio tower, which is still there.

Champa Tendar (Tibetan: *byams pa bstan dar*) (died 1921): A Tibetan monk-official appointed by the thirteenth Dalai Lama to run the war against the Chinese soldiers who had taken over Lhasa in 1910. He was appointed Governor-General of Kham in 1913 and drove Chinese troops out of most of central Tibet. See also **Tsarong**; **Tyengeling**.

Chamdo (Tibetan: *chab mdo*; Chinese: *Changdu* or *Qamdo*): Literally "the conjunction of two rivers"; an important town in eastern Tibet and the main town in Kham. It is west of the Drichu or Upper Yangtse river and so has been included since 1950 in the TAR and separated administratively from the eastern areas of Kham. The aristocrat-officials Yuthok, Lhalu, and Ngapö were among those sent to be the Governor-General (Tibetan: *spyi khyab*) of Kham during the 1940s and 1950s and were based at Chamdo. It was the site of the major battle that took place in October 1950, during the advance of the People's Liberation Army into central Tibet.

Champa Tenzin (Tibetan: *byams pa bstan 'dzin*) (1943–92): A monk from the Jokhang temple famous for running into a burning police station during a demonstration in Lhasa in October 1987 in order to help detainees escape; they were mainly monks who had been arrested during a small demonstration earlier that day. He was arrested two weeks later and held in solitary confinement for three months before being released. He was found hanged, allegedly by his own hand, in the Jokhang in February 1992.

Changngöpa (Tibetan: *byang ngos pa*): One of the more progressive aristocratic families in Lhasa. Changnöpa Ringang was among the four Tibetan boys sent by the thirteen Dalai Lama with Lungshar in 1913 to study at Rugby School in England. He obtained a degree in electrical engineering, the first graduate in Tibet. Ringang's son Dorje Ngodrup was a member of the Tibetan delegation that attended China's National Assembly (exiles say they went only as observers) in Nanjing in 1946. After persecution during the Cultural Revolution, he was given a position in the 1980s in the Education Bureau of the TAR. Another son,

Losang Namgyal, later became a mathematics teacher and a vice president of Tibet University. One of the sons is said by Kimura to have been among those who met with Phuntsog Wanggyal in Lhasa in the mid-1940s.

changthang (Tibetan: *byang thang*): The "northern plain," a vast area of high plateau grassland, much of it inhabited only by nomads, that stretches across upper northern and western Tibet.

Chengdu (Tibetan: *khreng tu'u*): The capital city of Sichuan province. Chengdu and Xining (Tibetan: *zi ling*), the capital of Qinghai province, are the Chinese cities nearest to Tibet.

Chiang Kai-shek (Chinese: *Jiang Jieshi*) (1887–1975): Chiang was the leader of the Chinese nationalist party, the Guomindang (also called the Kuomintang or KMT), from 1925 and leader of the Republic of China from 1928. He was involved in protracted conflict with the Chinese Communist Party from 1926 to 1949 and with invading Japanese troops from 1937 to 1945. Chiang defeated the Japanese, nominally with Communist assistance, but was in turn defeated by the Communists in 1949, when he fled with his followers to set up a government in Taiwan. Nanjing was the capital of the Republic from 1911 to 1925, 1927 to 1937, and 1945 to 1949; Chongqing was the capital during World War II.

chöd yön (Tibetan: *mchod yon*): The term used in official Tibetan texts before 1950 to describe the "priest-patron" relationship, in which a lama receives protection and support from a ruler, who in return receives spiritual guidance and endorsement. The fifth Dalai Lama, for example, received political protection and financial gifts from the first Qing emperor and in return recognized the emperor as an emanation of the Bodhisattva Manjushri (Tibetan: *'jam dpal dbyangs*). The term, which can be translated as "offering-wage," has often been interpreted by Tibetans as a description of equal status between two rulers and their nations, but official Chinese writers have not accepted that implication.

chögyal (Tibetan: *chos rgyal*): The Tibetan equivalent of the Sanskrit term *dharmarāja*, meaning "religious king"—in the Tibetan case, a monarch who defends and encourages Buddhism. The three Tibetan kings recognized as *chögyals* are Srongtsen Gampo, Trisong Detsen (742–97, crowned 755), and Tri Ralpachen (806–38).

Chongqing: A major Chinese city in Sichuan that was the base for the Chinese Nationalist Government during World War II.

Chumik Shenko (Tibetan: *chu mig shel sgo*): A hot spring near the shores of Lake Bam Tso in southern Tibet, not far from the border with Sikkim. This was the spot where the Tibetan *Depon* (General) Lhading had placed his troops to stop the British army in their march on Lhasa in 1904. The British killed some 500 Tibetans, most of whom were in retreat, in a few minutes with machine-gun fire. This followed a token attempt at negotiation by the British, which may have been intended as a stratagem to get the Tibetans to disarm. See also **Younghusband.**

Cultural Revolution (Tibetan: *rig gnas gsar brje*; Chinese: *wenhua gemin*): A mass movement that began when Mao Zedong called on China's youth in May 1966 to "bombard the headquarters"—in other words, to purge most of the party leaders and officials. Mao also called for the destruction of "the Four Olds," including culture and customs, which led to widespread persecution and factional warfare as competing gangs of Red Guards roamed the country destroying any cultural practices, objects, beliefs, or expertise that they considered nonproletarian or traditional. The movement lasted technically for three years before the PLA was sent in to suppress the violence, but China's leaders since refer to it as having lasted until 1976. In Tibet it is usually said to have continued till 1979. The party ruled in 1976 that the 10-year era had been an "extreme leftist" error and condemned the main leaders to lengthy terms of imprisonment.

Curzon, George Nathaniel (1859–1925): Lord Curzon was Viceroy of India from 1899 to 1905. He instigated the British invasion of Tibet, arguing that he needed to ensure the safety of British India by deterring Russia from obtaining influence in Lhasa, though no Russian presence was to be found in Tibet. He was British Foreign Minister from 1919 to 1923. See also **Younghusband.**

Dalai Lama (Tibetan: *Da la'i bla ma*): The reincarnated lama who became the leading figure in the Gelugpa school of Tibetan Buddhism, and after 1642 the political and spiritual leader of Tibet. The title of Dalai Lama was first conferred posthumously on Gendun Drub (1391–1474), a close disciple and nephew of Tsongkhapa. The Dalai Lamas are popularly regarded as emanations of Chenrezig (Tibetan: *spyan ras gzigs*), the Bodhisattva of Compassion. The fifth Dalai Lama (1617–82) was the first to be given the role of political leader, a position he held initially at the behest of his military supporter, the Mongolian leader Gushri Khan (d. 1655). Most of the Dalai Lamas after him, besides the seventh, thirteenth, and fourteenth, died in adolescence, four of them in suspicious circumstances. The thirteenth Dalai Lama (1876–1933) went into exile in 1904 and again in 1910 to avoid invading armies from Britain and China, respectively. The fourteenth Dalai Lama (b. 1935) has lived in exile in India since 1959.

danwei (Tibetan: *las khung*): The Chinese term for a work unit, meaning an enterprise or office that is part of the government or the party. A work unit in China or Tibet is usually a large compound including a number of buildings, often surrounded by a wall or other enclosure with a single entrance, and can vary in size, housing from a few dozen occupants to several thousand. Until the 1990s, all state workers lived in their work units. These were the basic-level unit of administration for state employees, controlling the allocation of housing, food rations, permission to marry and bear children or to change employment, and so on.

darchen (Tibetan: *dar chen*): A tall wooden pole, some 30 feet high, draped in *lungta* or prayer flags of five colors. There is still a *darchen* at each of the four corners of the Barkor pilgrimage circuit that runs around the Jokhang temple in Lhasa.

Dekyi Lingka (Tibetan: *bde skyid gling kha*): The compound near the Norbulingka that housed the British mission in Lhasa from 1937. It housed the Indian mission from 1947, but later was handed over to the Nepalese for use as their consulate. See also **Richardson**.

Demo (Tibetan: *bde mo*): The name of a line of lamas of *hutuktu* rank whose seat was at Tengyeling monastery in Lhasa. The ninth Demo served as regent from 1886 to 1895, but in 1899 he and his attendants were found guilty of conspiring to assassinate the thirteenth Dalai Lama. The Demo was banned from recognition in future incarnations (the ban was later recanted) and died while under house arrest, reportedly from being immersed in a copper vat full of water. His estates were confiscated and many of his monks fled to China. Those who remained later supported Chinese troops during the 1910–12 occupation of Lhasa.

democratic reform: See *minzhu gaige*.

densasum (Tibetan: *gdan sa gsum*): The "three seats," a term for the three monasteries of the Gelugpa school that were founded by Tsongkhapa or his disciples in the early fifteenth century in the vicinity of Lhasa—Sera, Drepung, and Ganden.

Dharamsala: A hill station in the state of Himachal Pradesh in northern India. The Indian government allowed the Dalai Lama and the former Tibetan government to establish their exile base there shortly after they fled Tibet in 1959.

dobdobs (Tibetan: *ldab ldob*): Monks retained before 1959 in certain large monasteries to maintain order. The *dobdobs* trained in weight-lifting and wrestling, and carried large metal keys that could be used as weapons. Melvyn Goldstein estimates that there were 2,000 to 3,000 of these trained "fighting monks" in Lhasa in the 1950s.

Dode (Tibetan: *rdog sde*): A village in a valley north of Lhasa, just east of Sera monastery.

dorje (Tibetan: *rdo rje*): The most frequently seen implement in Tibetan Buddhist iconography and ritual, derived from the Indian *vajra*, a short, two-headed instrument wielded as a scepter by the Hindu god Indra and said to be made from a material that is indestructible and unchangeable. It is sometimes translated as adamantine or, more commonly, as a thunderbolt, since deities and adepts are said to be able to transmit energy through it. It is used by Tantric practitioners for many rituals. In Tibetan Buddhism it represents the third "vehicle" or form of Buddhist teaching, the Tantric teachings, and specifically symbolizes the means for attaining wisdom.

Dorje Yuthok (Tibetan: *rdo rje gyu thog*) (born 1912): Dorje Yudon Yuthok was the sister of Surkhang Wangchen Gelek, an important *kalön* in the 1940s who later became Tibet's last prime minister. She was married to Yuthok Tashi Dondrup, the Governor of Kham from 1942 to 1946 who befriended *Baba* Phuntsog Wanggyal. After fleeing to India in 1959, and thence to the United States in 1965, Dorje Yuthok wrote an autobiography called *The House of the Turquoise Roof* (Ithaca, NY: Snow Lion, 1990).

Dram (Tibetan: *'gram*; Chinese: *Zhangmu*): A border town in southern Tibet, also known as Dram-mo, 70 miles by road north of Kathmandu, that since 1959 has been the only significant crossing point between Tibet and Nepal. Since tourists were allowed to enter Tibet in about 1980, it has been the only entrance point allowed for foreigners coming from Nepal, apart from occasional groups allowed to cross at Humla in western Nepal after the late 1990s. See also **Friendship Bridge**.

Drepung (Tibetan: *'bras spungs*; Chinese: *Zhai bang*): One of the three great monasteries of the Gelugpa school in the Lhasa area. It was founded by Jamyang Chöje, a follower of the Buddhist reformer Tsongkhapa, in 1416. Drepung—the name means literally "the Heap of Rice," a rendering of the name of an ancient Buddhist temple in India—is situated some 5 miles west of Lhasa at the foot of the mountain known as Gamphel Ri. It housed about 10,000 monks in 1951. Much of the monastery was destroyed in the Cultural Revolution, and many of the monks who joined or rejoined after the liberalization policies of 1980 were expelled in "patriotic re-education" purges in 1996. It is now reported to have about 700 monks. See also **Sera**; **Ganden**.

Drichu (Tibetan: *'bri chu*; Chinese: *Chiang jiang*): The upper reaches of the river known in Chinese as the Chiang Jiang or Yangtse, running east from the northern Tibetan plateau toward the China plains. Its source is in an area known in Chinese as Tuotuohe (Tibetan: *tho tho hu* or *dmar chu*), situated in the northernmost part of the Tibetan plateau just south of Golmud. Part of the river, running north-south, is used as the current boundary between the TAR and Sichuan province, and the parts of Kham west of the Drichu are now part of the TAR, while Kham east of the Drichu is in Sichuan.

dri-dug (Tibetan: *gri gug*): A curved knife, one of many ritual objects seen in Buddhist or Bonpo iconography, usually said to represent the ability of the mind to "cut through" a spiritual obstacle such as ignorance or to destroy a passion such as desire. The objects are usually shown as being held by a buddha in wrathful form, or by a protector deity. See also *dorje*.

Dzungars (Tibetan: *jun gar*): A subgroup of Mongols who had settled before the seventeenth century in the eastern Turkestan areas now known as Xinjiang. The Dzungars (also spelled Jungar) were the principal military threat to the early Qing (Manchu) emperors of China, particularly under their leader Gaden until his death in 1696. They had become devotees of the Dalai Lamas and in 1717, led by Gaden's nephew Tsewang Rabden, they invaded Tibet to support the claim of their candidate as the seventh Dalai Lama. They destroyed and ransacked non-Gelugpa monasteries and institutions. Chinese forces drove them out of Lhasa in 1720.

Ford, Robert (born 1923): A junior British air force radio officer who was recruited by the Tibetan government to work as a radio officer in Tibet in 1948, along with Reginald Fox. Earlier, from 1945 to 1947, he had worked for the British mission in Lhasa. The Tibetan government sent Ford to Chamdo in summer 1949 to operate radio communications with Lhasa, and he was captured by the PLA in October 1950. He spent five years in prison in Sichuan, accused of spying and of involvement in poisoning a Chinese representative in Chamdo, accusations he has consistently denied. His book about his experiences is called *Wind Between the Worlds* (New York: David McKay, 1957) or, in the UK, *Captured in Tibet* (Oxford: Oxford University Press, 1957).

Fox, Reginald (1899–1953): A junior British officer recruited by the Tibetan government to train its staff in operating radio equipment in the 1940s and one of the five Westerners living in Lhasa at the time of the Chinese invasion. He lived in the Tibetan capital from 1937 until 1950, learned fluent written and spoken Tibetan, and married a Tibetan. Chinese histories describe him as a spy for the British and claim that he was reporting to Hugh Richardson.

Friendship Bridge: The bridge built by the Chinese authorities across the river that separates Nepal from Tibet, some 5 miles below the border checkpoint at Dram (Chinese: *Zhangmu*). The border lies halfway across the bridge. The road from Kathmandu to Lhasa, which crosses the bridge, is called "the Friendship Highway" by the Chinese.

Gampa-la (Tibetan: *gam pa la*): The high mountain pass that is crossed by the road leading from Gyantse to Lhasa, until 1950 the main route for traders and travelers journeying between India and the Tibetan capital. The pass separates the Ü (central) area around Lhasa from the Tsang (central-western) area around Shigatse.

Gamphel Ri (Tibetan: *dge 'phel ri*): A mountain on the western side of the Lhasa valley, one of the eight "auspicious mountains" around Lhasa, and one of the four noted in Wencheng's geomantic reading of the Lhasa landscape. Drepung monastery was built on the southern flank of Gamphel Ri in 1416.

Ganden (Tibetan: *dga' ldan*; Chinese: *Gan dan*): The first of three great monasteries near Lhasa founded by the monastic reformer Tsongkhapa and his followers in the early fifteenth century. The name means "Having Happiness" or "the Place of Bliss," a translation of the Sanskrit name for the heavenly realm known as Tushita. The monastery, some 20 miles east of Lhasa, was established by Tsongkhapa in 1409. It had 3,300 monks officially, but in practice there were about 5,000 monks resident before 1959. It was destroyed during the Cultural Revolution but has been reconstructed gradually since 1980. At least 100 monks were imprisoned or expelled in 1996 after refusing to remove pictures of the Dalai Lama from the precincts, and it now has only about 200 monks. See also **Sera**; **Drepung**.

Gelugpa (Tibetan: *dge lugs pa*): The dominant school of Tibetan Buddhism, literally "the Way of Virtue." Also known as "the Yellow Hat school" (sometimes considered pejorative), this tradition was established by Tsongkhapa in the early fifteenth century. The school is led by the Ganden Tripa (Tibetan: *dga' ldan khrid pa*), a senior monk from Ganden monastery who is chosen by election every three years, but its best-known teachers are the Dalai Lamas and the Panchen Lamas. See also **Karma Kagyü**.

Gendun Chöphel (Tibetan: *dge 'dun chos 'phel*) (1905–51): The most famous of Tibetan radical scholars and artists. Gendun Chöphel was a monk from Rebkong in Amdo who studied at Drepung monastery in Lhasa and produced innovative and controversial works of poetry, history, painting, and philosophy. He spent twelve years in India after 1934, becoming fluent in English, Hindi, and other languages. He was influenced by Indian communism and helped Rabga Pangdatshang start the Tibetan Improvement Party, which planned a Tibetan republic, in Calcutta in 1946. He returned to Lhasa in 1946 and was imprisoned for three years; he died shortly after his release in 1951. See also **Tharchin**.

Gesar (Tibetan: *ge sar*): The hero of the Tibetan epic *King Gesar of Ling*, believed to have been composed in about the tenth century and said to be the longest epic in the world. Traveling bards throughout Tibet still recite sections of the text from memory or while in trance.

Geshe (Tibetan: *dge bshes*): The title given in the main Gelugpa monasteries to a monk who has completed a rigorous training course and a series of examinations in Buddhist studies, usually lasting fifteen to twenty years.

Golmud (Tibetan: *sgor mo*): An industrial city in the far western area of Qinghai province that is the last Chinese city on the road from the north to Lhasa, the most important of the four major roads that link Tibet to China. From 2006

Golmud will be the main terminus for the new railway that will connect Lhasa to the Chinese rail network.

gön-khang (Tibetan: *mgon khang*): A small temple or chapel dedicated to *mgon po* or protector deities, figures in the Tibetan Buddhist pantheon that are always depicted in wrathful forms and often given offerings of alcohol. The protector deities are particular to Tibetan religion, and usually associated with Bonpo or other pre-Buddhist religious practices. They are often forms of local deities who are linked to a particular mountain or place in Tibet and who are said to have been tamed or converted to Buddhism in earlier times.

gönpa (Tibetan: *dgon pa*): The Tibetan term for a monastery, originally meaning "a deserted place."

Gumalingka (Tibetan: *rku ma gling kha*): Literally "Thieves' Island," one of two islands in the Kyichu river that were traditionally used by Lhasans as picnic spots. The island was formerly named Jamalingka (Tibetan: *'jag ma gling kha*), referring to a type of grass found on it, though some say the name "jama" referred to the two German-speaking Austrians, Aufschnaiter and Harrer, who lived in Lhasa in the late 1940s and who built the new dikes that finally protected the city from the risk of annual floods. The island was renamed Zhonghe International City in the 1990s after it was redeveloped as a densely constructed modern leisure resort. The second island has been renamed Xianzudao (Tibetan: *lha zhabs gling*) and was developed in about 2000 with a walled picnic park in Tibetan style.

gya ma bod (Tibetan: *rgya ma bod*): Literally "not Chinese, not Tibetan," a colloquial Tibetan phrase for a person of mixed Chinese and Tibetan parentage.

Gyalo Thondup (Tibetan: *rgya lo don grub*) (born 1928): The elder brother of the fourteenth Dalai Lama. Fluent in Chinese as well as English, he was the main person handling relations between the Dalai Lama's government and the CIA in the 1950s and 1960s, and running the Tibetan guerrilla forces that were based in Nepal until 1974. Until about 2002 he was also responsible for maintaining extensive contacts with Taiwan and, after 1978, with Beijing.

Gyanag (Tibetan: *rgya nag*): The traditional Tibetan word for China. The term does not include Tibet, and since 1951 Tibetans in Tibet have been limited to using it as the equivalent of the Chinese word *neidi*, which means "the inland area." There is no word in Tibetan for China including Tibet, and since 1951, Tibetans within Tibet have had to use the Chinese word *Zhongguo* ("Central Kingdom") in its Tibetan form, *krung go,* to refer to China including Tibet.

Gyantse (Tibetan: *rgyal rtse*; Chinese: *Jiangzi* or *Gyanze*): a Tibetan town about 150 miles southwest of Lhasa, halfway to the border with Sikkim and India. It was the site of important battles with the British army during the invasion of 1903–4. See also **Chumik Shenko**.

Han (Tibetan: *han* or unofficially *rgya mi*): The term used in modern Chinese to refer to the majority ethnic group in China, usually referred to in English as "Chinese"; this usage was invented in the late nineteenth century by campaigners against the Qing emperors. The term has become controversial because its use appears to be understood by Chinese officials to constitute tacit recognition that "non-Han" peoples such as Tibetans are citizens of China. Use of the term "Chinese" (or *Gyami* in Tibetan) for ethnic Chinese can similarly be taken to imply that Tibetans and others are not citizens of China.

Harrer, Heinrich (born 1912): An Austrian mountaineer who spent seven years in Tibet after escaping in 1944 from a British prison camp in northern India where he had been interned at the start of World War II. Harrer's book about his experiences, *Seven Years in Tibet* (London: Hart-Davies, 1953), became the most popular Western account of Tibet before the Chinese invasion. Harrer was given a position as a minor official in the Tibetan government, helping with construction and technical work, and had some contact with the young fourteenth Dalai Lama before leaving Tibet in spring 1951. See also **Aufschnaiter**.

Hedin, Sven (1865–1952): A Swedish explorer who produced numerous accounts of his travels in central Asia and northern Tibet in the 1890s. Hedin traveled in southwestern Tibet in 1906–8, but was never able to get permission to enter Lhasa.

hutuktu (Tibetan: *ho thog thu* or *hu thug thu*): A Mongolian term used in the Qing era as a title of high rank for eight lamas and their successors in central Tibet who were entitled to serve as regent during the minority of a Dalai Lama. The full term is *gyetru* (Tibetan: *rgyal sprul* or "royal incarnation") *hutuktu*. It was also used for certain high lamas in Mongolian and other areas. See also *trulku*.

Jamyang Sakya (Tibetan: *'jam dbyangs sa skya*) (born 1934): A Tibetan woman from the aristocratic family of Sakya who moved to the United States in 1961, where she co-wrote an account of her life, *Princess in the Land of Snows* (with Julie Emery; Boston: Shambala, 1990). The family is named after Sakya ("Gray Earth"), a famous monastery founded in 1073 about 100 miles southwest of Shigatse by road. It became the seat of the Sakya school of Tibetan Buddhism, one of the four main schools. Its leaders ruled Tibet on behalf of the Mongol emperors in the thirteenth century, who later became the Yuan rulers of China. The school is led by lamas of the Sakya family who are not monks and who do not reincarnate as *trulkus*. The leadership position alternates each generation between two branches of the Sakya family.

Jokhang (Tibetan: *jo khang* or *gtsug lag khang*, Chinese: *Dazhaosi*): The seventh-century temple around which the city of Lhasa is built, widely regarded as the most important Buddhist site for Tibetans. The main chapel is called the Jokhang ("House of the Jowo") because of its most famous statue, known as the Jowo, depicting the Buddha when he was eight (some say twelve) years old. The temple was built at the time of the Tibetan king Srongtsen Gampo, with the assistance of Newari craftsmen brought from Nepal by his Nepalese wife Bhrikuti.

junqu (Tibetan: *cun chu'u* or *dmag khul khang*): The Chinese term for military headquarters; in Lhasa, it often refers to the compound on the south side of the Lingkor that has been the major Chinese military base in the city since the 1950s.

Kabshöpa (Tibetan: *ka shod pa chos rgyal nyi ma*) (1902–86): A Tibetan from a small landholding family who was given noble rank after he pulled the Nepalese consul from his horse in order to force him to make way for the thirteenth Dalai Lama's entourage. In 1945 he was made a *kalön* in the Tibetan cabinet. Kabshöpa became infamous for having denounced Lungshar's reform plans in 1934 and for having cooperated later with the Chinese authorities.

Kalachakra (Tibetan: *dus 'khor dbang chen*): A Tibetan Buddhist ritual performed by the current Dalai Lama on special occasions. The name means "the Wheel of Time." The Kalachakra initiation is based on a specialized tantric text dealing with a millenarian struggle to attain the utopia of Shambhala, but is nowadays said to be useful in promoting world peace.

Kalimpong (Tibetan: *ka lon sbug*): A hill station in northeastern India near the Sikkimese and Tibetan borders. The town was on the route from Tibet to Calcutta, and until 1959 was an important trading post for Tibetan traders, as well as a refuge for Tibetan intellectuals and radicals who had had to leave their country.

kalön (Tibetan: *bka' blon*): One of the four ministers in the cabinet or Kashag (Tibetan: *bka' shag*; Chinese: *ka xia*) from the time the Tibetan government was reorganized in 1721 until 1959. The *kalöns* were addressed as *Shapé* (Tibetan: *zhabs pad*) and were of third rank (*rim gsum*) in the hierarchy. Three of the four were laymen and the fourth was always a monk. See also *zasak*.

Karma Gönsar (Tibetan: *karma dgon gsar*): Formerly the site of the only temple of the Karma Kagyu school in Lhasa, but now the name of a new suburb on the east side of Lhasa. It is situated just north of the Kyichu river, beside the site where the Dalai Lama's birthday celebrations were held illicitly after 1980 for some 15 years. In the mid-1990s the area was rapidly developed with largely Chinese shops and also with new Tibetan-style or *simsha* residential buildings. The name is sometimes misheard by foreigners as "Karma Kusang."

Karma Kagyü (Tibetan: *karma bka' rgyud*): The best known of the eight sub-schools of the Kagyü (or Kagyüpa) school of Tibetan Buddhism, based on a set of teachings that date back to the eleventh century and emphasize mystical practices rather than, or as well as, monastic affiliation. The school, which also dates back to the eleventh century, is headed by a lama known as the Karmapa, regarded as the first Tibetan lama whose successor was recognized as a *trulku*.

Kham (Tibetan: *khams* or *mdo smad*; Chinese: *kang*): The eastern and southeastern parts of the Tibetan plateau. The region is now divided into various parts administered by different Chinese provinces or regions—the Chamdo area is within the TAR, the Kardze (Tibetan: *dkar mdzes*; Chinese: *Ganzi*) area is within Sichuan, Dechen (Tibetan: *bde chen*; Chinese: *Deqing* or *Deqen*, recently *Shangelila*) is within Yunnan, and Jyekundo (Tibetan: *skye rgu mdo*; Chinese: *Yushu*) is within Qinghai. See also **Amdo**; **central Tibet**; **Drichu**; **Chamdo**.

Khampas (Tibetan: *khams pa*): Tibetans from Kham. The men often wear their long hair braided with red yarn (as do men from some other regions), and have a reputation for forcefulness and courage. The area is also said to produce many religious adepts and scholars, as well as warriors. Khampas do not use honorifics in their dialect of Tibetan and regard themselves as much more forthright in manners and behavior than Lhasa people.

Kimura, Hisao (1922–89): A Japanese spy who was sent to discover if arms were being smuggled through Tibet to supply the Chinese military. Kimura was trained for several years in Japanese-occupied Mongolia, where he became fluent in Tibetan, before traveling on to Lhasa disguised as a Mongolian pilgrim and petty trader. He became close to radical Tibetans in Lhasa, such as Phuntsog Wanggyal, before returning to Japan in 1945. His memoir, *A Japanese Agent in Tibet* (London: Serindia, 1990), written just before his death, is one of the most important foreign accounts of 1940s Lhasa.

Kirey (Tibetan: *skyid ras*): An area in the northeastern section of the Old City of Lhasa adjoining the Banakshöl area.

Kongpo (Tibetan: *kong po*; Chinese: *Gongbu*): A region of southern Tibet, about 150 miles east of Lhasa.

kuai (Tibetan: *sgor mo* or *gor mo*): A Chinese term used colloquially for the *yuan*, the main unit of Chinese money. The Chinese currency was fixed at 8.26 *kuai* to a dollar from the early 1980s until 2005.

Kunphel (Tibetan: *kun 'phel*) (1905–63): A Tibetan monk born into a peasant family in Nyemo who became the leading attendant and favorite of the thirteenth Dalai Lama. The honorific "-la" (Tibetan: *lags*) is usually added to his name, since he had no formal title. He worked to modernize the military and set up a machine-gun unit, as well as running an electrical plant in Lhasa that powered the armory and the mint. He was the most influential figure in Tibet after the ruler until he was arrested, imprisoned, and then exiled for a trumped-up offense by other aristocrats following the Dalai Lama's death in 1933. He lived in India and was active with other progressives in setting up the Tibet Improvement Party in 1946, but was then expelled by the British to China, where, impoverished, he had to take a position with the Republican government in Nanjing. In 1947 he returned to Lhasa and after 1951 worked as an official for the Chinese administration there.

Kyicho Kuntun (Tibetan: *skyid phyogs kun mthun*): Literally "All Who Are United on the Side of Happiness"; the secret group of officials and young aristocrats formed by Lungshar in 1934 to introduce changes into the Tibetan governmental system. The members were accused by political opponents of a conspiracy to seize power and were arrested in 1934. See also **Kabshöpa**.

Kyichu (Tibetan: *skyid chu*): The river that runs through Lhasa from the east; the city lies on the north bank. Its name means "River of Happiness." The Kyichu turns to the south at Töelung Dechen, just past Lhasa, and joins the Yarlung Tsangpo near Chushul, about 30 miles south of Lhasa.

Kyishöd Ö-tso (Tibetan: *skyid shod 'o mtsho*): Literally "the Lake of Milk in the Lower Kyichu Valley," this was the body of water that lay at the center of the Lhasa valley floor when Srongtsen Gampo decided to build his capital there. Located immediately below the Jokhang temple, the lake was said to be the belly of the demoness identified by Princess Wencheng in the 640s as stretched across the landscape of Tibet. See also **Srinmo**; **Thandul**.

Kyitöpa (Tibetan: *skyid stod pa*): A former aristocratic mansion on the southwest corner of the Barkhor built by the Kyitöpa family. It was owned in the 1930s by Lungshar's common-law wife Lhalu, and Lungshar used it in 1933 as a viewing station for the public humiliation of Kunphel. It was the base for officials of the Chinese nationalist government in the 1940s, and the center of their spying operations, as well as their school. In the 1990s it was demolished and rebuilt as a tourist guesthouse called the Mandala Hotel.

Labrang (Tibetan: *bla-brang*): The estate or residence of a *trulku* or lama, and the goods inherited by his or her successors. Often a labrang is within a monastery, although technically not a part of it.

lama (Tibetan: *bla ma*; Chinese: *la ma*): A title in Tibetan Buddhism that is a translation of the Sanskrit word *guru* or religious teacher. In both India and Tibet the term is used for highly regarded teachers, not necessarily monks, who are considered to be spiritually accomplished to an exceptional degree and who are objects of devotion for their disciples. In China the word is used erroneously to refer to any Tibetan monk. In some cases in eastern Tibet it is used to show respect for monks even though they might not be high teachers. See also **Geshe**.

Lamrim (Tibetan: *lam rim*): Literally "the Graduated Path," the Tibetan term for a set of teachings in the Gelugpa school that is said to lead by stages to enlightenment. It was also the name given to a famous Geshe from Drepung monastery who was probably the only person in Lhasa allowed to give public religious teachings in the 1980s, which he did each summer. He died in 1997.

Landon, Perceval (1869–1927): The correspondent for *The Times* of London who accompanied the British expedition in the 1903–4 invasion. He wrote a book about his impressions of Tibet called *LHASA: An account of the country and people of central Tibet and of the progress of the mission sent there by the English Government in the year 1903–1904* (London: Hurst and Blackett, 1905), published in the United States as *The Opening of Tibet: An account of Lhasa and the people of central Tibet* ... (London: Doubleday, Page & Co., 1906).

lha ma yin (Tibetan: *lha ma yin*): Literally "not a god, not a being," a term used most often to describe the inhabitants of the demigod realm in Sanskrit cosmology, known in Sanskrit as *āsuras*. They are one of the six types of beings and are located in the Buddhist cosmological system between gods and humans. They are said to be consumed with jealousy of the happier life led by the gods.

lhakhang (Tibetan: *lha khang*): The Tibetan term for a temple or shrine room, usually lined with statues of deities and spacious enough for monks to assemble for ceremonies. Literally "a house of the gods." See also **gönpa**.

Lhalu (Tibetan: *lha klu*; Chinese: *La lu*): An area of the Lhasa valley just northwest of the city that traditionally belonged to the Lhalu family and consists mostly of a broad expanse of marshland. The area is currently a wetlands preserve. The best-known member of the Lhalu family today is Lhalu Tsewang Dorje (Tibetan: *lha klu tshe dbang rdo rje*, born 1915). He is the son of Lungshar, though after his father's blinding and humiliation in 1934 he formally claimed different paternity in order to have the chance of a government appointment. He was made a *kalön* in 1946 and was Governor of Chamdo from 1947 until September 1950. He led a delegation to Beijing in 1955 but was imprisoned from 1959 to 1965 after the Tibetan Uprising and made to do hard labor for twelve years during the Cultural Revolution, until 1977. He recanted his "crimes" and was made a vice chairman of the Tibet Branch of the Chinese People's Political Consultative Conference in 1983. At least one of his sons was also given a leadership position.

Lhatotori Nyentsen (Tibetan: *lha tho tho ri gnyan btsan*) (374–460?): Said to have been the twenty-eighth of the forty-two Tibetan kings, and the first to receive some Buddhist teachings, which were said to have fallen from the sky (indicating that they could not be translated at that time). It is believed that he had a meditation cave on Marpori, one of the reasons the Tibetan kings moved their capital to Lhasa, and why the fifth Dalai Lama had the Potala built on that site.

Lhazang Khan (Tibetan: *lha bzang klu dpal h'an* or *khAng*) (1658?–1717): A Qoshot (or Hoshot) Mongol, the great-grandson of Gushri Khan (Tibetan: *sgo bzhi*).

Lhazang Khan was the secular ruler or king of Tibet under Qing hegemony from 1703 to 1717. The name is sometimes spelled Lhabzang or Lajang.

liberalization, reform, and opening up (Tibetan: *rang dbang chan gyi lam lugs; gyur chos sgo dbye ba'i srid jus*; Chinese: *zi you hua; gaige kaifeng*): The main policies of Deng Xiaoping after 1978, which led the Communist Party to encourage first "household responsibility" and later private trade in China, together with much greater contact with the outside world. The policies included declarations that many previous "leftist" policies had been excessive, that China would remain in the "primary stage of socialism" for the forseeable future (so there was no need to have communes), and that accumulating personal wealth was compatible with socialism. See also *Cultural Revolution*.

lingka (Tibetan: *gling ga* or *gling ka*): A park or pleasure garden, usually a grassy area surrounded by trees beside a stream.

Lingkor (Tibetan: *gling skor*): The sacred outer *korwa* (Tibetan: *skor ba*) or circuit running around the traditional city of Lhasa and a major pilgrimage route. The Lingkor runs around, and therefore pays respect to, the Jokhang temple, Chakpori, Marpori (and the Potala Palace), and the Ramoche. Buddhist pilgrims walking the Lingkor always go in a clockwise direction; Bonpo pilgrims circumambulate in the opposite direction.

Lubu (Tibetan: *klu sbug*): An area in the southwestern part of Lhasa.

Lukhang (Tibetan: *klu khang*): A temple on a small island in an ornamental lake constructed in a park on the north side of the Potala Palace. It was built primarily by the sixth Dalai Lama (1683–1706).

Lungshar, Dorje Tsegyal (Tibetan: *lung shar rdo rje tshe rgyal*) (1881–1939): A leading Tibetan aristocrat-official who was a favored official of the thirteenth Dalai Lama from 1925 to 1931, especially as commander in chief after 1929, when he led efforts to modernize the military. Lungshar, trained as a physician, had visited Britain and other European countries as the guardian of four Tibetans sent to study at Rugby in 1913, and had developed considerable interest in Western democratic systems. In 1934 he established a secret group called Kyicho Kuntun that aimed to introduce reforms into the Tibetan traditional system of government. The plan was denounced by Kabshöpa, who claimed it was a conspiracy to assassinate the regent; Lungshar was convicted of planning a coup and on May 20, 1934 was blinded. He died in Lhasa five years later. His son, Lhalu Tsewang Dorje, became a leading Tibetan dignitary in both the traditional government and the later Chinese administration.

Ma Lihua (born 1953): A Chinese official who was sent to Lhasa in the 1970s as a writer and cultural worker. She was made a vice president of the Tibet Writers Association in 1976. She produced television documentaries and published numerous books in Chinese about her impressions of Tibetan landscape and folklore, several of which were translated into English by official publishing houses, including *Glimpses of Northern Tibet* (Beijing: Panda Books, 1991) and *Old Lhasa: A Sacred City at Dusk* (Beijing: Foreign Languages Press, 2003).

Manchus: A warrior tribe from the area that is now northeast China, known until about 1635 as the Jurchen. Under their leader Noruhaci (1559–1626) and his son Hong *Taiji* they conquered China, defeated the ruling Ming emperors, and established their successors as the Qing emperors of China from 1644 to 1911.

Maraini, Fosco (1912–2004): A distinguished Italian explorer, photographer, and writer who accompanied the Italian Tibetologist Giuseppe Tucci to Tibet in 1937 and 1948. Maraini wrote a popular and influential account of his travels, *Secret Tibet* (London: Hutchinson, 1952).

Marpori. See **Red Hill**.

menkhang (Tibetan: *sman khang*): The Tibetan word for hospital or clinic.

mGar Tongtsen (Tibetan: *mGar stong btsan*) (died 667): The chief minister of the Tibetan king or emperor Srongtsen Gampo. mGar was sent in 641 to ask the Tang dynasty Emperor Taizong for a princess to marry the Tibetan king and in a series of tests is said to have outwitted all the other suitors for the hand of the princess.

Minyak Chökyi Gyaltsen (Tibetan: *mi nyag chos kyi rgyal mtshan*): A Tibetan lama based in Lhasa who used his knowledge of traditional Tibetan architecture to help in the restoration of Tibetan houses in the 1990s.

minzhu gaige (Tibetan: *dmangs gtsho bcos bsgyur*): A Chinese term meaning "democratic reform" but used as an official euphemism to describe a major policy move to redistribute land and to impose other radical reforms in society and culture. Chinese official historians say that the process began in central Tibet in March 1959, but this appears to be an attempt to downplay the Tibetan Uprising, which took place that month. Beijing in fact ordered "democratic reform" to be initiated in Tibet a few weeks after the uprising and its suppression.

Mönlam (Tibetan: *smon-lam*): Literally a prayer, but usually an abbreviation for *Mönlam Chenmo*, the Great Prayer Festival, held traditionally during the third week of the new year at the Jokhang temple in Lhasa since 1409. It was banned by the Chinese authorities in 1966 and reinstated in 1986 for three years. It has been banned as a public ceremony since 1989. See also **Tsongkhapa**.

Murray, Gilbert (1866–1957): A noted classics professor at Oxford University who became active in the League of Nations, established in 1919 to promote disarmament and the peaceful settlement of international disputes. Murray was the chairman of the League of Nations Union from 1923 to 1938. In the 1920s he contacted the Lhasa government to propose that Tibet join the league.

Murunyingpa (Tibetan: *rme ru rnying pa*): A small, secluded temple in the Old City of Lhasa located within the Barkor pilgrimage circuit, next to the northeast corner of the Jokhang temple.

nāgas (Tibetan: *klu*): The Sanskrit term for a category of spirits, often said to resemble serpents, which live in subterranean caverns or in bodies of water and are associated with long life and wealth.

Nanjing: A city in Jiangsu province in eastern China that was the capital of the Republic of China from 1911 to 1925, 1927 to 1937, and 1945 to 1949. Also known as Nanking. See also **Chiang Kai-shek**; **Chang ngöpa**.

Ngapö Ngawang Jigme (Tibetan: *nga phod ngag dbang 'jigs med*; Chinese: *Apei Awang Jimei*) (born 1910): A leading Tibetan aristocrat-official who was made a *kalön* in June 1950 and a month later was sent to Chamdo as Governor-General of Kham. Ngapö replaced Lhalu as leader of the Tibetan army and was in charge during the attack on Tibet by the People's Liberation Army in October of that year. He considered the task unwinnable and was rapidly defeated. After Chinese forces took over Tibet, he became the chief intermediary with the Chinese government and signed the surrender document known as the Seventeen-Point Agreement on behalf of the Tibetan government in Beijing in 1951. In 1952 he was made deputy head of the military forces in Tibet, in 1954 a deputy to the National Congress, in 1955 a lieutenant-general in the PLA, and Chairman of the TAR Congress after 1965. From 1981 to 1983 Ngapö was Governor of the TAR. He was not persecuted during the Cultural Revolution and, according to the historian Tsering Shakya, was made a secret member of the CCP, not normally permissible for an aristocrat. He was later made a vice chairman of the National People's Congress and worked closely with the Panchen Lama to revive Tibetan culture in the 1980s, becoming technically the highest-ranking Tibetan in the PRC after 1989. He had twelve children, of whom at least two were given leadership positions in China, one becoming Minister of Civil Affairs and another head of the TAR Tourism Bureau. Another defected to the United States in 1985 and runs the Tibetan branch of Radio Free Asia.

Ngawang Kesang (Tibetan: *ngag dbang skal bzang*) (born 1913): A Tibetan from Bathang who had been brought up in an orphanage there run by American missionaries. He worked closely with Phuntsog Wanggyal in establishing small communist cells and front organizations in Kham, Lhasa, and Dechen from 1939 to 1949 before these areas and their movement were incorporated into the Chinese Communist Party in 1949–50. He was arrested by the Chinese authorities in the late 1950s, possibly for suspected "rightism" or "local nationalism," and imprisoned for two and a half years, then sent to a labor camp in Sichuan to work on road construction for sixteen years.

Norbulingka (Tibetan: *nor bu gling kha*; Chinese: *Luobulinka*): Literally "the Jewel Park," this was the Summer Palace of the Dalai Lamas, about 2 miles west of the traditional city of Lhasa. It is now a park within the *Xiqiao* or western suburb of Lhasa, next to the former Holiday Inn, built in 1985, now the Lhasa Hotel. The Norbulingka was established by the seventh Dalai Lama (1708–57).

Nyangdren (Tibetan: *nyang bran* or *nyang re*; Chinese: *Niang re*): A valley northwest of Lhasa, now partly a suburb of the city.

Pabongka (Tibetan: *pha bong kha*): A monastery about 5 miles northwest of Lhasa that is said to have been used by Srongtsen Gampo as a meditation site in the seventh century.

Panchen Lama (Tibetan: *pan chen rin po che*; Chinese: *Banchen erdeni*): The second most prominent *trulku* line in the Gelugpa school, dating from the fifteenth century, whose incarnations are said to be emanations of the buddha Amitabha. The Panchen Lamas, based at Tashilhunpo (Tibetan: *bkra shis lhun po*) monastery in Shigatse, sometimes acted as tutors to the Dalai Lamas and oversaw the discovery of their incarnations, and vice versa. The ninth Panchen Lama (born 1883, often numbered before 1950 as the sixth, and referred to as the "Tashi Lama" by earlier foreign visitors) fled central Tibet in 1923 after a conflict with Lhasa over taxation obligations. He lived in eastern Tibet or China until his death in 1937. The child recognized by China as the tenth Panchen Lama was born in Dowi (Tibetan: *rdo sbis*) in Amdo in 1938. The Lhasa authorities agreed to recognize him as part of the Seventeen-Point Agreement with China in 1951. The tenth Panchen Lama was given high office by the Chinese authorities in the new administration in Tibet and replaced the Dalai Lama after the latter fled to India in 1959. After writing an internal petition criticizing Chinese policy in 1962, the tenth was removed from office and spent most of the next sixteen years under house arrest or in prison. He was released in 1978 and given a nominal position as vice chairman of the People's Congress in Beijing, which allowed him to become a major factor in reviving Tibetan religion and culture until his early death in 1989. In 1995 there was a major controversy between Beijing and the Dalai Lama over the recognition of the eleventh Panchen Lama, with Beijing enthroning its selected child while holding the child recognized by the Dalai Lama in "protective" custody, where he remains at the time of writing.

Pasang (Tibetan: *pa sangs*; Chinese: *Basang*) (born 1937): A Tibetan woman from a farming background who was promoted to a high leadership position during the Cultural Revolution. She was the only woman in the TAR leadership from 1978 until 2002, when she retired. See also **Ragti**.

pa-wo (Tibetan: *dpa' bo*): The Tibetan term for a hero.

Peaceful Liberation (Tibetan: *zhi ba'i bcings 'grol*; Chinese: *heping jiefang*): The official Chinese term for the events of 1950–51, when Chinese troops defeated the Tibetan army in Chamdo and seven months later, on May 23, 1951, persuaded the Tibetan government to surrender sovereignty by signing the Seventeen-Point Agreement.

Pemá Chöki (Tibetan: *pad ma chos skyid*) (1926–69): The Princess of Sikkim, daughter of the Maharaja of that country at the time of Fosco Maraini's visit in 1948. She was renowned for her intellect as well as her beauty, and had graduated from high school at 14. Also known as Ku-la, she married the stepson of Dorje Yuthok in 1949. The Sikkimese royal family and elite were Tibetan in culture and ethnicity and had close links with Lhasa. Sikkim (Tibetan: *'bras ljongs*) was in effect an independent country under Indian protection until it was annexed by India in 1975, but its status was disputed by China until 2004. Earlier, it had sometimes been considered part of Tibet.

Phala (Tibetan: *pha lha*): An aristocratic Tibetan family whose estates were based mainly in or near Gyantse.

Phari (Tibetan: *phag ri*): A small town in southern Tibet close to the borders with Sikkim and Bhutan. It was the first town that a traveler would reach if entering Tibet by the shortest route from India to Lhasa.

Phuntsog Tashi Takla (Tibetan: *phun tshogs bkra shis stag lha*) (1922–99): A childhood friend of the family of the fourteenth Dalai Lama, which came from the village of Taktser (Tibetan: *stag tsher*) in Amdo, now Qinghai, in the far northeastern area of the Tibetan plateau. Takla went with the Dalai Lama's elder brother Gyalo Thondup to Nanjing in 1946 and was an interpreter in the 1951 Sino-Tibetan negotiations that led to the signing of the Seventeen-Point Agreement. He later became head of the Dalai Lama's bodyguard, and, after fleeing into exile in 1959, married Tsering Drolma (Tibetan: *tse ring sgrol ma*), a sister of the Dalai Lama, and became a minister in the Tibetan government in exile in India.

PLA (Tibetan: *bcings 'grol dmag*, Chinese: *jiefangjun*): The People's Liberation Army, formerly the Red Army, of the Chinese Communist Party. It defeated the nationalist forces of Chiang Kai-shek in 1949 and became the national army of the People's Republic of China.

Potala Palace (Tibetan: *po Ta la'i pho brang* or *rtse pho brang*; Chinese: *Budala gong*): The palace that dominates the Lhasa skyline, used as the primary residence of the Dalai Lamas and as the seat of the Tibetan government from 1649 to 1959. One part, called the White Palace, was built on the Marpori or Red Hill overlooking Lhasa by the fifth Dalai Lama in 1645–49, reputedly adding to a palace constructed there in the seventh century by Srongtsen Gampo. An extension known as the Red Palace was built by the fifth Dalai Lama and his regent or *Desi*, Sangye Gyatso, between about 1682 and 1694, using some 7,000 workers. The palace is said to have more than 1,000 rooms, and to have been built without the use of any nails or iron. The Chinese authorities spent large amounts on conservation efforts in the 1990s. The palace and its surroundings were named a World Heritage Site by UNESCO in 1994.

Public Security (Tibetan: *spyi dbe cus;* Chinese: *gonganju*): The term for the police force in post–1949 China. See also **State Security Bureau.**

Qing (Tibetan: *ching*): The Chinese dynastic name taken by the Manchu leader Hong *Taiji* after he conquered China in 1644. The dynasty collapsed in 1911.

Qinghai (Tibetan: *mtsho sngon*): A province in western China that includes part of the Tibetan plateau. It is named after a famous lake, "the Blue Lake," and is better known by its Mongolian name, Kokonor. Much of the western and southern part of Qinghai province consists of "Tibetan autonomous prefectures" that formerly constituted most of the traditional northeastern province of Amdo. About 20 percent of the population is Tibetan, mostly nomadic. The capital of Qinghai is Xining (Tibetan: *zi ling*).

ra ma lug (Tibetan: *ra ma lug*): Literally "not goat, not sheep," a term implying that something is mongrel, confused, or hybrid. It is used most commonly to describe language that is a mixture of Tibetan and Chinese.

Ragti (Tibetan: *rag ti*; Chinese: *Raidi*) (born 1938): A Tibetan from a nomadic community in Biru county in Nagchu who joined the CCP in 1961 and was promoted to a leadership position in the TAR during the Cultural Revolution, becoming a deputy secretary on the TAR party committee in 1975. Ragti retained that position until 2002, when he was promoted to a token but prestigious position in the National People's Congress in Beijing that makes him technically one of the seniormost Tibetan officials in the PRC. See also **Pasang.**

Ramoche (Tibetan: *ra mo che*; Chinese: *Xiaojiaosi*): One of the two principal Buddhist temples in Lhasa. It was built on the northern edge of the city by Wencheng, the Chinese wife of Srongtsen Gampo, in the mid-seventh century.

Red Hill (Tibetan: *dmar po ri*): One of three small hills, each about 300 feet high, that stand close together at the center of the Lhasa valley floor. Marpori, the Red Hill, is the most famous because the Potala Palace stands on its peak and because it includes caves used as sacred sites by the early Tibetan kings Lhatotori Nyentsen and Srongtsen Gampo. The latter is said to have built an early version of the Potala on the hill. The other two hills, connected by spurs, are Chakpori (the Iron Hill) and Bemari (the Hill of Rocks). Marpori and Chakpori lie within the Lingkor or outer pilgrimage circuit.

Retring, Thubten Jampel Yeshe Tenpa'i Gyaltsen (Tibetan: *rwa sgreng* or *ra sgreng thub bstan 'jam dpal ye shes bstan pa'i rgyal mtshan*) (1912 or 1919–47): One of the lamas of *hutuktu* rank, eligible to be the regent during the minority of a Dalai

Lama. The fifth Retring was appointed as regent in 1934, but in 1941 he handed over his position to his tutor Taktra Rinpoche, supposedly so he could go into retreat but probably to avoid having to become the formal tutor of the young fourteenth Dalai Lama, since Retring had not maintained his vows of celibacy. In 1947 Retring, who had expected Taktra to hand back the regency to him after three years, was implicated in a plot to assassinate Taktra and an attempt to get the Chinese to invade Tibet. He was imprisoned in the Potala and was found dead there a few days later, probably murdered.

Richardson, Hugh (1905–2000): The most famous of the British residents in Lhasa, who for nine years represented either Britain or, after 1947, India in Tibet. Richardson was a fluent speaker of Tibetan and is ranked among the leading Western experts in Tibetan culture, scholarship, and history. Richardson learned Tibetan while stationed in Bengal in 1933 and was British Trade Agent in Gyantse from 1936. He was the first resident head of the British mission in Lhasa from 1937 till 1940, and again from 1946 till Indian independence in 1947. He stayed in Lhasa as India's representative until August 1950.

Rinchen Lhamo (Tibetan: *rin chen lha mo*): A wealthy Khampa woman who married Louis King (born 1886), a British diplomat stationed in western China. She moved with him to London in the 1920s and wrote an account of the Tibetan people and their customs, published as *We Tibetans* (London: Seeley Service & Co., 1926).

rinpoche (Tibetan: *rin po che*): A Tibetan term of respect, literally meaning "precious." It is added to the names of important Tibetan lamas.

ru (Tibetan: *ru*): Literally "horn"; the term used at the time of Srongtsen Gampo for the administrative areas into which he divided the central part of the Tibetan kingdom. Each *ru* had to produce a certain number of troops in times of war.

ru-nön (Tibetan: *ru gnon*): Literally "the Suppression of the Horns," a set of four temples, each between 60 and 220 miles from Lhasa, said to have been built by Srongtsen Gampo in the seventh century to pin down the shoulders and hips of the *srinmo* or demoness lying across Tibet. See also **Thandul; Yangdul.**

sa dra (Tibetan: *sa dgra*): A term in Tibetan geomancy for features in the landscape that are antagonistic and have to be subdued or suppressed through a ritual.

Samye (Tibetan: *bsam yas*): The earliest Buddhist monastery in Tibet, established by the Tibetan king Trisong Detsen (born 742, reigned 755–97) in about 779, with the help of the Indian tantric master Padmasambhava, known to Tibetans as Guru Rinpoche. Samye, largely reconstructed in the 1980s after being destroyed in the Cultural Revolution, lies on the north bank of the Yarlung Tsangpo river near the town of Tsethang (Tibetan: *rtse thang*; Chinese: *Ze dang*), the capital of Lhokha (Tibetan: *lho kha*; Chinese: *Shannan*).

Sera (Tibetan: *se ra*; Chinese: *Se la*): One of the three monastic seats in the vicinity of Lhasa that were central institutions for the Gelugpa school of Tibetan Buddhism. Sera, founded in 1419 by Sakya Yeshe, a principal disciple of Tsongkhapa, lies some 2 miles north of the Old City of Lhasa. Before 1959 it held 5,000 monks officially, but in fact in 1951 had about 7,000. Since the 1990s it is believed to house about 600 monks. See also **Drepung**; **Ganden**.

Sera Je (Tibetan: *se ra byes*): One of the three *dratshangs* (Tibetan: *grwa tshang*) or colleges of Sera monastery, a main Gelugpa center 2 miles north of Lhasa. In 1947 the monks of this college, mainly from Kham and with links to China and to the former regent Retring, took part in an armed revolt against the Tibetan government that lasted a week.

sha 'mdre (Tibetan: *sha 'bras*): Rice with meat and curry, a dish that has become common in contemporary Tibetan restaurants. See also *thupa*.

Shakabpa, Wangchuk Deden (Tibetan: *zhwa sgab pa dbang phyug bde ldan*, Chinese: *Xiageba*) (1908–89): A Tibetan aristocrat-official who was a *tsipön* or finance minister for the Tibetan government during the 1940s. He was a leading figure in a delegation sent by the Lhasa government to India, the United States, and the United Kingdom in 1948 to ask for support and funds. After he went into exile in 1959 he wrote a comprehensive history of Tibet supporting its claim for independence, the main Tibetan-language history published in the last half century, published in English as *Tibet: A Political History* (1967; reprint, New York: Potala, 1984).

Shangri-la (Chinese: *Shang ge li la*): A term invented by the American novelist James Hilton in 1933 to refer to an imaginary Himalayan domain whose inhabitants (except for one Russian) apparently enjoyed eternal youth, high culture, and endless harmony. It was adopted by Chinese officials in 2002 as the official name for Zhongdian county in the Tibetan autonomous prefecture of Dechen (Chinese: *Deqing* or *Diqing*) in China's Yunnan province in a deliberate attempt to attract tourists. There is no such term in Tibetan, although Hilton might have intended a reference to Shambhala (Tibetan: *sham bha la*), a name given in certain Tibetan scriptures for a mythical utopia, which, according to fifteenth-century texts, was supposed to be located northwest of Tibet.

Shatra (Tibetan: *bzhad sgra*): A former mansion in Lhasa, in the area south of the Barkor, that once belonged to the Shatra family. Shatra Wangchuk Gyalpo (1795–1864) was a lay official who founded the National Assembly (Tibetan: *tshogs 'du*) in 1860, and was then appointed as the regent. Shatra Ganden Paljor (c. 1860–1919) was a prime minister of Tibet in 1910 and headed the Tibetan negotiating team that signed the Simla agreement with the British in 1913.

Shigatse (Tibetan: *gzhis ka rtse*; Chinese: *Xigaze* or *Rikaze*): The second most important town in Tibet, about 150 miles west of Lhasa. It is the center of Tsang, the central-western region of Tibet, and its most important feature is Tashilhunpo monastery, the seat of the Panchen Lamas. See also **Gyantse**.

Shingra (Tibetan: *shing ra*): A small doorway set into an alcove in the front, or western, face of the Jokhang temple. Literally "wood-enclosure," the door was so called because traditionally it was where wood was handed out to the poor during the annual Mönlam Chenmo or Great Prayer Festival (*q.v.*).

Shöl (Tibetan: *zhol*): A village situated at the foot of the Potala Palace, on its southern side. In 1995, much of the village was cleared and its inhabitants were moved to an area north of the city.

Sichuan (Tibetan: *si khron*): A province in western China that now includes the eastern areas of Kham, which are now known as Ganze (Tibetan: *dkar mdzes*, pronounced "Kardze") Tibetan Autonomous Prefecture, as well as the southern area of Amdo, now called Ngaba (Tibetan: *rnga ba*; Chinese: *Aba*) Tibetan Autonomous Prefecture. From 1939 to 1955 the Kardze area was known as Xikang province, making it separate from and of equal status to both Sichuan and the TAR.

simsha (Tibetan: *gzim shag*): The honorific term in Tibetan for the house or room of an important person; also used in the late 1990s to refer to a new, Tibetanized style of architecture. See also **Karma Gönsar**.

Spencer Chapman, Frederick (1907–71): An English ornithologist, mountaineer, and photographer who was stationed at the British mission in Lhasa as its diplomatic secretary from 1936 to 1937. Chapman wrote a book about his time in Tibet called *Lhasa: The Holy City* (London: Chatto & Windus, 1938).

Spring Tide (Tibetan: *dbyid ka'i rba rlabs*; Chinese: *chun chao*): A political movement initiated by Deng Xiaoping in early 1992 that called on Chinese officials to introduce high-speed market reforms in the economy. It was taken up by Chen Kuiyuan, then the new party secretary in the TAR, and used to justify removing restrictions on the movement of Chinese traders and job seekers into the Tibetan region.

srinmo (Tibetan: *srin mo*): A demoness, particularly the one said to have been identified by Princess Wencheng in the mid-seventh century as lying supine across Tibet. See also **Kyichö**; **Jokhang**; **Chagpori**; **Red Hill**.

Srongtsen Gampo (Tibetan: *srong btsan sgam po*) (617 or 618–649): The thirty-third and most famous of the early Tibetan kings. He was born in Medrogongkar, northwest of present-day Lhasa, in about 617 and became king in 629. He moved the Tibetan capital from the Yarlung valley to Lhasa in the mid-seventh century and conquered vast areas, including parts of Nepal and the regions now known as western and eastern Tibet. He sent scholars to India to collect texts and to develop a script (not necessarily the first one) for writing Tibetan. He is regarded as the first of the three *chögyals* or "religious kings" and credited with the introduction of Buddhism from India to Tibet, though modern historians date the spread of the religion beyond court circles as happening many decades later. He had several wives, including after 632 the Nepalese princess Bhrikuti, who helped him build the Jokhang temple, and the Chinese princess Wencheng, who built the Ramoche temple. See also **Thandul**; **Yangdul.**

State Security Bureau (Tibetan: *rgyal khab bde 'jags bu'u*, Chinese: *an quan bu*): The Chinese government agency that handles cases involving the security of the state, including activities supporting Tibetan independence. It was established in 1983 by merging the previous Central Investigation Department with the counterintelligence sections of the Public Security Bureau.

Sungchöra (Tibetan: *gsung chos ra ba*): Literally "the Enclosure for Speeches About Religion," the open area on the southwest side of the Jokhang temple that traditionally was used for public talks by lamas. The Sungchöra is now used as an entrance to the temple, and as a part of the Barkor market.

Surkhang Wangchen Gelek (Tibetan: *zur khang dbang chen dge legs*) (1910–1977): A famous *kalön* in the Tibetan cabinet in the 1940s and 1950s who is often described as Tibet's last *silön* or prime minister before the Chinese authorities took over direct control of the Tibetan government in 1959. Surkhang had been in favor of the Dalai Lama fleeing to the United States at the time of the Chinese invasion in 1950, but a majority of National Assembly members had called for the ruler to return to Lhasa. After the 1959 flight to India, Surkhang moved to the United States and is said to have written an important history, of which only fragments have emerged. See also **Dorje Yuthok**; *Baba* **Phuntsog.**

Taizong: The Emperor of China during the Tang dynasty from 626 to 649 who gave Wencheng, a princess from the imperial family, to Srongtsen Gampo. See also **mGar.**

Taktra, Ngawang Sungrab Thutob (Tibetan: *stag brag ngag dbang gsung rab mthu stobs*) (1874–1952): A scholar and lama who was appointed as acting Regent of Tibet in 1941 when Retring stepped down from the regency. Retring later claimed that Taktra had agreed to hand back the position after three years, and armed conflict broke out over the dispute in 1947. Taktra retained his position as regent until the Dalai Lama took over the throne in 1950.

Taring, Jigme (Tibetan: *phreng ring 'jigs med*) (1908–91): A Tibetan aristocrat and modernizer related to the Sikkimese royal family who had been educated in British India. Taring was brought to Lhasa in 1932 from his estate at Gyantse to establish and train a machine-gun regiment in modern military techniques, but it was disbanded within two years. He was married to Rinchen Dolma (1909–2000), also educated in India and sometimes known as Mary Taring, who wrote a biography in English, *Daughter of Tibet* (London: John Murray, 1970). He and his wife fled to India in 1959, where they established schools and relief projects for Tibetan refugees.

Tashi Tsering (Tibetan: *bkra shis tshe ring*): The name of three figures in recent Tibetan events: (1) a member of the Dalai Lama's dance troupe as a child in 1942 who later fled to India and then studied in the United States before returning to Tibet in the 1960s, and who later co-wrote his autobiography in English, *The Struggle for Modern Tibet* (Armonk, NY: M. E. Sharpe, 1997); (2) a famous Tibetan historian based in Dharamsala in India; (3) a builder who staged a one-man protest during an official celebration in the New Potala Square in August 1999 and died in Chinese custody six months later.

Tengyeling (Tibetan: *bstan rgyas gling*): One of the four main monasteries or *trulku* estates in Lhasa, the names of three of which end in "ling," the Tibetan word for a place or island. The other three "lings" were Kundeling, Tsechogling, and Tsemonling (Tibetan: *kun bde gling, tshe mchog gling,* and *mtsho smon gling* or *tshe smon gling*); some sources replace Tsechogling with Retring. The chief incumbents of Tengyeling, the Demo line of *trulkus*, were lamas of the *gyetru hutuktu* rank, and were thus eligible to hold the position of regent until the ninth was convicted of an assassination plot in 1895. Tengyeling was stripped of its possessions and razed to the ground in 1913 for its support of the Chinese troops and officials during their occupation of Lhasa in 1910–12.

Tethong, Tomjor Wangchuk (Tibetan: *bkras mthong stobs 'byor dbang phyug*) (1924–1997): A young and progressive aristocrat whose father, Tethong Gyurme Gyatsho (Tibetan: *bkras mthong 'gyur med rgya mtsho*) (1890 or 1892–1938), was a *kalön* from 1922 until his death. Tomjor Wangchuk joined the radical group around *Baba* Phuntsog Wanggyal in Lhasa in 1944. The latter says in his biography that Tomjor was inducted into the "inner circle," a secret communist group, and most of its meetings took place in the Tethong mansion. In 1950 he went to India and, strongly anti-Communist, refused to cooperate with the new regime. Three of his sons and his brother became ministers in the exile Tibetan government, and his nephew, Jamyang Norbu, became a leading exile writer and intellectual.

Thandul (Tibetan: *mtha' 'dul*): The "border subduing" temples, a set of four temples said to have been built by Srongtsen Gampo in the seventh century to pin down the elbows and knees of the *srinmo* or demoness lying across Tibet. See also *ru-nön*; **Yangdul**.

Tharchin, Gergan Dorje (Tibetan: *mthar phyin*) (1890–1976): An ethnic Tibetan from Kinnaur in northern India who produced a weekly paper in Tibetan for more than thirty years, beginning in October 1925, called the *Sargyur Melong* (Tibetan: *gsar 'gyur me long*) or *News Mirror*, the only Tibetan paper of that time. Tharchin had been converted to Christianity by Moravians and became a minister of the Church of Scotland mission in Kalimpong, West Bengal. He was often called Tharchin *Babu*, a term of respect in Hindi. His base in Kalimpong became an important meeting place for Tibetan intellectuals and progressives throughout the mid-twentieth century. Tharchin, Gendun Chöphel, Rabga Pangdatsang, and other prominent Tibetans published articles on Tibetan history and modern politics in his paper.

Thieves' Island: See **Gumalingka**.

Third Plenary (Tibetan: *gros tshogs thengs gsum pa*): Usually refers to the third full session of the 11th Congress (Tibetan: *tshogs chen skabs bcu gcig pa*) of the Chinese Communist Party, convened in Beijing in 1978. That meeting passed resolutions that affirmed the overall authority of Deng Xiaoping and that were said to have decisively ended the era of Maoist and extreme leftist policies in China.

thupa (Tibetan: *thug pa*): A common Tibetan dish consisting of noodles in broth.

Tibet (Tibetan: *bod*, Chinese: *Xizang*): The Chinese term *Xizang* and modern Chinese uses of the English word "Tibet" always refer only to the area now termed the "Tibet Autonomous Region." Tibet in this usage therefore does not include the eastern Tibetan regions. The name (versions of which are found in Arabic and Indian texts of the tenth century) may be related to the name *purgyal* (Tibetan: *spur rgyal*), used in the early Tibetan histories to describe the Tibetan royal dynasty. The name given for the Tibetan imperial line in Tang dynasty Chinese sources is *Tubo*. The Tibetan term *Bod* is sometimes defined as having referred to the central Tibetan area, roughly the area that was directly administered by Lhasa up to 1950, but classical and premodern Tibetan texts routinely describe it as "the three circles of Ngari in the upper [western] area, Amdo and the six regions of Kham in the lower area, and the four horns of Ü [Lhasa] and Tsang [Shigatse] in between." This is a description of the area that Hugh Richardson later termed "ethnographic Tibet"—the area traditionally inhabited by Tibetans. It includes the former eastern Tibetan provinces known as Kham and Amdo and is commensurate with the Tibetan plateau (Tibetan: *sa mtho*), which is referred to in Chinese as the *Qingzang gaoyuan* or "the Qinghai-Tibetan Plateau." *Bod*, along with the English equivalent "Tibet," is used by exile Tibetans and by many foreign writers to refer to this larger ethnographic Tibetan area.

Tibet Autonomous Region or **TAR** (Tibetan: *bod rang skyong ljongs*; Chinese: *Xizang zizhiqu*): The area roughly equivalent to the territory directly ruled by the Dalai Lama's government in 1950. Chinese official sources say that the Chamdo region, or western Kham, was not ruled by Lhasa at that time, but it was included within the TAR anyway. The TAR thus includes the central and western areas of traditional or ethnographic Tibet, plus Kham west of the Drichu (the Upper Yangtse river). It was declared an "autonomous region" in 1965, until which time Chinese sources used the term *Xizang* or "Tibet" for that area.

Tibetan Uprising: In March 1959 Tibetans in Lhasa, supported by a Tibetan rebel army that had been fighting the PLA in eastern Tibet since at least 1956, staged a major armed uprising against Chinese rule. It was triggered by rumors that the Dalai Lama was about to be kidnapped by Chinese officials. The Lhasa uprising was put down within ten days by the Chinese, using heavy artillery support. Some 80,000 Tibetans fled with the Dalai Lama to India. The uprising was followed immediately by a major campaign called "The Elimination of the Rebellion," combined with "democratic reforms," meaning the imposition of radical land redistribution. These led to thousands of arrests and deaths among the Tibetan population. See also *minzhu gaige*.

Tromsikhang (Tibetan: *grom gzigs khang*): A mansion on the northern side of the Barkor or middle circuit in Lhasa. It was built as a residence for the sixth Dalai Lama in the late seventeenth century and used as a residence by the Mongol ruler Lhazang Khan until his death in 1717. Later it was used as a residence for the *ambans*, two of whom were assassinated in their rooms in 1751 after they murdered a Tibetan ruler. Except for the façade, the building was largely demolished in 1997, despite having been designated for preservation three years earlier.

trulku (Tibetan: *sprul sku*): The Tibetan term for a lama whose spiritual accomplishments are sufficiently advanced that his or her reincarnation can be identified—literally "manifested body." The first lineage of *trulkus* is said to have been that of the Karmapa, whose reincarnation was recognized after the death of the first Karmapa, Dusum Khyenpa, in 1193. The term is also written in English as *tulku*. The Chinese translation, *huofu* or "living buddha," is incorrect and considered disparaging by some Tibetan scholars. See also *hutuktu*; *rinpoche*.

tsampa (Tibetan: *rtsam pa*; Chinese: *qingke*): Roasted barley flour, the staple food of Tibetans, usually eaten with tea and butter.

Tsang (Tibetan: *gtsang*): The area of southern Tibet that has Shigatse at its center. It is one of the traditional areas of Tibet and in Tibetan, is usually referred to along with the central province of Ü (the Lhasa area) as the central Tibetan region. People from Tsang speak a slightly different dialect of Tibetan and are sometimes mocked by Lhasans. See also **central Tibet**; **Tibet**.

Tsarong, Wangchuk Gyalpo (Tibetan: *tsha rong dbang phyug rgyal po*) (18??–1912): A Tibetan aristocrat-official who became a *kalön* in 1903. Along with his son, he was executed, or according to some, murdered, in 1912 by ministers loyal to the thirteenth Dalai Lama for having cooperated with Chinese forces during the occupation of Lhasa, which began in February 1910. The more famous Tsarong, Dazang Dramdul (Tibetan: *zla bzang dgra 'dul*) (1888–1959), sometimes called "new Tsarong," known at the time as Jensey (Tibetan: *spyan gsal*, or "favorite") Namgang, was a Tibetan peasant who became a favorite of the thirteenth Dalai Lama. As a reward he was ennobled, appointed to the rank of *zasak*, and married into the "old Tsarong" family in 1913, thus acquiring the Tsarong name. He was a *kalön* from 1914 to 1929. He also served as commander of the army and was an important force for modernization in the Tibetan government in the 1920s. A biography has been published by D. N. Tsarong, *In the Service of His Country: The Biography of Dasang Damdul Tsarong, Commander General of Tibet* (Ithaca, NY: Snow Lion, 2000).

Tsashagpa (Tibetan: *tsha shag pa*): A Tibetan aristocrat-official who was executed in 1912 by Sera monks, possibly at the behest of Tibetan officials, for having cooperated with the Chinese occupation forces in Lhasa in 1910–12. Tsashagpa had been a *kadrung* (Tibetan: *bka' drung*) or cabinet secretary. Other senior Tibetan officials who were executed or killed for cooperation with the Chinese were Tsarong *shapé* and his son, Punrabpa (Tibetan: *phun rab pa*); Mondrong (Tibetan: *smon krong*); and Lobsang Dorje (Tibetan: *slob bzang rdo rje*).

tsipön (Tibetan: *rtsis dpon*): The Tibetan term for one of the four ministers in the *Tsigang* or revenue office of the Tibetan government before 1959. The ministers were in charge of collecting and adjudicating taxes. They also co-chaired the meetings of the National Assembly (consisting of representatives of the main monasteries, officials, and military officers) along with the four ministers of the *Yigtsang*, the office in charge of religious affairs.

Tsongkhapa (Tibetan: *tsong kha pa*) (1357–1419): A Tibetan monk and scholar from Tsongkha in Amdo who initiated a major reform movement in Tibetan Buddhism that led to the founding of the Gelugpa school. Tsongkhapa spent most of his adult life teaching and meditating in central Tibet, including Lhasa. In 1409 he established the annual Mönlam festival at the Jokhang temple and founded the monastery of Ganden. See also **Sera**; **Drepung**; **Gelugpa**.

Tuanjie xincun (Tibetan: *mthun sgril grong gsar*): The Chinese name for a new suburb created to the north of the Potala Palace. It means "New Unity Village."

Tucci, Giuseppe (1894–1984): A prominent Italian Tibetologist, an expert on Tibetan art and religion, who traveled to Tibet in the 1930s and 1940s.

Ü (Tibetan: *dbus*): Literally "the center," a traditional Tibetan term referring to the region around Lhasa. It does not include the areas around Shigatse (known as Tsang), Ngari, Kham, Amdo, or other regions. See also **Tsang**; **central Tibet**.

Uighurs (Tibetan: *yu gur*): An ancient people of Turkic descent who inhabit the easternmost desert areas of central Asian Turkestan. The areas have been claimed since the Tang dynasty by Chinese emperors and are known to the Chinese as Xinjiang. The people disappeared as a distinctive group, becoming known either as "Turks" or "Muslims," until the name reemerged in the early twentieth century, along with efforts to create and sustain the independent state of East Turkestan. That effort has continued but was successful only from 1944 to 1949. Like the Tibetans and the Mongols, the Uighurs had been promised the option of independence by the Chinese Communist Party in 1931, but in 1949 they were named as one of China's 55 "minority nationalities" and reintegrated with the People's Republic of China. In the 1950s and again after the late 1980s, major settlement of ethnic Chinese farmers was promoted in their area, officially known since 1955 as the Xinjiang Uighur Autonomous Region.

Waddell, L. Austine (1854–1939): A British military officer and physician who had been a professor of chemistry and pathology in Calcutta from 1881 to 1886. Waddell became a scholar of Tibetan language and culture at the turn of the twentieth century and later professor of Tibetan at the University of London. He traveled to Lhasa with the Younghusband expedition in 1903 as its medical officer and scholarly adviser, and was chiefly responsible for collecting Tibetan cultural heirlooms to bring back to Britain.

Wencheng (Tibetan: *rgya bza'*): The Chinese princess given in 641 by the Emperor Taizong to the Tibetan king Srongtsen Gampo, noted in Tibetan accounts for her skill in divination and her support of Buddhism. In contemporary Chinese accounts she is noted for introducing advanced knowledge and techniques to Tibetans. See also **Jokhang**; **Ramoche**; *srinmo*.

work unit: See *danwei*.

Xianzudao (Tibetan: *lha zhabs gling*): Literally "the Island of the God's Foot," the Chinese name for a park constructed in traditional Tibetan style in about 2003 on an island in the Kyichu river. See also **Gumalingka**.

Xi'an: A major city in western China that, under the name Chang'an (Tibetan: *khrang an*), was the capital of China in the eighth century. A Tibetan army raided the city in 763 and briefly set up a puppet emperor there before withdrawing to Tibet. Xi'an is now the capital of Shaanxi province.

Xinhua (Tibetan: *shin hwa*): The official news agency of the Chinese government since 1949.

Xizang Ribao (Tibetan: *nyin re'i tshags bar*): The Chinese name for *Tibet Daily*, the newspaper produced in Lhasa that is the official organ of the Tibet Branch of the Chinese Communist Party. It appears in a Chinese-language edition every day, and the following day the previous day's Chinese news appears in Tibetan translation, occasionally with additional articles written by Tibetans. It has been published since April 1956 and until 2004 was the only daily paper in the TAR.

Yamen (Tibetan: *ya smon*): The Chinese residency, a compound used by the ambans during the nineteenth and early twentieth centuries. It was situated just within the Lingkor, southwest of the main city of Lhasa, near the area known as Lubu.

Yangdul (Tibetan: *yang 'dul*): A set of four temples, called "Subduing Beyond the Borders," said to have been built by Srongtsen Gampo in the seventh century to pin down the hands and feet of the *srinmo* or demoness lying across Tibet. See also *ru-nön*; **Thandul.**

Yarlung (Tibetan: *yar klungs* or *yar lung*): A fertile valley in Lhokha in southern Tibet, near the town of Tsethang, about 50 miles southeast of Lhasa, or 100 miles by road. The Tibetan royal dynasty is said to have originated in the area and ruled from there until it moved to Lhasa in the mid-seventh century. The main river in Tibet, the Yarlung Tsangpo (*tsang po* means "river" in Tibetan), runs in an easterly direction through almost all of southern Tibet, including this area, before arcing sharply to the south and becoming the Brahmaputra river in Bangladesh and India.

Younghusband, Francis (Chinese: *Rong he peng*) (1863–1942): Colonel Younghusband led the British invasion of Tibet in 1903–4. His efforts attracted considerable criticism in the British parliament at the time, but he had strong popular support and was knighted. He had earlier traveled as an explorer in Manchuria and northwestern India, and later made three attempts to climb Everest. He became an advocate of eclectic spirituality after the Tibet episode and founded the World Congress of Faiths in 1936.

Youtai (Tibetan: *yu tha'e*): The name of the *amban* or imperial commissioner in Lhasa at the time that the British invading force arrived in the city in 1904.

Yuan (Tibetan: *yon*): The Chinese dynastic name taken by the Mongolian leader Kubilai Khan after he conquered China in 1271. The dynasty collapsed in 1368 and was replaced by the Ming. Tibet had become part of the Mongol empire, through an arrangement brokered by the head of the Sakya school with the Mongol leader Godan Khan, in 1247.

zasak (Tibetan: *dza sag*): *Zasak* or *dzasa* is a Mongolian term used as a title for certain high-ranking lay officials in the traditional Tibetan government. A *zasak* ranks immediately below a *kalön* and above the fourth-rank (*rim bzhi*) officials, and so is one of the highest ranks other than cabinet minister.

Zhang Yintang: A Chinese official who had worked in the United States as a diplomat before being sent to Lhasa for seven months in 1904–5, where he served as the amban or imperial commissioner shortly after the British invasion.

Zhongguo (Tibetan: *krung go*): The Chinese term for China, literally "the Central Kingdom," now used to refer to the People's Republic of China. Since 1959, Tibetans in Tibet have been required to use the term in its Tibetanized form, *krung go*, in order to describe China including Tibet. This is because the only word in Tibetan that exists for China, *Gyanag* (Tibetan: *rgya nag*), does not include Tibet.

Gyanag is still used, but officially it now means "inland China" or "China apart from Tibet."

Zorge (Tibetan: *mdzod dge*; Chinese: *Zoige* or *Ruergai*): A Tibetan town in Ngapa prefecture in the former eastern Tibetan area of Amdo, now within Sichuan province.

ASIA PERSPECTIVES

HISTORY, SOCIETY, AND CULTURE

A series of the East Asian Institute, Columbia University, published by Columbia University Press
Carol Gluck, Editor